Roger of Salisbury

VICEROY OF ENGLAND

Roger of Salisbury

VICEROY OF ENGLAND

by
Edward J. Kealey

University of California Press

BERKELEY, LOS ANGELES, LONDON, 1972

University of California Press
Berkeley and Los Angeles, California
University of California Press, Ltd.
London, England
Copyright © 1972, by
The Regents of the University of California
ISBN: 0-520-01985-7
Library of Congress Catalog Card Number: 78-92681
Printed in the United States of America

To My Mother

Contents

List of Plates

(following page 176)

Abbreviations

AHR	*American Historical Review*
Anglo-Saxon Chronicle	*The Anglo-Saxon Chronicle,* ed. Benjamin Thorpe, RS 23(1861), 2 vols.
Annales Monastici	*Annales Monastici,* ed. Henry Richard Luard, RS 36(1864–1869), 5 vols.
CHJ	*Cambridge Historical Journal*
DNB	*Dictionary of National Biography*
Eadmer, *H.N.*	*Eadmeri Historia Novorum in Anglia,* ed. Martin Rule, RS 81(1884).
EHR	*English Historical Review*
Florence of Worcester	*Florenti Wigorniensis Chronicon Ex Chronicis,* ed. Benjamin Thorpe (London, 1848–1849), 2 vols.
Gesta Stephani	*Gesta Stephani,* ed. and trans., K. R. Potter, Nelson's Medieval Texts (London, 1955).
Henry of Huntingdon	*Henrici Huntendunensis Historia Anglorum,* ed. Thomas Arnold, RS 74(1879).
JEH	*Journal of Ecclesiastical History*
John of Worcester	*The Chronicle of John of Worcester, 1118–1146,* ed. John R. H. Weaver (Oxford, 1908).

Orderic Vitalis *Orderici Vitalis Historiae Ecclesiasticae Libri Tredecim,* ed.
August Le Prévost (Paris,
1838–1855), 5 vols.

PBA *Proceedings of the British
Academy*

PL *Patrologiae Cursus Completus:
Series Latina,* ed. J. P. Migne
(Paris, 1844–1864), 221 vols.

PMLA *[Publications of the Modern
Language Association of Amer-
ica]*

Regesta *Regesta Regum Anglo-Normannorum,* vol. 1, ed. H. W. C.
Davis (Oxford, 1913); vol. 2, ed.
Charles Johnson and H. A.
Cronne (Oxford, 1956); vol. 3,
ed. H. A. Cronne and R. H. C.
Davis (Oxford, 1968); vol. 4,
(facsimilies), ed. H. A. Cronne
and R. H. C. Davis (Oxford,
1969).*

Richard Fitz Nigel *The Course of the Exchequer
by Richard Son of Nigel,* ed.
and trans. Charles Johnson,
Nelson's Medieval Texts (London, 1950).

RS *Rolls Series*

Symeon of Durham *Symeonis Monachi Opera
Omnia,* ed. Thomas Arnold, RS
75(1882–1885), 2 vols.

TRHS *Transactions of the Royal Historical Society*

VCH *The Victoria History of the
Counties of England*

William of Malmesbury, *G.P.* *Willelmi Malmesbiriensis Monachi de Gestis Pontificum Anglorum,* ed. Nicholas E. S. A. Hamilton, RS 52(1870).

William of Malmesbury, *G.R.* *Willelmi Malmesbiriensis Monachi de Gestis Regum Anglorum,* ed. William Stubbs, RS 90(1887–1889), 2 vols.

William of Malmesbury, H.N. *The Historia Novella of William of Malmesbury,* ed. and trans. K. R. Potter, Nelson's Medieval Texts (London, 1955).

William of Newburgh *Historia Rerum Anglicarum of William of Newburgh,* ed. Hans Claude Hamilton (London, 1856), 2 vols.

Preface

SOMEWHERE amidst the clutter of his office and the clouds of tobacco which always enveloped him, the late Sidney Painter, a merry man and a serious scholar, first urged me to write about Roger of Salisbury. His successor at The Johns Hopkins University, John W. Baldwin, and Joseph R. Strayer of Princeton University guided me throughout the early versions of this study. R. H. C. Davis now of the University of Birmingham very kindly read my preliminary typescript of the viceroy's charters, and Brian Kemp of the University of Reading offered valuable suggestions about Reading Abbey. Hugh de S. Shortt, curator of the Salisbury and South Wiltshire Museum, helped me become familiar with the ruins at Old Sarum and obtained several photographs for me. Edward Maszewski Kemp entertained me in his home, Devizes Castle, and Frederick Marsden and James Gibb graciously introduced me to Sherborne Old Castle. Peter R. White of the Inspectorate of Ancient Monuments of the Department of the Environment showed me his excavations at Sherborne and explained his preliminary conclusions. Miss Pamela Stewart readily assisted me in using the archives of the Salisbury Diocesan Record Office, and Ralph B. Pugh, general editor of the Victoria History of the Counties of England, and the staffs of the British Museum Manuscript Room, the Institute of Historical Research, London, and the many other record depositories and libraries where I worked all courteously and quickly came to my aid. None of these scholars has seen the final draft of this book, nor indeed can be held accountable for any part of it, but it is better for their generous interest, and I am deeply grateful. The editors of the University of California Press have also made a genuine contribution to the quality of this study, and in some measure all my students and colleagues have helped it mature. In the earliest stages of research I was supported by a Danforth National Foundation Fellowship, and the charters and writs were edited while I was on sabbatical leave from the College of the Holy Cross, Worcester, Massachusetts.

Although Bishop Roger's career also lends itself to a solely administrative study, it is really the mixture of his many roles which gives us the best appreciation of his intensely personal and surprisingly complex Anglo-Norman world. I have tried to establish the complete record of his life, and therefore some documentation is necessarily greater than I might have wished. Dating revisions have been accepted into the text, but detailed argumentation has usually been carried in the notes.

The New Bishop and
the New King,
1100–1107

ROGER OF SALISBURY (1065?–1139) was a complex, vibrant individual and an ambitious, resourceful statesman. Born amidst change and opportunity, gifted with enterprise and administrative genius, he, like so many other Normans, found scope for his special talents in conquered England. King Henry I acknowledged his brilliance by making Roger chancellor, bishop, and, ultimately, second only to himself in authority and power—a veritable viceroy. For more than a generation thereafter he imaginatively and successfully governed the kingdom under Henry and his successor, King Stephen. Nevertheless, despite triumphs as churchman, politician, and viceroy, Bishop Roger died in disgrace, deserted by all who knew him. The value of his works sometimes overshadows the drama of his life, but he is, as recent historians have observed, "an outstanding, a mighty figure in English history." [1]

Contemporary writers who remembered the excitement of Roger's career described it as a turn on the wheel of fortune, thereby suggesting the classic case of a gradual rise from obscurity to fame, followed by a sudden dash to tragedy and death. [2] This stock analysis is correct as far as it goes, but there was greater significance to his existence, and

1. Henry G. Richardson and George O. Sayles, *The Governance of Medieval England from the Conquest to Magna Carta* (hereafter cited as Richardson and Sayles, *Governance of England*), p. 165.

2. Henry of Huntingdon, pp. 266–269; William of Malmesbury, *H.N.*, p. 5.

his legacy is much more than a warning to ambitious men. Roger made many positive contributions to Anglo-Norman affairs, and the island kingdom prospered in the order he encouraged. He inaugurated the exchequer system, centralized royal justice, created a trained bureaucracy, and still found time to govern his own large diocese and be an active patron of art, education, and learning. Throughout a long life he not only strove to accommodate his lord's will but also fought to maintain his own advantage over more established men and institutions. Like other strong leaders who simultaneously master spiritual and temporal responsibilities, he was sometimes torn by conflicting loyalties and thus alternately protected and exploited his church. His deeds were not always popular with the monastic chroniclers who recorded them, and he occasionally faced episcopal and baronial opposition in the royal council, but his plans usually prevailed. In the long run Bishop Roger was a model for later political prelates and ecclesiastical statesmen, and he even founded a clerical dynasty which produced governmental servants and church officials for almost a hundred years.

Roger's career is inseparable from those of his royal lords, Henry I (reigned 1100-1135) and Stephen (reigned 1135-1154).[3] Fat, ruddy King Henry was certainly the major force in Roger's life, and it was as his alter ego that the bishop became such a dominant and influential figure in the kingdom. Lacking charismatic qualities and inspiring or farsighted ideas, Henry was instead a clever politician, a skillful manager, and a stern taskmaster. The earlier Norman monarchs—Henry's brother, William II, or William Rufus

3. For Henry I, see Richard W. Southern, "The Place of Henry I in English History." C. Warren Hollister is preparing a biography of the king. For Stephen, see R. H. C. Davis, *King Stephen,* and John Appleby, *The Troubled Reign of King Stephen.* A third study, H. A. Cronne, *The Reign of Stephen, 1135-1154: Anarchy in England* (London, 1970), appeared too late to be used in this biography.

as he is sometimes called, and his father, William the Conqueror—were cruel, avaricious, unpleasant individuals, who were also exceptionally able rulers, shrewd judges of other men, valued allies, and vengeful, implacable enemies. Henry shared all these characteristics and appears different only in that he added unbridled lust to his other unattractive personal traits.

Governmental success in Henry's reign was largely the achievement of his carefully chosen ministers. The king's prestige and personality could easily overawe his subordinates, but he usually gave them great independence and support and promised future rewards for faithful service. Many of these men, like Roger, came from western Normandy; few held great fiefs or belonged to prominent baronial families. Though not impoverished, they were completely dependent upon Henry for patronage and made excellent instruments for effecting his programs against entrenched feudal privilege. The contemporary chroniclers —frequently spokesmen of reaction—criticized this royal policy of raising unknown men "from the dust" to be the principal officials of the realm.[4] In the long view the tide ran with these "new men," but it is only recently that their great contributions have been recognized.

The first roads obscure men take to greatness are frequently hidden paths, and Roger's early history, like those of so many important medieval men, survives only in legend. The best known tale of his origins comes from the pen of an Augustinian canon, William of Newburgh, who wrote sixty years after the bishop's death. His gossipy report is a blend of imagination, prejudice, and limited research, and it illustrates some of the difficulties of constructing an accurate record from chronicle sources:

Since the opportunity offers itself a few things must be said about the origins and career of this Roger in order that in

4. Orderic Vitalis, 4:164; *Gesta Stephani*, pp. 15–16; Richard of Hexham, *Historia de Gestis Stephani et de Bello Standardii*, p. 140.

his miserable end, the depths of divine judgment may be considered. In the reign of William the younger, he was a poor priest in the suburbs of Caen living, as it is said, on his benefice. At one time when Henry the younger was campaigning against his brother the king, he happened to turn aside with his companions to the church where Roger was officiating and asked him to celebrate mass for them. The priest agreed and was as prompt to begin as he was quick to finish. In both these respects he so pleased the soldiers that they claimed that a more suitable chaplain for military men could not be found. And when the regal youth said, "Follow me," he stuck as closely to him as Peter once did to the Lord of Heaven when He uttered a similar invitation. Peter left his boat and followed the King of Kings, but this man left his chapel and followed the prince. At his own choice Roger became chaplain to him and his troops, the blind leading the blind. Although he was practically unlettered, he nevertheless so shrewdly managed things by his innate astuteness that within a short time he became dear to his master and conducted his most confidential affairs.[5]

This widely quoted story is plausible enough in itself, but it is completely unsupported by other evidence. Although it is quite likely that Roger could and did offer fast masses, no contemporary commentator referred to his origins. The petty allusion to his being unlettered (*fere illiteratus*) might pass if it only means that he was not a truly learned man; if it indicates more than that, its falsehood is betrayed by Roger's latter career.

William of Newburgh's tale should be contrasted with a much more objective reference to Roger's early life, the official diocesan certification of his election as bishop of Salisbury. This document, which still survives, is a fairly standard ritual formula testifying to the newly-elected prel-

5. William of Newburgh, 1:35–36; see also Kate Norgate, "The Date of the Composition of William of Newburgh's History." Gervaise La Rue in *Essais Historiques sur la Ville de Caen et son Arrondissement*, 1:293, identified the chapel as being at Vaucelles, but no evidence supports this.

ate's character, eloquence, learning, orthodoxy, and virtue, and it therefore cannot be said to describe Roger's individual attainments precisely; but it does offer a very different evaluation. Furthermore, it identifies him as "a priest of Avranches," and this definitely establishes that in 1101 Roger was associated with the diocese of Avranches in western Normandy.[6] Considering that he was elected bisop in 1101 and that he died in 1139, the date of Roger's birth can be roughly approximated between 1065 and 1070. Although nothing definite is known about the viceroy's education and formative years, Avranches was a considerable intellectual center in the mid-eleventh century, at one time even boasting the famed Lanfranc among its teachers.[7] The fact that Roger quickly became a priest in an age when many clerics long deferred ordination, is some slight indication of his piety and sense of responsibility. He had at least one brother, Humphrey, about whom little is known.[8] Their numerous and well-placed descendants will appear later, but, for the moment, some slight confirmation of the obscurity of the viceroy's beginnings is found in the writings of his grand-nephew, Richard Fitz Nigel, who suggested in passing that Roger was indeed poor and unknown as a youth.[9]

Other leading figures of the early twelfth century, men like Abelard and Anselm, fascinate us by the charm and brilliance of their writings, but Bishop Roger is known largely through legal records and chronicle accounts. None of his letters or sermons is extant, and I have uncovered only thirty-one charters and writs from the hundreds he may have written.[10] His mind and motivation therefore remain somewhat enigmatic. However, Roger was frequently men-

6. British Museum Manuscript, Harley Roll, A 3, no. 4.
7. Eadmer, *The Life of St. Anselm, Archbishop of Canterbury,* p. 8.
8. Charter 4 in Appendix 2.
9. *"Ignotus non tamen ignobilis,"* Richard Fitz Nigel, p. 42.
10. For a critical edition of all Roger's known charters, see Appendix 2; hereafter his charters are referred to by their number in this appendix.

tioned in royal documents which can at least be usefully employed to flesh out his biography and recreate his itinerary.[11]

The twelfth century, which has so justly been called a renaissance, fortunately witnessed a great resurgence of historical writing. England, in particular, felt this impulse, and most monasteries there housed resident chroniclers and commentators. Government records were also better organized and preserved than elsewhere in Europe. No biographer detailed Roger's life, however; and, although most contemporary historians recognized his stature and power, no one really analyzed his personality or policies or took the full measure of the man. Perhaps this was because most authors tended to attribute all important works directly to the king, while at the same time being unsympathetic to his ministers. Furthermore, many of the historians were monks living in quiet cloisters where they were dependent upon chance visitors for detailed information about current events. Some wrote from well-developed prejudices of their own, and others received biased accounts of the viceroy's activities from bishops, barons, and monks who chafed under his rule. It is interesting, for example, that the more impersonal financial and legal records appear to support Roger's push for governmental centralization, while the chroniclers condemned the policy.

Some of the chroniclers knew Roger quite well and probably had extended contact with him. William of Malmesbury, clearly the greatest English historian since Bede, lived in an abbey in the bishop's diocese. This monk's deserved reputation for accuracy has been challenged recently, but his reports can usually be confirmed by other authorities.[12] Among his many works William wrote three books which

11. See Appendix 1 for Bishop Roger's itinerary.
12. Robert B. Patterson, "William of Malmesbury's Robert of Gloucester, a Re-evaluation of the *Historia Novella*."

discussed Bishop Roger: *De Gestis Regum Anglorum,* a general history of England to about 1120, parts of which were later revised; *De Gestis Pontificum Anglorum,* an ecclesiastical history finished in 1125; and *Historia Novella,* actually a concluding chapter of the first book, completed about 1142, three years after Roger's death.[13] William's evaluation of the viceroy became more critical over the years, but his remarks are the most valuable narrative sources for Roger's biography.

Some of the other accounts of Roger's world might also be briefly introduced.[14] The Canterbury monk Eadmer was a secretary to Archbishop Anselm and knowledgeable about many English affairs. Anonymous Canterbury and Peterborough monks recorded entries in the *Anglo-Saxon Chronicle* and were well informed in an unsystematic way, as was Orderic Vitalis who wrote his lengthy church history in a Norman monastery. The *Gesta Stephani,* which was probably composed by the monastic bishop, Robert of Bath, is filled with detailed descriptions of events after 1135, but it is also quite critical of Roger.[15] A more favorable interpretation was offered by Henry of Huntingdon, a secular priest and archdeacon in Lincoln, the diocese of Roger's nephew. Modern historians have called Roger both an ecclesiastical schemer [16] and the architect of the Anglo-Norman administration [17] and have tended either to accept old chronicle

13. For an analysis of his works, see Hugh Farmer, "William of Malmesbury's Life and Works."

14. At the end of his recent biography, *King Stephen,* R. H. C. Davis provided a very useful appendix, which discussed many of the original sources of this period.

15. R. H. C. Davis in "The Authorship of the *Gesta Stephani*" suggests that the parts dealing with the first twelve years of the reign were probably written in 1148.

16. Donald Nicholl, *Thurstan Archbishop of York, 1114–1140,* p. 183.

17. S. B. Chrimes, *An Introduction to the Administrative History of Medieval England* (hereafter cited as Chrimes, *Administrative History*), p. 50.

evaluations rather uncritically or to concentrate almost exclusively on the bishop's administrative accomplishments. Perhaps the full story of his life will now suggest a more balanced judgment.

William of Newburgh, who represented a tradition two generations removed from Roger, concluded his gossipy report of the viceroy by declaring him to have been industrious, wealthy, distinguished in the church and second in the realm, but greedy, vainglorious, and overly concerned with such worldly ostentations as castle-building.[18] Some of these ideas also appeared in William of Malmesbury's contemporary and more responsible accounts. This monk's first extended discussion of the bishop does not include anything about his origins, but it does offer a quick review of his first quarter-century in England:

King Henry had among his counsellors Bishop Roger of Salisbury on whose advice he principally relied; before his accession he placed him in charge of his household. Having experienced his ability, after Henry became king he made Roger first his chancellor and then a bishop. The able discharge of his episcopal functions gave rise to a hope that he might be deserving of a higher office. He therefore committed to his care the administration of the whole kingdom, whether he might himself be in England or absent in Normandy. But the bishop would have refused to assume so onerous a task had not the three archbishops of Canterbury, Anselm, Ralph, and William, and finally even the pope, enjoined on him this duty under obedience. Henry was very eager to achieve this because he knew that Roger would work everything for his advantage. Nor were the royal hopes misplaced, for Roger conducted himself with such integrity and diligence that no spark of envy was kindled against him. Moreover the king was frequently detained in Normandy, sometimes three, sometimes four years, or possibly longer; when he returned he laid it to his justiciar's discretion that he could find little or nothing to disturb him. Yet even amidst these cares, Roger did not neglect his ecclesiastical responsibilities, but carefully

18. William of Newburgh, 1:36–38.

attended to them in the morning so that he might be ready and undisturbed for other business.[19]

Seventeen years later William of Malmesbury's last book still acknowledged Roger's faithful adherence to religious obligations, but it no longer saw him as a reluctant administrator and rather said that he was extremely ambitious and would not hesitate to use force if other means failed to achieve his ends. Moreover, according to this changed view, "Roger was a man who knew well how to adapt himself to any situation according as the wheel of fortune changed." [20] This mature evaluation is closer to William of Newburgh's much later image of Roger as a timeserver, but it is not clear which perspective better represents the truth. Perhaps the Malmesbury monk felt less constrained when writing after the bishop's disgrace and death, or perhaps he was prejudiced by changes in his own abbey and the whole country. On the other hand, Roger himself may well have changed over the years.

William of Newburgh's portrait, while greatly overdrawn, is not incompatible with the fact that Roger was a priest of Avranches. According to the Newburgh canon, the encounter between him and young Henry occurred while the prince was fighting against his brother William Rufus. If true, this suggests a date in the spring of 1091 shortly after King William and his elder brother, Duke Robert Curthose of Normandy, had joined forces to eject Henry from lands he had purchased in the Avranchin and the Cotentin.[21] Henry was twenty-three, and Roger was probably not much older. Although Henry did not regain all these Norman lands for some years, by autumn of 1091 chivalry and family

19. William of Malmesbury, *G.R.*, 2:483–484. For a thirteenth century confirmation of this testimony, see Ralph de Diceto, *Historical Works*, 1:432, 2:77. Master Ralph cited Roger's conduct of civil affairs as a good example for other bishops.

20. William of Malmesbury, *H.N.*, pp. 5, 38.

21. Austin Lane Poole, *From Domesday Book to Magna Carta, 1087–1216*, pp. 99–113.

ties had prevailed, and the three sons of the Conqueror had united to repel a Scottish invasion of northern England. The next year Henry was again in southern Normandy ruling his few remaining subjects from Domfront and using that stronghold as a base for recapturing his lost territories.

Whenever and wherever they may have met, Henry, evidently discovering that his new chaplain was blessed with special administrative talents, soon placed Roger in complete charge of what remained of his paternal inheritance of five thousand silver pounds.[22] By curbing court expenses and carefully collecting revenues, Roger soon brought order to the prince's finances and quickly became one of his most trusted confidants. William of Malmesbury noted that Roger diligently studied Henry's character and was thereby able to anticipate his wishes.[23] A gulf of rank and profession, and probably of personality, separated these two striking individuals, and one cannot be sure that they were intimate friends; but they certainly respected one another and were most effective co-workers.

The restricted roles these men played as clever chaplain and small beseiged Norman landowner suddenly evaporated on August 2, 1100, when King William Rufus was slain while hunting in the New Forest in southern England. Whether Rufus was shot accidentally or whether Walter Tirel was an assassin is still a mystery, but Tirel's Clare relatives were certainly well favored in the new reign.[24] Henry's role in his brother's death was also ambiguous, for he, too, had been in the hunting party and he stood most to gain. The smooth execution of the next few days' events makes him doubly suspect. From the tragedy he dashed straight for Winchester, seized the royal treasure, and had himself proclaimed king. Three days after Rufus's death Henry was hastily crowned at Westminster. Duke Robert

22. David C. Douglas, *William the Conqueror,* pp. 360–361.
23. William of Malmesbury, *G.R.,* 2:483; *H.N.,* p. 37.
24. John Horace Round, *Feudal England,* p. 472. For the most recent study, see Duncan Grinnell-Milne, *The Killing of William Rufus.*

of Normandy had a better claim to England's throne, but he was conveniently off on crusade at the time. Moreover, although a renowned warrior, Curthose was a weak, self-indulgent ruler, and he seemed to lack the ruthlessness which was such a conspicuous trait of the other members of his family. Roger was probably in England during the change of monarchs, but there is no record to prove it. Once his master was enthroned, he entered the royal household, after which his movements become much easier to trace.

Chroniclers passed harsh judgments on the reign of William Rufus.[25] Showing scant regard for his subjects, his barons, or his church, according to them, the late king's pleasures had been morally reprehensible and his policies brutally oppressive. He had continually demanded money from his vassals and seized the revenues of vacant abbeys and bishoprics. His homosexual tendencies had alienated many supporters, and his quarrels with Archbishop Anselm of Canterbury about church liberties had sent that famed scholar abroad into exile. Despite his unpopularity with historical commentators, William II had been a strong sovereign who had tried to centralize his government in order to reduce feudal and baronial prerogatives and to increase his own revenues. Almost by accident temporary control of the large duchy of Normandy had fallen to his grasp when Robert Curthose had pawned it to make his crusading pilgrimage to the Holy Land. To William's credit, he had kept the peace and had skillfully administered both lands at once. On the whole, however, men hoped for better times under the new king.

At his coronation, which he said was made possible by the united will of the barons, King Henry promulgated a charter in which he promised to abolish the abuses of his late brother.[26] He swore that he would not despoil vacant church benefices, or make arbitrary exactions of lay lords.

25. Henry of Huntingdon, p. 232; *Anglo-Saxon Chronicle,* 2:176.
26. Richard of Hexham, *Historia de Gestis Stephani,* pp. 147–150; Eadmer, *H.N.,* p. 224.

To demonstrate good faith he imprisoned Rufus's clever administrative counselor, Bishop Ranulf Flambard of Durham, in the Tower of London. He also quickly recalled Archbishop Anselm, who returned to England in September 1100, longing for religious peace. In November the primate greatly enhanced the new king's rather shaky position by marrying him to Edith (or Matilda, as the Normans called her), the daughter of the king of Scotland and, through her mother, a descendant of the ancient Saxon house of Wessex.

The beginnings of the new reign offered a splendid opportunity for Henry's Norman retainers to take over the royal administration. Roger himself was considered a significant enough member of the king's household to be listed as a witness to a royal charter issued at Westminster during the first Christmas court. The text was signed "by (*per*) Roger the chaplain" indicating that he was a confidential messenger bearing the king's instructions; the attestation suggests that Roger was also probably already working in the royal chancery.[27]

A few months later, about Easter 1101, Roger was appointed chancellor of the realm succeeding William Giffard, who had received the bishopric of Winchester even before Henry's coronation.[28] Although the early twelfth-century chancellorship was not as powerful a position as it would become in later ages, this appointment was nevertheless a very important promotion for Roger. As chancellor he kept the king's seal and had a staff of two or three scribes who drafted letters and documents; these clerks also frequently served as royal chaplains.[29] Roger's salary was increased, for the chancellor received the highest wages of any member of

27. *Regesta,* 2, no. 507; Roger was apparently the first of a long line of such confidential messengers (p. *xxvii*). For his other attestations as chaplain, see nos. 521, 622. Another chaplain named Roger was also active at this time (nos. 544, 547).

28. *Ibid.,* no. 528.

29. *Regesta,* 3:*xiii–xvii;* Terrence A. M. Bishop, *Scriptores Regis,* p. 30; Thomas F. Tout, *Chapters in the Administrative History of Medieval England,* 1:127–132.

the royal household: five shillings a day plus gratuities, which included one lord's simnel loaf and two salted simnel loaves, one sextary of clear wine and one of ordinary wine, one fat candle and forty candle ends.[30] Ambitious chancellors could look to great rewards. Most bishops were selected from the royal household, and clerics who served as chancellors for a few years were regularly advanced to episcopal chairs.[31]

On September 3, 1101, a little more than one year after Henry's accession, a great assembly of lay and ecclesiastical barons, the curia regis, convened at Windsor Castle. Even Robert Curthose, recently returned from Palestine, was there. In the summer he had invaded England, claiming the crown as his own rightful inheritance, but, while brave as a warrior, he was feckless as a prince and at Alton was easily persuaded by a generous cash subsidy to acknowledge Henry's rule. At the Windsor meeting Roger the chancellor joined the duke and other great magnates in witnessing several royal charters.[32] In one addressed to the bishop of Bath Roger noted after his own name that he had dictated that charter himself.[33] This illustrates both chancery procedure and his own increasing importance.

At this curia regis Henry apparently announced that he had selected Roger to be the next bishop of the diocese of Salisbury. The precise date Roger became shepherd of Salisbury is uncertain. A charter of Archbishop Anselm which seems to have been issued about the time of the Windsor meeting bore the witness of the bishop of Salisbury, but the name space before the title was left blank.[34] This omission may have expressed some formal distinction between Roger

30. *Constitutio Domus Regis,* ed. and trans. Charles Johnson, p. 129. This was written some years after Roger's promotion, but it is doubtful that the salary varied much.

31. For more on episcopal promotions, see Chapter 4; see also Richard W. Southern, *Saint Anselm and His Biographer,* p. 146.

32. *Regesta,* 2, nos. 547–550; also, nos. 567, 592, 595, 599, 601–605, 850.

33. *"Que hanc cartam dictavi," ibid.,* no. 544.   34. *Ibid.,* no. 549.

and the other bishops, since he alone of the witnesses had not yet been invested with the insignia of his office. Roger evidently had not yet been properly elected to his see, either. Although the election notification sent to Archbishop Anselm was undated, chroniclers gave the year as 1102, with one thirteenth-century writer claiming April 13, 1102, for the election.[35] There may thus have been an interval between his nomination by the king and his election by the clergy and people of Sarum. Although Anselm was probably unhappy to have an unelected bishop attest an ecclesiastical charter, the king may have nominated Roger in September 1101, knowing full well that the Sarum canons were unlikely to oppose his choice.

Roger's elevation to the episcopal bench was adversely affected by a renewal of the religious controversies which had rocked England during the previous reign. The struggle between Anselm and William Rufus had arisen from local English problems, but it was really part of a wider effort of the reforming church to free itself from lay domina-

35. Matthew of Westminster in the *Flores Historiarum*, 2:36, gave the date April 13, 1102, for Roger's election. H. W. C. Davis, "Waldric, the Chancellor of Henry I," pp. 86–87, and the editors of *Regesta*, 2:*ix*, and no. 653, incorrectly cited this as April 13, 1103. Other thirteenth-century chroniclers, Matthew Paris, *Chronica Majora*, 2:124, and the "Annals of Margan," in *Annales Monastici*, 1:7–9, said Roger was elected in 1102, but the anonymous Margan annalist was extremely unreliable, also recording that Roger was consecrated in 1104 and ordained in 1107. The "Annals of Winchester," in *Annales Monastici*, 2:41–42, said that Roger the chancellor was made bishop in 1102 and consecrated in 1107. William of Malmesbury, *G.P.*, pp. 109–110, seemed to accept an 1102 date for Roger's election. Richardson and Sayles, *Governance of England*, p. 429 (citing Eadmer, *H.N.*, p. 141) agreed and on p. 159 said that he was nominated bishop in September 1102. Regesta, 2:*ix*, also referred to Roger's nomination in 1102, but in no. 549 (also citing Eadmer) placed his nomination in August or September 1101. Actually, Eadmer referred to Roger's investiture in 1102, not to his nomination or election. F. J. West, *The Justiciarship in England*, p. 17 (citing William of Newburgh, 1:36), strangely gave 1104 for Roger's episcopal promotion. For a study of the office of Bishop-elect, see Robert L. Benson, *The Bishop Elect* (Princeton, 1968).

tion. Pope Gregory VII (1073–1085) and his associates had launched a thoroughgoing attack on long-standing practices in the church which they considered to be terrible abuses; some historians have called their movement a veritable world revolution.[36] Clerical ignorance, marriage, nepotism, simony, and especially secular control of the choice of prelates, along with the symbols of that control—lay investiture and homage—were all forbidden. Investiture conveyed feudal properties and rights, but, since a king said "Receive the Church" when investing bishops and abbots, many felt that he was granting both temporal and spiritual powers. This inability to distinguish the offices of lay lord and ecclesiastical minister caused endless trouble as church and state competed for the primary allegiance of individual prelates.

Although Archbishop Anselm had cast his immense prestige behind Henry's usurpation of the throne, from the very beginning he refused to do homage to the king for the see of Canterbury or to receive it from Henry's hands. He had performed these ceremonies under William II, but in exile the old monk had personally heard the papal thunderings against lay investiture and now felt bound to carry out the reform decrees. Retiring by nature and scholarly by inclination, the archbishop was at best surely a reluctant Gregorian.[37] Moreover, he and the king respected each other's unique responsibilities, and both wanted to avoid a tragic confrontation like that of the last reign. They had therefore agreed to postpone any final decision about their differences until Easter 1101. Meanwhile, Henry gave the archbishop his temporalities without homage and Anselm agreed to appeal to the reigning pope, Paschal II, to mitigate

36. Norman F. Cantor, *Church, Kingship, and Lay Investiture in England, 1089–1135* (hereafter cited as Cantor, *Lay Investiture*), p. 7. For a recent analysis of the whole reform, see Gerd Tellenbach, *Church, State, and Christian Society at the Time of the Investiture Contest.*

37. Southern, *Saint Anselm and His Biographer,* pp. 180–182.

his prohibition of lay investiture and homage of priests in favor of traditional English usage.

Paschal, a fervent reformer, refused to change his decrees; his reply arrived in summer 1101, when Henry was preparing to face Robert Curthose's invasion. Since he was then not yet sure that his brother would accept a cash settlement, the king attempted to gain wide ecclesiastical support by promising to abolish lay investitures. In September, after having made peace with his brother, Henry went back on his word and asked Anselm to consecrate the bishop and abbots whom he had earlier invested. Anselm refused and suggested another embassy to Rome. This postponement also was acceptable to the king, and a second appeal was sent off. Roger's episcopal consecration was, of course, deferred by this action, but enforcement of the reform decrees had prevented even his investiture.

The envoys to the pope, led by Archbishop Gerard of York, returned to England at the end of August 1102. They alleged that, although Pope Paschal had written uncompromising letters to Anselm and Henry, he privately had confided to the messengers that he would not excommunicate anyone in England because of lay investitures.[38] Anselm's own representatives on the delegation denied this report, but he himself had discovered in exile how papal policy might adjust itself to external pressure. The story seemed conceivable, so he embraced it as a pretext for avoiding an open break with the king and suggested yet a third mission to the pope to confirm this latest guideline. Meanwhile, on the strength of the report, he granted Henry permission to invest ecclesiastics without fear of censure. The king quickly invested his chancellor, Roger, with the episcopal ring and pastoral staff of Salisbury; another Roger, the royal larderer, was given the symbols for Hereford. The ceremony occurred at the Michaelmas court, September 29,

38. Eadmer, *H.N.*, pp. 120–138; Cantor, *Lay Investiture*, pp. 147–180.

1102.[39] Shortly thereafter Roger resigned from his position as royal chancellor.[40]

At Michaelmas Anselm held a synod which the newly invested bishops attended. Setting aside the investiture problem for the moment, he focused on other aspects of church reform. Canons were promulgated which made celibacy mandatory for all clerics in holy orders, down to and including subdeacons; simony was condemned; and bishops were directed to avoid judicial responsibilities.

Although he associated with the new bishops, Anselm steadfastly declined to consecrate anyone but William Giffard, who had been appointed while Anselm was in exile. Henry wanted all three consecrated and impetuously decided not to await the return of the latest embassy to the pope. He asked Archbishop Gerard of York to consecrate the new bishops, even though this was clearly uncanonical since the men were suffragans of Canterbury. The bishops awaiting consecration reacted in diverse ways. Roger the larderer, elect of Hereford, had died, and Henry had quickly invested Reinhelm, the queen's chancellor, with his place. Rather than accept consecration by the archbishop of York, Reinhelm returned his ring and crosier to the king. Roger and William were to be consecrated at London, but, according to the Canterbury monk Eadmer, right before the ceremony William threw the assembled clergy into confusion by protesting the legality of the consecrations. Shortly thereafter he was exiled from the kingdom.[41] No protest by Bishop Roger was recorded, but William of Malmesbury said he acted so prudently that neither the king nor Anselm was offended.[42] It was no mean feat to retain the good graces of

39. Eadmer, *H.N.*, pp. 140–141; William of Malmesbury, *G.P.*, pp. 109–110; Symeon of Durham, 2:235; Florence of Worcester, 2:51.

40. Waldric was his successor (*Regesta*, 2, no. 618). For a short time Roger had served both as chancellor and as bishop (nos. 592, 593, 595, 596).

41. Eadmer, *H.N.*, pp. 141–142.

42. William of Malmesbury, *G.P.*, pp. 109–110.

both these men who were so ultrasensitive about the dignity of their positions. Shortly after this, on January 13, 1103, Roger paid his first recorded visit to Salisbury, where he may have accepted jurisdiction of his see; his sacramental powers, of course, still awaited consecration.[43]

Pope Paschal's answer in Lent 1103 gave the lie to the report of the previous embassy: he had never promised not to excommunicate anyone. Furthermore, to demonstrate his high regard for Anselm he reviewed a long-standing Canterbury-York dispute and ordered Gerard of York to recognize the superior dignity of Canterbury by making due submission to its archbishop. Emboldened by this papal support, Anselm again demanded that the king abandon lay investiture. Henry refused; but as a last measure to avert an absolute break with Rome, he entreated the weary archbishop to plead the royal side of the dispute before the pope. Anselm had little choice; shortly after Easter 1103 he sailed from England, beginning what proved to be his second exile. It lasted four winters. In a very petty act, Henry confiscated the revenues of Canterbury in 1104.

The years of waiting for episcopal consecration apparently made Roger careless of any written distinction between bishop and bishop-elect. When he witnessed charters he used the terms interchangeably, as, for example, on February 13, 1105, when from Romsey he bade farewell to the king, who was sailing for Normandy.[44] In March of the same year, Pope Paschal, out of exasperation at Henry's intransigence, excommunicated Count Robert of Meulan, Henry's principal lay adviser and a vigorous opponent of the clergy.[45] The papal intent was obvious; the anathema would touch Henry himself unless he changed his policy.

The pope's warning was well timed. Henry had gone to Normandy to pose as the savior of its oppressed people and

43. *Regesta*, 2, no. 626.   44. *Ibid.*, nos. 682, 683.
45. Anselm, *Opera Omnia*, letters 353, 354; Cantor, *Lay Investiture*, pp. 199–235.

church. His supporters were claiming that Duke Robert had forfeited the right to rule by his failure to maintain public order and protect the churches from rapacious lay lords.[46] The king had warned his brother, writing him to stop acting like a monk and to start governing like a duke.[47] Now Henry proclaimed that he would bring peace to the Norman church himself. To make his propaganda plausible, Henry first had to settle his own problems with the pope and the English hierarchy. He therefore sought out Anselm in Normandy, and at Laigle in July 1105 they arrived at a personal reconciliation.[48] The king indicated that he was willing to surrender investing bishops with the insignia representing the spiritual functions of their office, but that prelates must still perform homage for their lands and temporalities. He further agreed to treat with the pope before Christmas. Following this informal accord, Anselm released Robert of Meulan from his excommunication.[49]

Christmas came and went, and no royal rider left for Rome. Henry was clearly in no hurry to abandon lay investiture and the theocratic monarchy that implied. Furthermore, late in 1105, rumors circulated in the court that the old archbishop was about to give up the ghost. It would certainly be an opportune moment. An unnamed prelate, very possibly the ambitious bishop-elect of Salisbury, was already looking forward to leading the English church, it was said.[50] Unfortunately for his dreams and the king's plans, the ailing monk clung to life. Reluctantly, Henry sent his men off to the pope.

Word of the pope's acceptance of the Laigle compromise reached Anselm at Rouen in June 1106.[51] Receiving the news

46. Orderic Vitalis, 4:204–206.
47. William of Malmesbury, *G.R.*, 2:474.
48. Eadmer, *H.N.*, p. 166.
49. Perhaps Robert himself urged the compromise (see Cantor, *Lay Investiture*, pp. 236–237).
50. Anselm, *Opera Omnia*, letter 373; Cantor, *Lay Investiture*, p. 260.
51. Eadmer, *H.N.*, p. 177; Anselm *Opera Omnia*, letter 397.

in England a short while later, King Henry rewarded the messenger, William Warelwast, with the vacant bishopric of Exeter. Pope Paschal had expressed satisfaction with the abolition of lay investiture and reluctantly agreed that, even if prelates had done homage for their fiefs, they should not be deprived of benediction on that account. He thought of this as a temporary concession and prayed that the king's heart would soon soften and then also remit this objectionable ceremony; King Henry, however, continued to demand ecclesiastical homage throughout his reign. The pope may have yielded on this point in the hope of enlisting the king's support for a new crusade.[52] Henry had other conquests in mind, however. Archbishop Anselm was recalled to England, but, since he was too ill to travel, the king crossed to meet him at his former monastery at Bec on August 15, the feast of the Assumption of the Virgin. Their reunion was joyful and tearful in the manner of most medieval reconciliations, and the king promised to restore Canterbury's temporalities as soon as Anselm landed in England.

Six weeks later, on September 28, 1106, forty years to the day after the historic Norman invasion at Pevensey, King Henry and his English levies routed his brother's forces at Tinchebrai, capturing Duke Robert and most of his followers. It was a decisive victory, and both shores of the Channel were again to be ruled by one man. The king entrusted his priceless captive to Bishop Roger, who for the next twenty years kept Curthose in close but honorable custody in a great fortress at Devizes on the Salisbury Plain.[53] This was an extraordinary demonstration of royal confidence; it also suggests that at such critical times the king relied more on his bishops than on his lay barons, who might

52. Cantor, *Lay Investiture,* pp. 262–263.
53. Orderic Vitalis, 4:146; Charles W. David, *Robert Curthose, Duke of Normandy,* pp. 179–180, 186–189. For a more fanciful account of the duke's confinement, see Matthew Paris, *Historia Anglorum,* 1:206, 3:180. For more on Devizes, see Chapter 3.

be tempted to use someone like the duke for their own personal or feudal advantage.

It was about this same time that the king gave Roger the important marcher lordship of Kidwelly in southern Wales.[54] The bishop constructed a castle there, and a borough gradually rose in its shadow. Tower and town watched the frontier and pacified the area.

The king remained in Normandy until early April 1107, savoring his triumph and reorganizing his duchy. The official settlement of the investiture controversy was to have been celebrated at Easter but had to be delayed because of Anselm's continuing illness. At last, on August 1, 1107, the curia regis met in London to signify the end of the long struggle.[55] For three days the magnates of the kingdom, lay and spiritual, debated the issues. Then Anselm went to court, and he and the king drew up the agreement itself. The terms followed those of Laigle: henceforth no layman in England would invest any prelate with the spiritual symbols of his office; consecration would not be denied to those who must perform homage for their temporalities; the archbishop of York would promise obedience to Anselm of Canterbury.

To climax the settlement Archbishop Anselm consecrated Roger and the other bishops-elect who had waited so patiently. In a truly magnificent ceremony at Canterbury cathedral on August 11, 1107, Roger was anointed third bishop of Salisbury. A copy of his ritual submission to Anselm as Primate of All England still exists.[56] With him were consecrated Reinhelm for Hereford, William Giffard for Winchester (both now restored to the king's good graces), William Warelwast for Exeter, and Urban for

54. Lynn H. Nelson, *The Normans in South Wales, 1070–1171*, p. 122.

55. William of Malmesbury, *G.P.*, p. 117; Eadmer, *H.N.*, p. 187; Symeon of Durham, 2:239; Florence of Worcester, 2:56.

56. Charter 1.

Glamorgan. Contemporary chroniclers could not remember when so many bishops had been consecrated together.[57]

None of Roger's views about the Gregorian reform have been uncovered, but something of his attitude may be gauged from his mode of life. He had skillfully declined an illicit consecration by Gerard of York but apparently had made no dramatic protest at the king's attempt to circumvent Archbishop Anselm's policies. In later years he would dispute the king's choice of particular prelates, but it is doubtful that he ever questioned Henry's right to choose.[58] Many of his episcopal colleagues visited the popes, but there is no indication that Roger ever did. After becoming bishop, he tried to avoid governmental assignments, and shortly after his investiture in 1102 he resigned from the chancellorship, although, unlike Anselm, he did not believe that administrative and judicial work were basically incompatible with episcopal status.[59] Oddly enough, Anselm himself is said to have urged Roger to accept governmental responsibilities.[60] No hint of simony ever touched the bishop, but his records on clerical marriage and nepotism were quite un-Gregorian.

Several years after Roger's death the author of the *Gesta Stephani* vaguely criticized him for wanton living.[61] This was probably a veiled reference to his long association with Matilda of Ramsbury, the only woman known to have shared his life. Orderic Vitalis, writing in Normandy just after the bishop's death, was the sole chronicler ever to mention Matilda, but in his pages she appears as a devoted mother and an intelligent, determined woman.[62] Ramsbury was an episcopal manor near Salisbury and a few of the cathedral canons, possibly Matilda's relations, came from

57. See Note 55.   58. See Chapter 4.

59. The witnesses to *Regesta*, 2, nos. 898, 901, imply two persons, the bishop and the chancellor, not one man acting in two capacities. See also Note 40.

60. William of Malmesbury, *G.R.*, 2:483–484.

61. *Gesta Stephani*, p. 64.

62. Orderic Vitalis, 5:120–121; see Chapter 6 for her role in 1139 and Appendix 3 for more on her and her family.

there. She and Roger had at least one son, a lad whom later historians called Roger the Pauper who became chancellor of the realm under King Stephen. Another possible son of theirs, Adelelm, became a royal treasurer, Salisbury archdeacon, and dean of Lincoln cathedral. Matilda herself controlled the viceroy's huge castle at Devizes as late as the last year of his life, and it is obvious that their relationship was much more than a casual affair. Orderic called her a concubine, but this may have been because canon law considered a bishop to be married to his church. Evidently, other contemporary writers found Roger's behavior unexceptional, were ignorant of it, or were unusually discreet, even after his passing. Since the reforming church was so adamant about enforcing clerical celibacy and the Anglo-Norman bishops themselves were so strict about it, it is rather surprising to find Roger so deliberately, continuously, and successfully defying church law on this major issue.[63]

Nepotism was a common practice also under attack by the Gregorians, but in Roger's case and in the English church as a whole they were unsuccessful in preventing clerics from placing their sons and nephews in important, well endowed benefices. The word *nephew* was frequently used as a polite euphemism for illegitimate son; William of Malmesbury described Roger the Pauper in this fashion.[64] He also said that he was a young man, and that his father loved him very dearly. The fact that Roger the Poor was referred to as young in 1139 indicates that he was born after the bishop's consecration in 1107. Bishop Roger gave him and his probable brother, Adelelm, wealthy archdeaconries at Salisbury; they also seemed destined for brilliant governmental careers, for young Roger became the chancellor under King Stephen, while Adelelm was royal treasurer.[65] The viceroy's disgrace

63. The English episcopate was very strict about celibacy, but the Norman clergy was not (see C. N. L. Brooke, "Gregorian Reform in Action, Clerical Marriage in England," pp. 11–16).
64. William of Malmesbury, *H.N.*, p. 39.
65. For more on Roger and Adelelm, see Appendix 3.

cut short their professions, however. The specific meaning of the cognomen *Poor* or *Pauper* (never applied to Adelelm) is uncertain, but it may simply distinguish Roger from his cousins and from his father. Surely young Roger was not poor in any commonly accepted sense of the term. It was not a family name, and, despite the designation by later historians, there is no evidence that Bishop Roger himself was ever called Roger le Poer.[66]

Other nephews of the bishop, probably sons of his brother Humphrey, were also pushed up clerical and curial ladders to success and prominence. Alexander and Nigel were given good educations at the cathedral school of Laon, arch-deaconries and benefices at Sarum, and then bishoprics of their own. Alexander was made bishop of Lincoln in 1123; ten years later Nigel, after having been royal treasurer, was elected to the fenland see of Ely. William of Malmesbury considered them learned and industrious men.[67] Both Henry of Huntingdon and Geoffrey of Monmouth dedicated their histories to Alexander. Each nephew appears to have been a minor author, himself. Alexander may have compiled a dictionary of Anglo-Saxon legal terms, the *Expositiones Vocabulorum;* Nigel, writing about 1135, probably was the author of the *Constitutio Domus Regis,* a brief description of the royal household.[68] Before his consecration Nigel had a son, Richard Fitz Nigel, or Fitz Neal, who eventually served as a treasurer of King Henry II and later as bishop of London. Fitz Nigel's masterpiece, *The Dialogue of the Exchequer,* lavished praise upon his great-uncle, Bishop Roger, by describing in considerable detail his contributions to the financial organization of the kingdom.[69]

66. William Stubbs, *Historical Introductions to the Rolls Series,* pp. 145, 299–300; Brooke, "Clerical Marriage," p. 16; Richardson and Sayles, *Governance of England,* p. 158; see also Appendix 3.

67. William of Malmesbury, *H.N.,* p. 38.

68. See the introductions to the *Red Book of the Exchequer,* ed. Hubert Hall, 2:*cclxii–cclxiii,* and the *Constitutio Domus Regis,* ed. Charles Johnson, pp. *xlix–l.*

69. See Chapter 2 for Richard Fitz Nigel's remarks.

These relatives and their descendants form a dynasty of ecclesiastical and governmental servants the viceroy may be said to have founded.[70] By the time he bestowed these benefices on his family, the reform impetus in the church had lost much of its original thrust, and the bishop easily evaded religious censure. In fact, Roger's nepotism was not much different from that of most other bishops, and his continuing effort on behalf of his dependents reveals relatively little about his personality, beyond a determined persistence to protect and provide for his own. Nevertheless, William of Malmesbury was struck by it and noted with some surprise that Roger was quite modest in discussing his relatives' accomplishments and that he rarely boasted about his success in obtaining such high positions for them.[71]

In 1107 Roger was a new bishop who had raised himself by his talents and the king's favor. Experience as chaplain, chancellor, and bishop-elect prepared him for the additional responsibilities, status, wealth, and power which episcopal consecration conferred. These early experiences also highlight threads which can be discerned running through his whole life: a positive genius for administration; a deep, but not completely altruistic, involvement in the church; a calculated accommodation of his will to his lord's; and a continuing struggle to maintain his own standards and advantage. He was a pragmatic man of principle.

70. See Appendix 3 for an analysis of his family.
71. William of Malmesbury, *H.N.*, p. 38.

Second Only to the King,
1108–1135

ADMINISTRATION was a major part of Roger of Salisbury's lifework, and his ideas and actions reshaped the Anglo-Norman government and erected foundations for institutions and procedures which last to this very day. Oddly enough, the innovations of the reign of Henry I have tended to obscure the men who created the changes. If Roger's hand cannot be traced in every experiment and fluctuation of policy between 1100 and 1135, this is understandable. His contemporaries never doubted that his genius ultimately presided over the governmental accomplishments of the reign, and we would do well to accept their testimony.

Administration is not an exciting or romantic art, nor is its progress even necessarily marked by clear turning points. Its cumulative effect is more important than any one of its individual processes, and the temptation to discover perfected systems in mere trial efforts must be resisted. Viewed from the present, successful steps frequently seem to have been inevitable, but the reality is probably very different. Trial, error, and pragmatic development may well have been more significant than plan or purpose. Administration is a very human, temporal endeavor which urges men to become conscious of their own society and reflect on its institutions.[1] Above all, the attempt to create an effective, impersonal gov-

1. Marc Bloch, *Feudal Society,* pp. 106–108, suggests that the investiture controversy prompted men to become critical of their institutions.

ernment paradoxically relies on the initial influence of outstanding individuals.

Can the viceroy's achievements be evaluated, as well as described? If so, which standard should be used? Were his actions good for the king, for himself, for the country as a whole? Did he merely faithfully execute the king's commands or did he show independent initiative? Fortunately, several scholars have already devoted great attention to medieval adminstrative history.[2] By building on their research and emphasizing Roger's own activity, an approach might be made to some of these questions, and perhaps a larger picture of the reality of Anglo-Norman government may emerge. There are tensions within the sources, however. For example, many now think increased governmental centralization is a good thing; documentary collections and analyses tend to support this viewpoint. On the other hand, most twelfth-century writers, especially the monks, judged it a threat to local autonomy. This was especially true when Bishop Roger tried to systematize his diocese in the same way he was streamlining civil affairs. For the moment, it may be enough to suggest that some of his governmental reforms probably provoked even more opposition than the contemporary writers recorded.

Rational government had come a long way by 1100. The king no longer kept his records in his head and his treasures in a chest at the foot of his bed, but the early days of Henry's rule still reflected the informal, highly personal nature of his father's and brother's reigns. The royal court, or curia regis, remained the king and his friends, the officials of his household, and others whose advice he sought. Although some chronicles complained of long-haired dandies at court, most

2. For example, Richardson and Sayles, *Governance of England,* pp. 159–190, 216–250, who also give much attention to Bishop Roger's contributions, especially pp. 156–166; see also Chrimes, *Administrative History,* pp. 18–32; Jacques Boussard, "Les institutions financières de l'Angleterre au XIIe siècle." For a recent general treatment, see Norman F. Cantor, *The English,* pp. 22–35.

officials, whatever their dress, worked very hard.[3] The court
traveled ceaselessly throughout the country, and local barons
drifted in and out as it passed their way. When a major
decision was to be made or the king were to wear his ceremonial crown, as at Easter, Pentecost, and Christmas, greater
numbers of vassals might be summoned, but ordinarily the
court was fairly simple. Like his predecessors, Henry had a
passion for hunting, but otherwise he was no spendthrift,
and his magnificent displays were carefully calculated and
controlled.

The permanent members of the court, those who served
the king and rode with him (including a good number of
bishops), soon developed interests apart from those of the
barons who were only consulted on occasion. Some scholars
have seen these curialists forming almost a separate small
court distinct from the great curia regis into which it sometimes merged.[4] This is probably too formal a distinction for
Henry's reign, but even contemporaries recognized that the
king's close advisers and ministers were different from other
barons in background, education, and loyalty.[5] Despite this,
the kingdom was still essentially a feudal land, with most
people living far from government and sharing intensely
local concerns. Sheriffs and justiciars might bring royal
commands to the populace, but the barons of the countryside
were the real powers in the villages of England.

The first two Norman kings had made considerable efforts
to provide for the secretarial, financial, and judicial needs of
their governments, and trained clerks were already laying
the groundwork for a later bureaucracy. Domesday Book
is a monument to the self-effacing efforts of these men who
were steadily extending royal power at the expense of local
and feudal privilege. Approximately five hundred extant
charters and writs demonstrate the extent of royal rule be-

3. Eadmer, *H.N.*, p. 214.
4. For example, Bryce Lyon, *A Constitutional and Legal History
of Medieval England*, pp. 142–151.
5. *Gesta Stephani*, pp. 15–16; Orderic Vitalis, 4:164–165.

tween 1066 and 1100; from the thirty-five years of Henry's reign more than fifteen hundred writs remain as impressive testimony to the expansion of monarchial government and control.

The government was a complex of feudal and personal relations. William I had supervised most things himself, but when he sailed to Normandy he ordered his half-brother, Bishop Odo of Bayeux, to manage his kingdom. Later he found a more trustworthy viceruler in Archbishop Lanfranc of Canterbury. William Rufus rarely went abroad, but he still gave Ranulf Flambard wide administrative powers.[6] Nevertheless, until he was made bishop of Durham at the end of the reign, Flambard lacked any significant status or feudal eminence of his own. He was one of the first professional administrators, but, according to some scholars, not really a chief justiciar.[7]

Since he was frequently absent from his kingdom—at times for years on end—King Henry also needed a thoroughly reliable viceroy who could assume complete charge in his absence. He selected Roger of Salisbury and evidently never regretted his choice. The accident of chance and the interest of chroniclers have combined to preserve more evidence about the coordinated activity of Henry and Roger than about the bishop's independent role as viceroy, but there were long intervals when Roger's own judgment controlled English affairs.[8] Henry crossed to Normandy at least eleven times:

> August 1104–December 1104
> February 1105–August 1105
> August 1106–March or April 1107

6. Richard W. Southern, "Ranulf Flambard and Early Anglo-Norman Administration."

7. Richardson and Sayles, *Governance of England,* p. 164; West, *Justiciarship in England,* pp. 10–13. Orderic Vitalis, 4:107, however, said of him, *"Summus regiarum procurator opum et justiciarius factus est."*

8. See Appendix 1, where Henry's absences and Roger's activities are correlated.

July 1108–June 1109
August 1111–July 1113
September 1114–July 1115
April 1116–November 1120 (4½ years)
June 1123–September 1126 (3 years)
August 1127–July 1129
August 1130–August 1131
August 1133–December 1135 (death) [9]

In all, the king spent about half his reign abroad. He usually left and returned by Portsmouth harbor, where Roger frequently appeared to bid him farewell or greet him on his return. One can easily imagine the king's issuing last-minute instructions to his viceroy as he left and asking countless questions when he arrived back. Roger very rarely left the country, but a constant flow of writs kept them in continual touch; royal commands survived, but, unfortunately, viceregal replies did not.

Roger was not only the governor of an absent king, he was also Henry's administrative chief whenever the monarch was in England. The bishop did not step into an office which had established traditions or responsibilities. As Lady Stenton put it, "Roger of Salisbury is constitutionally an elusive figure. He was the king's alter ego in an age when the techniques of government were still experimental, and there was as yet no constitutional scheme into which he could be neatly fitted." [10] Sometimes he executed royal affairs at the king's direction: on other occasions he was given wide latitude and independence. His powers were obviously delegated, however, and always subject to withdrawal at the king's pleasure. The fact that Henry only increased Roger's authority is itself a demonstration of his ability and success, at least by one standard. He supervised the existing machinery of government and created new institutions to enhance its

9. *Regesta*, 2:*xxxix–xxxi*.

10. Doris M. Stenton, *English Justice Between the Norman Conquest and the Great Charter, 1066–1216* (hereafter cited as Stenton, *English Justice*), p. 60.

efficiency, cared for the myriad details of daily problems, and planned new directions for its operations. Justice and finance absorbed much of his attention, but little escaped him. There is no evidence that his authority ran beyond the island kingdom, and, since there was peace except for frontier expansion, military affairs were apparently of little consequence under him. Secretaries and sheriffs, farmers and knights, merchants and monks, lords and bishops, all dealt with him and received his commands, for he was the king's instrument, intermediary, and representative.

Roger's first appearance as second-in-command of the king's government left no dramatic imprint in the court records or contemporary accounts. Probably it was not an event at all, for Henry usually advanced men to authority and power gradually. When the king's seemingly endless series of voyages to Normandy began in 1104, he designated Queen Matilda as his formal regent. Although she took an active part in government, her husband undoubtedly directed some particular individual to be her principal assistant. Roger's earlier service as chaplain and chancellor and his later prominence as chief justiciar suggest that the king chose him. Certainly Matilda and Roger were working together by 1109 at the latest. The queen continued to act as regent during most of Henry's trips and, when he came of age, their son also briefly served.[11] Although the respective strengths of queen regent and appointed viceroy cannot be measured, their responsibilities apparently never conflicted. Matilda was more than a figurehead, but Roger's power does not seem to have been diminished by her title. By 1120 both Matilda and her son William had died and Roger's authority and position were obvious to all. In the first decade of the century, however, the pattern is more difficult to perceive. At one point Henry sought out Archbishop Anselm's advice

11. West, *Justiciarship in England*, pp. 14–15; Richardson and Sayles, *Governance of England*, pp. 162–163, 189. In 1106 or 1107 the queen went to Normandy, however (*Regesta*, 2, no. 809), perhaps this was when Roger's role first became evident.

and the primate seems to have been the man who urged Roger to assume control of the government.

After the settlement of the investiture controversy, the king asked Archbishop Anselm to become involved in the royal administration. In 1108, for example, the primate complained to the king that lay lords were mistreating the common people, and Henry ordered that such barons should be punished by mutilation.[12] The same year the king also took steps to upgrade his coinage and prevent counterfeiting. Again the penalty was severe—blinding and castration—but Anselm's friend Eadmer believed that the coinage reforms brought great good to the whole kingdom.[13]

When he sailed for Normandy in July 1108, Henry committed his kingdom to Anselm and declared that whatever he commanded should be law, whatever he forbade should be illegal.[14] A while later, writing to the archbishop from Normandy, Henry observed in passing that he had notified his other justiciars that they should act by Anselm's advice.[15] Apparently Henry was also trying to organize Normandy about this time, for as early as 1109 Bishop John of Lisieux seems to have headed the administration there. He usually acted in concert with the seneschal, however.[16] The greater independence of the Norman barons and the frequent rebellions which troubled the duchy prevented Bishop John from ever becoming as effective in Normandy as Bishop Roger was in England.

According to William of Malmesbury, Roger accepted control of the administration of the whole kingdom very reluctantly, and three successive archbishops of Canterbury —Anselm, Ralph, and William—and finally even the pope had to enjoin this duty on him under obedience.[17] This

12. Eadmer, *H.N.*, p. 193.   13. *Ibid.*   14. *Ibid.*
15. Anselm, *Opera Omnia*, letter 461; *Regesta*, 2, no. 910; Richardson and Sayles, *Governance of England*, pp. 159, 165.
16. Charles Homer Haskins, *Norman Institutions*, p. 99; West, *Justiciarship in England*, pp. 27–30.
17. William of Malmesbury, *G.R.*, 2:483–484. Richardson and Sayles, *Governance of England*, pp. 159–160, believe Roger was granted all his powers in 1109, but it seems much more probable

means that Roger must have accepted direction of the government by late 1108 or early 1109 at the latest, since Anselm died in March of the latter year. And if the Malmesbury monk's account is true—and there is nothing to refute it —Roger must have tried to resign his duties more than once. This intriguing insight into his character hardly fits the conventional picture of him as an ambitious, self-seeking timeserver. Nevertheless, in the same breath William also recorded that King Henry forced the issue "because he knew that Roger would do everything for his [Henry's] advantage." Henry's commitment of the kingdom to Anselm was probably more a formal courtesy than anything else.

The titles most frequently used by contemporaries and later historians to describe Roger's position as principal administrative official in the kingdom were justiciar, justiciar of all England, and chief justiciar.[18] Francis West has studied this office in great detail, particularly in the later twelfth and thirteenth centuries, and, because Roger's position and power were personal rather than clearly defined, he sees the bishop as a forerunner of later justiciars but not one of their lineal ancestors. For him, Henry's government was a period of experimentation, rather than final resolution of problems.[19] From the vantage point of later justiciars' more predictable roles all this is true, but in his day, earlier in the century, too much emphasis ought not be placed on titles or strict definitions; Roger's exercise of his powers was radically different from that of his predecessors, which is the main point.[20] He was a pioneer in government, both because of the things he did and because of the example he set for future leaders.

In the early twelfth century *justiciar* was a vague, widely

that his authority gradually increased; see also West, *Justiciarship in England,* pp. 17–18.

18. Henry of Huntingdon, p. 245; Richard Fitz Nigel, p. 15; *Chronicon Abbatiae Rameseinsis,* ed. W. Dunn Macray (hereafter cited as *Ramsay Chronicle*), p. 255.

19. West, *Justiciarship in England,* pp. 23, 30.

20. Richardson and Sayles, *Governance of England,* pp. 157, 164–165.

used general term meaning a minister, a justice, or an official. Royal representatives on the local level or men empowered for a single ad hoc purpose were frequently called justiciars; some were resident, and some traveled from place to place.[21] As early as 1106 Roger had served in such a purely local capacity when King Henry had sent him and the men of Dorset a writ instructing him and Alfred of Lincoln to act "as justiciars" to protect the abbot of Abbotsbury and guard his property.[22]

The other phrases were not applied exclusively to Roger, either. Ranulf Flambard was termed Justiciar of all England, but so were Roger's colleagues Bishop Robert Bloet of Lincoln, Bishop Herbert Losinga of Norwich, Ralph and Richard Basset, Geoffrey Ridel, and Aubrey de Vere.[23] This designation probably indicated that their authority was valid throughout several shires.[24] The other phrase, *chief justiciar* (*capitalis justiciarius*), may mean more to us than it did to contemporaries. It has been suggested, for example, that the Bassets held the great justiciarship themselves, but this seems an exaggeration of some vague primacy they may have exercised over itinerant justices.[25] The fact that others besides Roger had such titles reminds us that, although Roger was the principal governmental official, he was by no means the only one, and the king did not feel it necesary that all work be channeled through his viceroy. Even when abroad Henry sent his commands directly to many men; Bishop Roger, however, received the greatest number.

21. H. A. Cronne, "The Office of Local Justiciar in England Under the Norman Kings."

22. *Regesta*, 2, no. 754.

23. Christina of Markyate, p. 41; Henry of Huntingdon, pp. 245, 290, 299, 318; William de Vere mentions his father in *"Liber de Miraculis S. Osithae,"* quoted in John Leland, *Itinerary*, 5:172. For examples of these men acting as justiciars, see *Regesta*, 2, nos. 1094, 1129, 1608, 1882.

24. Richardson and Sayles, *Governance of England*, p. 174; West, *Justiciarship in England*, p. 23.

25. William T. Reedy, "The Origins of the General Eyre in the Reign of Henry I," pp. 694–695, reviewed this issue; see also West, *Justiciarship in England*, p. 23; Stenton, *English Justice*, pp. 60–65.

Roger apparently never used the word *justiciar* to describe his responsibilities. He was usually content to style himself simply as the bishop of Salisbury.[26] Once he was addressed as *Anglie provisori,* and twice he referred to himself as procurator.[27] Both expressions can be translated as administrator, regent, viceroy, or even justiciar.[28] The word *procurator* also seems to have had vague financial connotations.[29] I prefer the term *viceroy* and think this probably best conveys an understanding of the varied, quasi-royal nature of Roger's responsibilities, as it suggests a universally recognized, delegated authority, power limited only by the king, wide but unspecified duties, and complete direction of all facets of government. Roger's role as viceroy was a uniquely personal, cooperative arrangement. Elevation to the episcopacy gave him fiscal independence and rough social equality with the barons he would rule; intimate relations with King Henry gave his commands authority and force; genius and industry crowned his efforts with solid achievement.

Even if his position wanted definition and title, Roger certainly did not lack preeminence in his work. His contemporaries agreed that at his will "in the days of King Henry, all the business of the kingdom was conducted, for being second only to the king, he was exalted above all the judges and princes of the kingdom." [30] In 1125 when William of Malmesbury first wrote of Roger's position, he stressed the difficulty of the bishop's task, his diligence, in-

26. See his charters in Appendix 2. West, *Justiciarship in England,* p. 19, suggests that Roger may not have used another title because his position was well known through some public instrument, now lost.

27. British Museum Manuscripts, Egerton 3031, fo. 47; Harley 1708, fo. 195; Charters 9 and 10.

28. Richardson and Sayles, *Governance of England,* p. 161. The office was not mentioned in the *Constitutio Domus Regis* (written about 1135), indicating that it was not considered a household position.

29. Stenton, *English Justice,* p. 60.

30. John of Hexham, *Historia,* p. 302. The phrase "second only to the king" was also used in *Gesta Stephani,* p. 48, but Henry of Huntingdon also applied it to Robert Bloet, p. 299.

tegrity, and good, blameless reputation.[31] Power creates
enemies, however, and seventeen years later William's report
claimed that many men envied the viceroy's success.[32] Unless
there was a change in Roger's methods, it is hard to recon-
cile these conflicting observations except to suggest that, although he was clever, efficient, and eager to advance his
own family, the bishop was evidently less overbearing than
might have been expected. Although the Malmesbury monk
did not make the connection, Roger's reluctance about governmental service may have grown from a realization that
his great competence would eventually arouse hostility.

There is no clear pattern in Bishop Roger's viceregal activity, nor is there any indication that he himself ever devised
any master plan to isolate and solve major problems. His administrative concerns were largely financial and judicial, but
he seems to have met demands as they arose, sometimes finding solutions which lasted beyond the moment of need. His
first great undertakings, the collection of a marriage aid
for the king's daughter and the consequent creation of a
permanent exchequer, seem to exhibit these characteristics.
One of the most remarkable features about both these
achievements is the relative speed with which they were
accomplished so early after Roger became viceroy.

Like any baron, King Henry was concerned that his
children should marry well and that their weddings should
serve his purposes. Although more than thirty natural offspring sought his favors at one time or another, he had
only two legitimate children, William and Matilda. Wanting a firm alliance with the Holy Roman Empire after his
Norman victory, the king arranged for the betrothal of
eight-year-old Matilda to the German emperor, Henry V.
To provide a suitable dowry, the English king ordered that
a feudal aid be collected in her behalf.

31. William of Malmesbury, *G.R.*, 2:483–484.
32. William of Malmesbury, *H.N.*, p. 37. Richard Fitz Nigel, p.
50, later claimed that no one in England envied Nigel of Ely. This
filial wish was hardly a credible observation.

Traditionally, a lord could request an aid from his vassals when his eldest son was knighted, his eldest daughter was married, or he himself was captured and held for ransom. Although these aids were recognized feudal prerogatives and would later be enshrined in the Magna Carta, the particular gift for Matilda may be the first recorded instance of such an aid's actually being collected. It was a massive undertaking and Roger's first test as administrator of the realm. In 1110 the aid was paid throughout the kingdom at the rate of three shillings for each hide of land, a very heavy burden that year because severe storms had badly damaged the crops.[33] Nevertheless, a writ addressed to Roger noted that the aid had been formally granted by the barons themselves.[34] When King Henry gave young Matilda in marriage to Emperor Henry on January 7, 1114, with her went a dowry of forty-five thousand pounds, a tremendous sum and evidence of the successful work of the new justiciar.[35] No wonder William of Malmesbury said Henry knew Roger would work everything for his advantage.[36]

Little is known about the actual process of gathering the silver coins, but several writs testify to the legal suits which accompanied it as great magnates rushed to obtain individual exemptions. The king sent one writ to inform Roger that he had quitclaimed five hides of land of Abbot Faritius of Abingdon, a royal favorite and former court physician.[37] In 1110 the king also wrote to the "barons of the exchequer," declaring that he did not wish the land of Lincoln cathedral to be assessed for his daughter's aid.[38] Oddly enough, no evi-

33. Henry of Huntingdon, p. 237; *Anglo-Saxon Chronicle*, 2:182.
34. *Regesta*, 2, no. 959; *Chronicon Monasterii de Abingdon*, ed. Joseph Stevenson (hereafter cited as *Abingdon Chronicle*), 2:113.
35. Poole, *From Domesday Book to Magna Carta*, p. 416.
36. William of Malmesbury, *G.R.*, 2:483–484.
37. *Regesta*, 2, no. 959; *Abingdon Chronicle*, 2:113. The writ was also addressed to Herbert the chamberlain and Hugh of Buckland, sheriff of Berkshire.
38. *Regesta*, 2, no. 963; *The Registrum Antiquissimum of the Cathedral Church of Lincoln*, ed. Charles Wilmer Foster and Kath-

dence has survived indicating that Roger sought exemption for his own extensive holdings, but such quittance may have been included under a general privilege which freed exchequer barons from payments at the exchequer.[39]

Bishop Herbert Losinga of Norwich apparently paid the aid, but his legal training prompted him to request a written statement confirming his existing privileges and noting that the payment of this aid should not be a precedent for further demands. Henry sent Roger a writ to this effect in 1110 and observed that Herbert's manor of Thorpe was not "to be subject to any new custom, but is to be free as in the charters which the bishop has." [40] The king obviously assumed that Bishop Roger had ready access to a complete set of financial records.

Bishop Herbert wanted further clarification and additional action and sometime later, probably between August 1111 and July 1113 while the king was in Normandy, he wrote to Bishop Roger. The letter is worth quoting completely, partly to catch the flavor of Losinga's unctuous style, and partly because it is probably typical of the letters Roger frequently received, although the only one which has survived:

To his friend Roger, the pastor of Salisbury, Herbert, his sheep of Norwich, greeting.

Although, during the entire time of your justiciarship, solicitude for my infirmities has been necessary, yet more especially in this hour, when I am fast-bound with sickness and more grievous adversity afflicts me, do I implore your fatherly goodness that him, whom formerly you set upon his feet, you will not, in the press of business, disregard,

---

leen Major (hereafter cited as *Registrum Antiquissimum*), 1:26. This writ was witnessed by Roger and the chancellor. For other writs related to this aid, see *Regesta, 2,* nos. 940, 942, 945, 956, 962, 964, 968.

39. Richard Fitz Nigel, p. 48.

40. *Regesta, 2,* no. 946 (no. *LXIX*); for earlier charters freeing Thorpe from treasury exactions, see nos. 548, 591, 786, 787.

now that he is cast down. I appeal to you as a father, I appeal to you as a pastor, with such appeals as a wounded heart is wont to utter. Let the voice of my anxiety pierce, I beseech you, your fatherly breast. The sheepfold is broken and I am exposed to the teeth of savage beasts, and unless, in your mercy, you aid me with your protection, I am given over to my enemies who rush to rend me to pieces. What answer shall be returned to the representations of your sheep is for you to decide: I leave it entirely to your discretion to counsel me in my anxieties.

From my lands fifty pounds are demanded for pleas (although my tenants of those lands have offended neither in their response nor in deed), and another sixty pounds for knights, which I find it the more difficult to pay since my resources in recent years have seriously diminished. What is worst of all, my neighbors are seeking to bring under contribution Thorpe, which our lord the king granted for the fabric of the [cathedral] church, as free as ever the manor was when in his hands and as his other manors are. On this I must take my stand; this must be the burden of my complaint; and this I implore you, from the very bottom of my heart, that our church shall not lose her franchise which hitherto, by the king's grace and on your advice, she has retained in its integrity. Command, I pray you, that Thorpe may be quit, as is customary, or grant a respite until our lord the king comes [to England] or, if nothing else may be done, allow me a long enough term to communicate with our lord the king and request his indulgence. In conceding and doing these things, I am sure that, by the grace of God, you will not find our lady the queen difficult, for, out of her kindness, she has been a very mother to me and she takes advantage of your advice in everything.

If you give the order, I live; and with never-ceasing tears I beseech our Saviour that, in His mercy, you will give the order.

A certain brother of ours is requesting your mercy for his brother in prison; hear his prayer, I beg you, with the same compassion that you desire God to grant your prayers.[41]

41. Herbert of Losinga, *Epistolae,* letter 26. I have used the translation of Richardson and Sayles, *Governance of England,* p. 160.

Herbert described Roger's "whole period of justiciarship" or administration, with the word *procuration* (*omni tempore vestrae procurationis*), a flattering but imprecise term. He stated his case as one bishop to another, but reminded Roger that he should be familiar with Thorpe's freedoms because "he had seen the charter and repeated writs about it." Bishop Herbert asked that his church remain free or that he receive a long delay in order to appeal to the king. He may have been offering Roger a way to avoid a very difficult decision, for he clearly believed the Thorpe exaction was unjust. On the other hand, he did not protest the scutage payment (*pro militibus*), but merely complained that he could not find the money.[42] His politic suggestion that Roger consult the queen regent makes it obvious that he realized the viceroy was in actual control of affairs. Although the whole complex of issues was largely financial, Herbert closed with a postscript asking clemency for the brother of one of his monks who was in jail, evidently on a criminal charge. Evidently the monk sent a separate letter of his own, and Herbert obviously expected Roger to be interested equally in civil and criminal matters, in great and small issues.

On another occasion Bishop Herbert wrote to the viceroy with far greater trepidation.[43] Roger had heard that Losinga

42. Thorpe was still quit of geld in 1130, *Magnus Rotulus Scaccarii, vel Magnus Rotulus Pipae, Anno Tricesimo-primo Regni Henrici Primi,* ed. Joseph Hunter (hereafter cited as *Pipe Roll*), p. 95. For a discussion of scutage, for which this letter is early evidence, see Richardson and Sayles, *Governance of England,* pp. 85–86, 161–162; Round, *Feudal England,* pp. 249, 270; Frank Merry Stenton, *The First Century of English Feudalism,* pp. 180–181; C. Warren Hollister, *The Military Organization of Norman England,* pp. 196–197, 210; James W. Alexander, "Herbert of Norwich, 1091–1119," pp. 144–148. Barbara Dodwell in "The Honours of the Bishop of Thetford / Norwich in the Late Eleventh and Early Twelfth Centuries," p. 196, dates the letter 1111–1113 and suggests that Bishop Herbert was probably still in the process of reorganizing his military tenures.

43. Herbert of Losinga, *Epistolae,* letter 21; also, E. M. Gouldburn and Henry Symonds, *The Life, Letters, and Sermons of Bishop Herbert de Losinga,* letter 21. The letter closed with a request that Roger return Archdeacon Walter to the Norwich diocese, for without him Herbert believed he could not hold his episcopal synod.

was spreading tales about him, and he sent the local sheriff to ask the Norwich bishop what was going on. Herbert hastily wrote to Roger pleading illness, thanking him for past counsel and favors, and staunchly proclaiming his innocence. He confessed, however, that he had heard some malicious talk and, while he would never repeat such things to others, he would tell Roger all about it when next they met. Cautiously, he committed none of the gossip to writing. Wealthy, powerful, influential, with a mistress quietly secreted in his diocese, Roger was vulnerable on many fronts. His reaction to the criticism and gossip was quite straightforward and aboveboard, however; he simply asked the accused bishop to explain himself.

Roger's reply to Herbert's letter has not survived, but the bishop of Norwich remained apprehensive. Sometime between 1111 and 1118 he wrote to Queen Matilda. Apologizing for adding yet another burden to the business of the kingdom she was administering so well, he begged her in her kindness "to salute my lord, the bishop of Salisbury, for me and ask him in disdaining my poverty not to find opportunities for rebuking my regard, and not to believe his enemies in regard to his friends." [44] Although it does contradict William of Malmesbury's naive early assertion that few men envied the viceroy, such intrigue and factionalism were not unusual at court, but it is revealing that a well established bishop like Herbert Losinga thought it necessary to implore the queen's intercession with Roger. Matilda was nominally regent, but it was Roger whom Herbert feared.

Herbert's letters and the various writs addressed to Roger are understandable in themselves, but they are much more meaningful when seen against the background of the total administrative apparatus Roger was in the process of developing. As Losinga's inquiries suggest, Roger's administrative concerns were largely fiscal and judicial, and the Thorpe case certainly illustrates how intertwined those functions were.

44. Herbert of Losinga, *Epistolae,* letter 25.

The mingling of such operations was perpetuated in Roger's greatest achievement, the exchequer system. This improved method of collecting, judging, assaying, and accounting the royal revenue was first mentioned in the king's writ exempting Lincoln lands from the aid collected for little Matilda in 1110, probably the first large-scale financial undertaking of the new exchequer.[45] Extraordinary administrative techniques appeared in the first decades of the twelfth century, but frequently their origins and early development were overshadowed by more newsworthy events like the investiture controversy. Thus, when institutions such as the exchequer finally do reveal themselves in the records, they are relatively well perfected, and one is forced to guess about their first procedures.

A superb guide to the English exchequer was written about 1179 by Bishop Roger's grand-nephew, Richard Fitz Nigel. Unique in medieval institutional history, his careful analysis was called *The Dialogue of the Exchequer*.[46] In the treatise a young scholar asks his master how the finances of the kingdom are collected and recorded and what the functions and divisions of the exchequer are. Clear and analytical answers form a regular handbook of procedures. There are some errors in this guide, but on the whole it is extremely reliable and the best indication of contemporary practice.[47] Not everything described in 1179 functioned in the early years of the twelfth century when Roger presided, but the system largely remained as the bishop envisioned it.

Richard Fitz Nigel, motivated by family pride and immensely pleased with his great-uncle of Salisbury, introduced Roger to his readers in this manner:

45. Poole, *From Domesday Book to Magna Carta,* p. 416; Stenton, *English Justice,* p. 59, says that the exchequer was "in being" before 1108.

46. In the abbreviations, notes, and bibliography this is listed by the author's name, Richard Fitz Nigel.

47. Richardson and Sayles, *Governance of England,* pp. 243–250.

There arose a wise man, prudent in counsel, eloquent in speech and (by the grace of God) suddenly the chief mover in great matters. You might say that in him was fulfilled that which is written "The grace of the Holy Ghost has no slow movements." Called by Henry I to his court, unknown yet not unnoble, he exemplified the saying, "How fertile is the lean poverty of men." He grew in favor with the king, the clergy, and the people, was made bishop of Salisbury and held the most important and honorable posts in the kingdom, and had the profoundest knowledge of the exchequer; so much that it is clear beyond all doubt from the rolls that it flourished exceedingly under his direction. It is from the overflowing of his learning that I have received, in my blood, the little that I know. But I will not enlarge on this, because he has, as he deserved, left behind him a memory which attests to his noble mind.[48]

All students of the exchequer are in Fitz Nigel's debt, and his treatise is as valuable today as when first composed. Before following his direction, however, something should be said of the other financial bureaus.

At the start of Henry's reign two departments were charged with royal finance, the chamber and the treasury. The chamber, or camera, traveled with the king, receiving various revenues and meeting daily expenses, especially military payments, while he was on the road.[49] In those days there was no overall budget and no separation between the king's personal funds and his governmental receipts and disbursements. Since the chamber rode with the king, it naturally fell under direct royal control, but Roger can be found checking its operations as late as a few months before his death.[50] Some have suggested that the chamber played the dominant role in financial admistration, but Richard Fitz Nigel did not mention it, and its relation to the more

48. Richard Fitz Nigel, p. 42.
49. Richardson and Sayles, *Governance of England,* pp. 229–231; Chrimes, *Administrative History,* pp. 27–32; Geoffrey H. White, "Master Chamberlains Under the Norman Kings," *Notes and Queries* (1923):223–225, 245–246, 263–266.
50. William of Malmesbury, *H.N.,* p. 29.

stable exchequer is uncertain, although it may have occasionally drawn subsidies there.[51] The chancery staff also formed part of the king's entourage and usually handled the chamber's secretarial needs.

A permanent treasury had been established in the city of Winchester at least since the days of Edward the Confessor, and the conquering Normans leaned heavily on the highly developed Saxon techniques.[52] The treasury was a sophisticated institution with a trained staff which heard pleas as well as safeguarding the royal gold. In September 1111, for example, the influential Abbot Faritius of Abingdon appeared before Queen Matilda's court at Winchester and proved by consulting Domesday Book that his manor of Lewknor owed nothing to the hundred of Pyrton.[53] This is one of the earliest known references indicating that Domesday was preserved at the treasury, and it shows how useful that great survey proved to be.[54] Bishops Roger, Robert Bloet of Lincoln, Richard of London, and several other magnates attended this court, and Matilda, acting as regent, confirmed their decision. This was a time of transition; soon this type of plea would be transferred to the jurisdiction of the exchequer.

51. Richardson and Sayles, *Governance of England,* pp. 227–229, 239. Part of this debate was reviewed in Bryce Lyon and A. E. Verhulst, *Medieval Finance,* pp. 57–64. See also James H. Ramsay, *A History of the Revenues of the Kings of England, 1066–1399,* 1:52.
52. Chrimes, *Administrative History,* pp. 9–10; Douglas, *William the Conqueror,* p. 300.
53. *Abingdon Chronicle,* 2:115–116; *Regesta,* 2, no. 1000; it was called the *Liber de Thesauro.*
54. An earlier reference may be *Regesta,* 2, no. 976, where Domesday was called *carta Wintonie.* This charter has been dated between 1102 and 1111 by R. R. Darlington, ed., *The Cartulary of Worcester Cathedral Priory* (hereafter cited as *Worcester Cartulary*), no. 21. Another writ of Henry I—no. 41 in the *Worcester Cartulary* (omitted in the *Regesta*)—mentioned *carta mea de thesauro Wintonie.* This was witnessed by Bishop Roger and is datable to one of three periods, Whitsunday 1108, June 1109–August 1111, or June 1113–September 1114. In the Red Book of Worcester, a thirteenth-century compilation containing some earlier material, Domesday is referred to as *Rotulus Wyntone.* The dating is disputed, but it is probably in the twelfth century (*Worcester Cartulary,* p. xlvii).

There has been a great scholarly debate about the identity of King Henry's treasurers and chamberlains of the treasury.[55] The most recent account lists Herbert the Chamberlain, Geoffrey de Clinton, and Bishop Roger's nephew Nigel of Ely as treasurers. William de Pont de l'Arche, long considered a treasurer, is here viewed as the more powerful of the two chamberlains.[56] William of Malmesbury appeared to suggest that Roger actually kept the treasure himself, but it seems likely that this was actually a reference to the bishop's general control of all the realm's finances.[57]

Bishop Roger seems to have used the board of exchequer more than the treasury or the chamber as his principal agency for administering royal finances. With the advent of the exchequer, the expanding government centered its functions more in London and Westminster than in Winchester, although the treasury remained in that ancient Saxon center. The exchequer was really more an occasion than a place, and, as Fitz Nigel said, its main task was to hear pleas.[58] Thus it was a kind of sedentary court through which the sheriffs and other bailiffs paid the king the annual farm of their countries, the proceeds of justice, and national levies like Danegeld and feudal aids. It acted as a court to adjudicate complaints, as a board of collection to receive the levies, as an assay office to evaluate the coin offered to the king, and as a bureau to record debts, pleas, payments, and disbursements. The treasurer was an official of some

55. Geoffrey H. White, "Financial Administration Under Henry I;" Geoffrey H. White, "Treasurers in Normandy Under Henry I," *Notes and Queries* (1926):59–60; Chrimes, *Administrative History*, p. 28; Tout, *Chapters in Administrative History*, 1:76–91; Richard Fitz Nigel, p. 50; Charles Homer Haskins, *Norman Institutions*, pp. 107–108; Richardson and Sayles, *Governance of England*, pp. 216–218; *Regesta, 2:xiv*.

56. Richardson and Sayles, *Governance of England*, p. 200. Nigel was definitely mentioned as treasurer in Richard Fitz Nigel, p. 50; *Regesta*, 2, no. 1691; and British Museum Manuscript, Egerton 3031, fo. 36.

57. William of Malmesbury, *H.N.*, p. 40.

58. Richard Fitz Nigel, p. 16; Richardson and Sayles, *Governance of England*, p. 228.

importance at the exchequer, and treasury clerks probably carted the coin to Winchester for safekeeping, but the chief justiciar presided.[59]

Although the first mention of the exchequer appeared in 1110, Richard Fitz Nigel admitted that he himself did not know when it began.[60] Ruling out the possibility that it may have existed under the Saxon kings, he suggested that it may have originated with the Conqueror in practices borrowed from a Norman exchequer. If he was referring to a formal exchequer, he was in error because there is no evidence for the existence of such a Norman board until Henry's reign.[61] He may, however, have been thinking of the early curia regis, sitting as a court judging financial pleas, and this could go back as far as the compilation of Domesday Book in 1086.[62] The treasury sat like this to decide Abbot Faritius's case in 1111. Thus the essence of the exchequer may well precede its name, for it was really a permanent board of royal officials who checked the sources of revenue which flowed into the treasury and judicially determined what was due to the king from his lands and subjects.

The use of the word *exchequer* (*scaccarium*) in 1110 does, however, indicate something new. Reginald Lane Poole, who studied the exchequer intensively, declared that the word "indicated a revolution in the method of auditing the account; it means the introduction of a precise system of calculation worked out by counters on a chequered table and recorded on rolls. Thenceforward the treasury was limited to the payment and storage of money; the business of account and the higher work of judicature passed to the exchequer."[63] The word signified that a novel agency would

---

59. Richard Fitz Nigel, pp. 28–29.   60. *Ibid.*, p. 14.
61. *Ibid.*, p. *xxxxv;* Douglas, *William the Conqueror,* pp. 300–301.
62. Felix Liebermann's review of Reginald Lane Poole's *The Exchequer in the Twelfth Century,* EHR 28(1913):153–154.
63. Reginald Lane Poole, *The Exchequer in the Twelfth Century,* pp. 40–41.

henceforth administer, judge, receipt, and account the king's revenue.

The old name for the financial administration was "the tallies." [64] This was based on the Saxon method of receipting payments on wooden tally sticks, a method retained in the new system. A tally was usually an eight-inch stick of hazelnut bored at one end so that it could be hung on a rod; incisions on its edges indicated payments. A thousand pounds made a cut "wide enough to hold the thickness of the palm of the hand, a hundred that of the thumb, twenty pounds that of the little finger, a pound that of a swelling barley corn, a shilling smaller, but enough for two cuts to make a small notch. A penny is indicated by a single cut without removing any of the wood." [65] Payments were also written on the sides. The stick was then split lengthwise, and the sheriff and the treasury clerk each retained a piece —sort of carbon copies—to prevent forgery. The longer piece, the stock, was given to the depositer; the shorter piece was kept at the exchequer as a record.

More impressive than the tallies was the five-by-ten-foot accounting table which gave the name *exchequer* to the new system. Some think it resembled a giant chessboard, but actually it consisted of the white columns of an abacus painted on a black tablecloth.[66] On this huge abacus the columns represented pence, shillings, pounds, scores of pounds, hundreds of pounds, thousands of pounds, and tens of thousands of pounds.

The abacus had been known in medieval Europe since at least the tenth century, when Gerbert (later, Pope Sylvester II) wrote a treatise about it. Controversy still exists on who first introduced it into England, with the schools of Lorraine and Laon contending for the honors. Apparently the laurels go to Lorraine, for Bishop Robert of Hereford (1079-1095),

64. Richard Fitz Nigel, pp. *xxv*, 7.   65. *Ibid.*, p. 23.
66. *Ibid.*, p. 7; Urban T. Holmes, *Daily Living in the Twelfth Century*, p. 271.

a native of that area, evidently first carried knowledge of this wonderful device to the court of William Rufus.[67] Nevertheless, the more important point is when the abacus became widely known, and here the great cathedral school of Laon comes into its own.

In the early twelfth century, Laon was probably the greatest intellectual center in Europe. Master Anselm, a renowned theologian, but no relation to the venerable archbishop of Canterbury, headed the school, and his brother Ralph, who wrote about the abacus, taught mathematics there.[68] Another famous mathematician, the Englishman Adelard of Bath, lectured at Laon until about 1109. A world traveler and Arabic scholar, he also composed a learned analysis of the abacus.[69] Like a magnet Laon drew the best students of its time and numbered on its rolls many future leaders of Christendom. Abelard, ever brilliant and controversial, studied there about 1113 when he was thirty, but characteristically he criticized Master Anselm, calling him an eloquent fool.[70] William of Champeaux and Gilbert de la Porré, both men of fine, exacting minds, studied at Laon, as did the future abbot of Reading and archbishop of Rouen, Hugh of Amiens.

Bishop Roger was well connected with this exciting school. Waldric, his successor as royal chancellor, was elected bishop of Laon in 1106; six years later he died there in a bloody uprising of the town commune.[71] Guy of Étampes, master of Bishop Roger's own schools at Salisbury, was a

67. Charles Homer Haskins, *Studies in the History of Medieval Science*, pp. 327–335.
68. Poole, *Exchequer in the Twelfth Century*, pp. 52–55. A Ralph of Laon witnessed a Bath charter in 1121 (*Two Cartularies of the Priory of St. Peter at Bath*, ed. William Hunt, p. 51).
69. Charles Homer Haskins, "Adelard of Bath," p. 497; Poole, *Exchequer in the Twelfth Century*, pp. 46–57. Adelard claimed that King Henry had supported him while he studied abroad. This may be, but it sounds more the type of thing his viceroy would do; see Adelard's *Natural Questions* quoted in C. Warren Hollister, *The Twelfth Century Renaissance*, p. 144.
70. Abelard, *The Story of My Adversities*, pp. 20–23.
71. Davis, "Waldric, the Chancellor of Henry I," p. 87.

Laon product.[72] Ranulf, who followed Waldric as chancellor, sent his sons there to Master Anselm, where for a while their tutor was William of Corbeil, a future archbishop of Canterbury.[73] Laon canons visited Salisbury cathedral in the spring of 1113 and were very well received because Bishop Roger's nephews, Alexander and Nigel, had previously studied at Laon for a long time.[74] The town had a mint of its own, and the school trained many of the secular clerks who gradually were replacing monks as the bureaucratic servants of feudal governments. Alexander and Nigel thus had joined a stimulating and important group of students who were to exercise a profound influence on Anglo-Norman society.[75] The school's fame did not last long, however, because Abelard soon attracted the most talented young minds away to what was fast becoming the university of Paris.

Laon's influence on the early exchequer can only be inferred, but seems extremely probable. Bishop Roger, for example, would have been thoroughly acquainted with its curriculum through his nephews and his local schoolmaster. Roger must have known Adelard of Bath fairly well, for he held lands near Salisbury and in 1130 may even have served as an exchequer official.[76] It would be fascinating to discover what one of the greatest medieval translators and scientists

72. For more on Guy, see Chapter 3.

73. Herman of Tournai, *De Miraculis S. Mariae Laudunensis*, col. 977.

74. *Ibid.*, col. 983. Perhaps they returned to England during the communal riots at Laon in 1112. Alexander's witness does not appear for some time, but Nigel attended the consecration of Bishop Bernard of St. David's at Westminster in September 1115, see J. Conway Davies, *Episcopal Acts Relating to Welsh Dioceses, 1066–1272* (hereafter cited as Davies, *Episcopal Acts*), 1:264.

75. Others who studied there included Robert of Chichester, bishop of Exeter; Robert Bethune, prior of Llanthony and bishop of Hereford; and Norman, prior of Holy Trinity. For the Flemish students there, see Galbert of Bruges, *The Murder of Charles the Good, Count of Flanders*, p. 114.

76. *Pipe Roll*, p. 22; Haskins, *Medieval Science*, p. 345. An Adelard witnessed a grant to Bury St. Edmunds abbey between 1135 and 1141, see David C. Douglas, *Feudal Documents From the Abbey of Bury St. Edmunds* (hereafter cited as Douglas, *Bury Documents*), no. 57, p. 80.

had to say to this bishop who was trying to order government on a rational basis, but unfortunately no such conver-
sation has survived. Adelard credited King Henry with un-
derwriting his studies abroad, but he was very critical of
royal officials' claiming that when he returned to England
he had learned that his country's "chief men were violent,
the magistrates wine lovers, and the judges mercenary." [77]
Despite this severity by an academician exposed to rude politics, there is every reason to believe that Adelard would have
helped the developing exchequer and that through him and
other Laon students knowledge of the abacus would have
spread in England.

The exchequer use of the abacus was simple but ingenious.
In later years, the exchequer met twice a year, at Easter and
at Michaelmas (September 29), and most likely these sessions date back to its earliest days. In the great hall William
Rufus had built at Westminster the officials convened to
receive the payments from the royal manors entrusted to the
various sheriffs. These obligations were usually farmed—that
is, each sheriff did not pay rents and profits as he obtained
them, but rather deposited a definite fixed lump sum, or
composition, previously agreed upon between him and the
exchequer. Danegeld, scutages, and murder fines were accounted separately. The sheriff's office was a lucrative one,
and profits in excess of the stated farm must have been frequent.

At both the Easter and Michaelmas sessions there was a
"proffer" at the Lower Exchequer, or Exchequer of Receipt,
when the sheriff paid his money and received a tally receipt.
At Easter the "view" of the account took place at the Upper
Exchequer, or Exchequer of Account. Here the sheriff made
a verbal declaration of what allowances and charges were
due him for his own expenses, and a balance was recorded
as a memorandum for the Michaelmas session. At this fall

77. Adelard of Bath, *Natural Questions,* quoted in Hollister, *The
Twelfth Century Renaissance,* p. 144.

meeting a completion of the account was demanded, and all the particulars were recorded on parchment sheets called pipe rolls, of which the earliest extant dates from 1130, although it clearly had many predecessors.

Richard Fitz Nigel detailed the functions of each exchequer official, but, basically, at the Upper Exchequer, the justiciar, treasurer, clerks, other ministers, barons, and the sheriff, all gathered round the great abacus board to play the game of the exchequer. As a clerk read out what the sheriff owed to the king, counters were placed on the great black board in the columns individually denoting pounds and their multiples and shillings and pence. The sheriff's deposit in the Lower Exchequer was similarly announced and represented. Then, leaning over the board, everyone watched a clerk move the counters to perform the simple addition and subtraction required to strike a balance. Deposit counters canceled debt counters, and the remainder indicated a surplus for the future or a payment still due. Although the sheriff could probably read, he nonetheless witnessed a clear visual demonstration of his debt, and the exchequer clerk, who knew how difficult it was to calculate with Roman numerals, performed his computations easily.

The chief justiciar's particular function at the exchequer board was described this way by Richard Fitz Nigel:

At it there sits the king's chief justiciar, second only to the king by virtue of his jurisdiction, and all the barons of the realm who are the king's privy counsellors, in order that the decrees made in such an important assembly may be inviolable. But some sit *ex officio,* others by the king's command alone.

Sitting *ex officio,* in the chief place, and presiding is the first subject in the realm, the chief justiciar. . . .

SCHOLAR: What is the duty of this most eminent member of the court?

MASTER: The best way of describing it is to say that he supervises everything that is done either in the Lower or in the Upper Exchequer, and that all the inferior offices are always at his entire disposal; provided always that the king's advantage is duly consulted. But the most exalted of all his privileges is that he can cause writs to be issued, either of *liberate,* for the payment of money out of the treasury, or of *computate,* for the allowance of expenditure to accountants, in the king's name with his own as witness, or, should he so prefer, in his own name with other witnesses, to the same effect.

SCHOLAR: He is indeed a great personage, seeing that he is trusted with the care of the whole realm, and indeed with the king's very heart. For it is written, "Where your treasure is, there will your heart be also." [78]

This description obviously applies to a time when the justiciar's exchequer duties had become part of a pattern and routine, but essentially it could also apply to Bishop Roger's own early activity.

The viceroy's achievement was not to preside over an already perfected system, but to initiate and enlarge its procedures. Take, for example, the manner in which payments were made at the Lower Exchequer. Although this was increasingly uncommon by King Henry's time, payments might be made in kind.[79] If silver pennies (the only circulating medium of exchange) were used, they could be paid by tale (*ad numerum*), which simply involved counting out the required number of coins. Most of the payments recorded on the pipe roll of 1130 were made in this fashion. Many of the coins were defective, clipped, or counterfeited, however, so this method offered no guarantee that the king would receive full value.

A third method, payment *ad scalam,* attempted to insure valid deposits by automatically charging a certain rate, usually six pence per pound, for coinage deterioration. Fitz Nigel said one could often find such payments in the old

78. Richard Fitz Nigel, pp. 14-15.
79. *Ibid.,* pp. 41-42; Robert S. Hoyt, *The Royal Demesne in English Constitutional History, 1066–1271* (hereafter cited as Hoyt, *Royal Demesne*), p. 94. Payments in kind continued longer in Europe, Lyon and Verhulst, *Medieval Finance,* p. 94.

pipe rolls of Henry I, but none was recorded in 1130.[80] This method may have been discontinued by then, for Bishop Roger effected a major coinage reform in 1125, and it might have been at that time that yet another method was introduced, payment by weight (*ad pensum*). The clerk simply weighed the sheriff's pennies to fulfill the debt; payments of this type were enrolled in 1130.

Most interesting is a fifth method whose invention Richard Fitz Nigel attributes directly to Bishop Roger:

By the king's command, he took his seat at the exchequer, and after sitting there for some years, perceived that the treasury was not completely satisfied by this method of payment. For though the tale and the weight might be correct, the standard might not. For it did not follow that if a man paid in a pound for twenty shillings by tale, and actually weighing a pound, he therefore paid a pound of silver. For it might be alloyed with copper or bronze of some kind, seeing no assay was taken. In order therefore to protect both the king and the public, it was ordered, after discussion in the council, that the combustion of the assay should be made.

SCHOLAR: How did this protect the public?

MASTER: The sheriff, finding that he suffers on account of the loss on inferior money, when he has to pay his farm, takes good care that the moneyers who work under him do not exceed the established proportion of alloy. And if he catches them, they are so punished as to discourage the others.[81]

There is a rather puzzling suggestion that Roger "took his seat" at some already well-established exchequer. Fitz Nigel never claimed that Roger began the exchequer, but surely this was because it evolved from preexisting institutions. The observation that assayed payments benefited the public as well as the monarch is a good indication that Roger's reforms were intended for more than the convenience of the king.

Assayed, or blanch, payments were also recorded in 1130,

80. Richard Fitz Nigel, p. 42.   81. *Ibid.*, pp. 42–43.

but this fifth method was as old as Domesday Book, despite Fitz Nigel's specific denial that it could be found there.[82] Some historians have felt that this mistake leaves his whole treatise open to mistrust but the most recent scholarship indicates that that passage may well have been an interpolation.[83] Blanch payment was certainly the most scientific method of securing a true exchequer yield, and the *Dialogue* explained in great detail that at the Lower Exchequer a random sampling of the sheriff's coins was carefully melted and assayed; if there was any deficit in the assay, the sheriff was fined an extra charge. Even if Bishop Roger did not originate this method, he ordered it generally enforced—a considerable improvement.

A series of royal writs concerning an annual grant to the canons of Holy Trinity in London illustrate the experiments in this period. Sometime before 1118, when she died, Queen Matilda gave the canons twenty-five pounds blanch from the farm of the city of Exeter; about 1127 the king wrote to Bishop Roger and the barons of the exchequer confirming this gift.[84] At the same time Henry sent another writ to the bishop, the reeve, and the burgesses of Exeter declaring that, on behalf of the soul of Queen Matilda, he granted the Holy Trinity canons twenty-five pounds *ad scalam* from the Exeter revenues she had given them in her lifetime; the money was to be paid by the sheriff of Devonshire.[85] In 1130 it was recorded on the pipe roll that the Devonshire sheriff was allowed twenty-five pounds, twelve shillings, six pence *numero* for a payment from the Exeter farm to the Holy

82. *Ibid.,* p. 14.

83. *Ibid.,* p. xl; Poole, *Exchequer in the Twelfth Century,* pp. 31, 65; John Horace Round, *The Commune of London and Other Studies,* pp. 66–67.

84. *Regesta,* 2, no. 1514. In 1912 Poole (*Exchequer in the Twelfth Century,* pp. 39–40) dated this writ 1110–1118 and declared it to be the earliest evidence for the exchequer. In 1950 Charles Johnson's edition of Richard Fitz Nigel (p. *xxxix*) accepted that date, but in 1956 his edition of *Regesta,* 2, gave the date as 1127.

85. *Regesta,* 2, no. 1493.

Trinity canons.[86] This last, of course, represents an addition of six pence in each pound, the *ad scalam* rate to secure full value for one's money. Apparently payments *ad scalam,* blanch, and *numero* were coming to be regarded as convertible terms.[87]

Since the queen's original grant was made before 1118, blanch payments were evidently accepted early in Henry's reign, but not until a few years after 1109, for Fitz Nigel said Roger devised the system after some years at the exchequer. This method had apparently first been enforced on royal manors where the central government could expect the least opposition to its policies.[88] It is rather confusing that in 1130 payments of old farms were often indicated blanch and the new farms, *ad pensum.*[89] This would suggest that the latest reform was in the direction of preferring payments by weight, although blanch deposits also had to be of full weight.[90] Perhaps the year 1129/1130 was one of particular experimentation.[91] Richard Fitz Nigel favored assayed payments, and in his day the rolls of Henry II indicated a uniform system of blanch payments.

The various methods would have been unnecessary if men had had confidence in the value of the royal coinage, but Roger had to wage continual campaigns against minters who tried to debase the king's silver. At the very beginning of the reign, Henry had ordered all the townsmen in his

86. *Pipe Roll,* p. 153.

87. Credit must be given to John Horace Round, who in *The Commune of London,* p. 92, traced down this *ad scalam* payment recorded as *numero.*

88. Hoyt, *Royal Demesne,* pp. 66–68.

89. In Berks, Hants, Wilts, Kent, Lincoln, and Warwickshire (William A. Morris, *The Medieval English Sheriff to 1300,* p. 86).

90. Ramsay, *A History of the Revenues of the Kings of England,* 1:19; Richard Fitz Nigel, p. *xxxix.*

91. Some important sheriffs, Restoldus of Oxford, for example, were dismissed in that year (*Pipe Roll,* p. 2), and at Easter 1130 Geoffrey de Clinton was charged with treason, but not dismissed; see Henry of Huntingdon, p. 252; Orderic Vitalis, 3:403–404. See also Chapter 5.

realm, Norman and English, to swear not to falsify his money.[92] Eight years later it was deemed necessary to carry through a major reform of the coinage. As already indicated, in 1108 Henry ordered that all his coins should be round and that anyone who debased them should be blinded and castrated.[93] A further reform was attempted between 1112 and 1128. Traders frequently cut a slit in the edge of Henry's coins to test their authenticity. The public feared such coins, so the government ordered that all coins should be snicked in order that none would be refused in commerce.[94] Henry's silver pennies were an unattractive, crudely ornamented lot, and at least fifteen different types were struck. Fifty-three-odd mints operated at one time or another, and the names of almost two hundred forty coiners are known, of which a very high percentage seems obviously Saxon.[95]

The most important reform occurred at Christmastide 1124/1125. It had been an extremely bad year; famine was widespread, and prices were rising sharply. Henry of Huntingdon, for example, complained that a horseload of wheat cost as much as six shillings.[96] Hunger drove men to crime. Ralph Basset, an important judge on circuit in Leicestershire that year, hanged forty-four men and blinded and emasculated six others. The first victims were thieves and the second probably counterfeiters. The monk who wrote the *Saxon Chronicle* groaned that Basset chose a year of debased

92. *Regesta,* 2, no. 501.

93. Eadmer, *H.N.,* p. 189; Symeon of Durham, 2:239; Florence of Worcester, 2:57.

94. The most convenient analysis of the coins of Henry I and Stephen is found in George C. Brooke, *English Coins,* pp. 86–101.

95. *Ibid.,* pp. 86–101, 255. According to the "Winton Domesday" —that is, between 1112 and 1115—five mints were closed at Winchester by order of the king (*Domesday Book,* 4:534).

96. Henry of Huntingdon, p. 246; William of Malmesbury, *G.P.,* p. 442. In 1179 enough wheat to bake bread for one hundred men cost only one shilling (Richard Fitz Nigel, p. 41). The bad weather and hard times also affected Flanders (see Galbert of Bruges, *The Murder of Charles the Good, Count of Flanders,* p. 85).

coinage and inflated prices to hang more thieves than ever before recorded.[97]

King Henry, away in Normandy suppressing another rebellion, spent vast sums paying his mercenary knights, and these roughnecks soon began complaining that their wages were worthless coins made two-thirds of tin. The enraged king wrote commanding Roger to punish the false minters immediately. The justiciar was swift and terrible. Ninety-four minters were summoned to Winchester, where almost all were reportedly blinded and castrated. A Winchester annalist boasted that only three coiners from his own town were exempted.[98] It was a revolting penalty, harsh in any age, but unfortunately regular practice in the twelfth century. Chroniclers writing from Normandy where so much of the defective coin had circulated, praised this stern justice, especially considering that the king might have greatly profited by permitting the coiners to ransom their penalty.[99] Bishop Roger finished his grim task by Twelfth Night, January 6, 1125; his own views on this work are not known, but no English writer praised it. The wonder is that things were so much out of hand in the first place and that all the minters had to suffer for the guilt of some of their number. No further counterfeiters are to be heard of in the remainder of the reign, however.

A less painful and more successful reform was Roger's system for recording exchequer payments. Two parchment sections were sewn together to make a sheet about one foot wide by four feet long; the filled sheets, bound at the top, rolled, and tied for storage, looked like pipes and were

97. *Anglo-Saxon Chronicle*, 2:191.

98. "Annals of Winchester" in *Annales Monastici*, 2:47. The minter at Bury Saint Edmunds was not spared (*Regesta*, 2, no. 1430).

99. Robert of Torigni, *Opera Omnia*, PL, 202:1307. See also William 'Calculus,' *Historica Northmannorum*, PL, 149:894; and J. A. Prestwick, "War and Finance in the Anglo-Norman State," pp. 33–34.

therefore called pipe rolls. It was not their shape that was remarkable, but the fact that they were permanent, orderly, complete, easily used records of all exchequer receipts, expenditures, and judgments; they were better registers than those of any other contemporary European government. Their first noted appearance dates from 1114, when Roger witnessed a royal writ granting the abbot of Westminster ten shillings, "as it is in my rolls." [100]

Unfortunately, only one roll survives from Roger's long supervision of the exchequer, the pipe roll for the thirty-first year of the reign of Henry I, which gives the financial details of 1130.[101] Although fiscal pardons were generally issued by royal command, Richard Fitz Nigel indicated that the chief justiciar could issue such writs in his own name and right. The pipe roll of 1130 shows Roger doing just that, acquitting a large debt of the abbot of Westminster.[102] A very great sum, eight hundred marks, was involved—eloquent testimony to the king's confidence in his viceroy. The orderly format of this pipe roll bespeaks many years experience. It recorded a royal income of more than sixty-six thousand pounds, but King Henry's actual total annual revenue was far greater than this, for several counties are missing from the pipe, as is any mention of the monies collected by the itinerant chamber.[103]

It is difficult to relate England's financial reforms to those appearing on the continent, but Bryce Lyon and A. E. Verhulst have recently made an important contribution to this study.[104] After 1106 England and Normandy were both ruled by Henry I, and, as Charles Homer Haskins pointed

100. *Regesta,* 2, no. 1053; Poole, *Exchequer in the Twelfth Century,* p. 37.
101. Richard Fitz Nigel (pp. 42, 58) referred to other rolls; some of these were still extant in the thirteenth century (*Pipe Roll,* p. *v*).
102. *Pipe Roll,* p. 150.
103. C. Warren Hollister, *The Military Organization of Norman England,* p. 170; Benedict of Peterborough, *Chronicle,* ed. William Stubbs, RS 49(1867)2:*xcix.*
104. Lyon and Verhulst, *Medieval Finance.*

out years ago, many of their institutions developed along similar lines.[105] Indeed, the king's household, chancery, and chamber followed him everywhere, and the same personnel were active on both sides of the English Channel. Even the more stationary departments like the treasury and the exchequer frequently interchanged officials and payments; Roger's own nephew, Nigel, can be seen paying large sums into the Norman exchequer in 1130.[106] By and large, however, the Norman departments had their own staffs, and Roger's supervision was directed to English affairs.[107]

The men who directed continental governments were like Roger in some ways. John of Lisieux was a bishop, and he had served in the English chancery before becoming Norman justiciar. While most Capetian counselors were nobles, Abbot Suger of St. Denis, the adviser and viceroy of Louis VI and Louis VII of France, came from an obscure background and rose by his administrative ability.[108] Bertulf, the provost of St. Donation's at Bruges, who acted as chancellor to the dukes of Flanders, was part of a dynasty of curial servants.[109] Several officials at the Norman court in Sicily came from England and maintained connections with the Anglo-Norman administration.[110] The English chief justiciar, however, had no real equal in other kingdoms.

105. Haskins, *Norman Institutions,* pp. 85–122.
106. *Pipe Roll,* pp. 54, 63; for other payments to the Norman exchequer, see pp. 7, 13, 37, 39. See also Haskins, *Norman Institutions,* pp. 107–108, for a short discussion of Nigel as treasurer in Normandy.
107. Richardson and Sayles, *Governance of England,* p. 223. The bishop did, however, have extensive holdings in Normandy, and many of the writs he enforced also concerned overseas possessions of English monasteries (see Chapter 3).
108. For his biography, see Edwin Panofsky, *Abbot Suger, the Abbey Church of St. Denis and its Art Treasures* (Princeton, 1946). Suger wrote about his own king, *Vie de Louis VI Le Gros,* ed. and trans. Henri Waquet (Paris, 1929). See also Robert Fawtier, *The Capetian Kings of France, 987–1328,* pp. 41, 171.
109. James Bruce Ross, "The Rise and Fall of a Twelfth Century Clan."
110. For the government of Sicily, see Charles Homer Haskins, "England and Sicily in the Twelfth Century," EHR, 26(1911):433–

Documentation for continental governmental and administrative progress is much less extensive than that for England. For example, only three hundred fifty-nine charters remain from the thirty-nine-year reign of Louis VI, and the earliest extant financial rolls of Normandy, Flanders, and France date as late as 1180, 1187, and 1202, respectively.[111] Fundamentally, government was organized in similar ways in these three lands, probably because of a Carolingian heritage. In each country the treasury was distinct from the financial administration, and revenues were farmed out with receipts being recorded on rolls.[112] Financial reorganization seems to have occurred first and most completely in Normandy under the stimulus of the English state. In Flanders the word *exchequer* (*scaccarium*), first appeared in the early thirteenth century, but it is logical to assume that the annual Flemish audit session, the *redeninge,* was using an abacuslike table much earlier.[113] Effective financial reforms did not come to France until the reign of Philip Augustus.

Bishop Roger must certainly have known what these governments were doing, and doubtless they were aware of his improvements. It is not possible, however, to trace any direct connection between his activity and theirs. Perhaps the greatest factor in the similar administrative experimentation in these four states may have been that each relied upon clerical bureaucrats trained in the same cathedral schools.

Collecting, enrolling, and assaying revenues were but parts of the work of the exchequer. As Richard Fitz Nigel put it,

---

447, 641–665. The Sicilian chancellor Robert, who died about 1150, has been identified both as Robert of Salisbury and as Robert of Selby because of an unclear manuscript reading of *Salesb'ia,* later changed to *Salesbia.* It seems impossible to determine which is correct. See John of Hexham, *Historia,* p. 318; DNB, 16:1251–1252; *The Letters and Charters of Gilbert Foliot,* ed. Adrian Morey and C. N. L. Brooke (hereafter cited as *Foliot Charters*), pp. 28–29.

111. Fawtier, *The Capetian Kings of France,* p. 8; Lyon and Verhulst, *Medieval Finance,* p. 45.

112. Lyon and Verhulst, *Medieval Finance,* pp. 41–52.

113. *Ibid.,* pp. 38–39.

"the highest skill at the exchequer does not lie in calculations, but in judgments of all kinds." [114] In 1119, for example, the litigious monks from Abingdon abbey appeared before the exchequer, claiming that their demesne lands should be free from geld payments. The court, consisting of Bishop Roger, Bishop Robert Bloet, Ranulf the chancellor, and Ralph Basset, sent the case back to the local shire court, where the exemption was proved. [115]

In another case, monks of Lewes Priory, a Cluniac house in Sussex, complained that inroads were being made upon some of their lands. Roger checked the testimony of the relevant charters and from Westminster ordered that nothing further be done against the monks until the king returned from overseas, laconically adding that he did not want to hear anything else about this problem. [116] In this instance his writ may have merely postponed a final decision, because the king was so personally interested in Cluniac affairs that he sometimes reserved judgments relating to such houses to himself.

At Winchester in 1127 Bishop Roger commanded the sheriff, Richard Fitz Baldwin, to acquit the canons of Plympton of any money due for the gelds and assizes of Ralph Basset. The bishop declared that such a payment was not recorded in the hidage of the charters of King William and therefore he did not demand it. [117] Shortly after this Henry ordered the same sheriff to leave the canons in peace because the bishop of Salisbury had acknowledged in a charter from the royal treasury that their church was free of any such dues; furthermore, his writ also indicated that the lands were not divided into hides. [118] Roger himself witnessed this royal writ, a confirmation of his own decree. Evidently

114. Richard Fitz Nigel, p. 16.
115. *Regesta,* 2, no. 1211; *Abingdon Chronicle,* 2:210. This is one of those rare times when all the judges in a court action were named. See also Henry G. Richardson, "Richard Fitzneal and the *Dialogus de Scaccario,*" p. 329.
116. Charter 15.   117. Charter 11.
118. *Regesta,* 2, no. 1515; the writ was sent from Westminster.

Ralph Basset was hearing pleas and checking revenue collections when he ordered the canons to pay this assessment.
The canons then appealed to the king, who referred the case
to a meeting of his exchequer court. Bishop Roger searched
the Conqueror's records at the treasury and decided that the
Plympton canons were right after all. He then wrote telling
the sheriff to recognize their claim, and the king confirmed
the whole judgment the next time he was in Westminster.

These cases demonstrate a few of the ways judicial problems came to the central government's attention. The local
judicature, however, was really the backbone of the system,
for most cases were heard locally, while only important or
difficult civil disputes reached the chief justiciar or the exchequer bench. On the other hand, practically all cases involving serious crimes were reserved to the judgment of royal
courts during Henry's reign. Early royal writs were normally
sent to sheriffs for execution, but gradually they surrendered
their power to hear pleas of the crown to locally resident
royal justiciars.[119] There has been considerable scholarly
debate over the relative importance of the royal and local
judicature, but it is evident that the king was eager to enlarge
his control.[120] Justice was, after all, an instrument both for
collecting great profit and for curbing baronial independence.

Although they did hear pleas at the exchequer and when
they traveled with the migratory royal court, Roger and
his colleagues could not handle all the cases themselves.
Other justiciars, including great barons, bishops, and minor
lords, were therefore sent out from the curia to local areas
to judge disputes and perform commissions. Precedents for
local and traveling justices can be found back as far as the
Conqueror's reign, and one cannot therefore claim that

119. Morris, *The Medieval English Sheriff to 1300*, pp. 102–103;
Cronne, "The Office of Local Justiciar," p. 93; Stenton, *English Justice*, pp. 65–67.

120. Reedy in "General Eyre," pp. 688–689, reviewed this issue.

Roger introduced itinerant justice to the country.[121] Many of his excellent improvements were prompted by the ideas of other men, for his role was to experiment with such concepts, systematize their use, and make them effective methods of government.

From the very beginning of Roger's tenure, justiciars served on ad hoc and local commissions. In 1110 a group from the curia regis, including Ralph Basset and Geoffrey Ridel, heard the sworn testimony of eighty-six burgesses in a case involving the size of the demesne lands of Edward the Confessor.[122] In 1111 Roger witnessed a writ sending Geoffrey Ridel and others to determine whether the abbot of Thorney should hold pleas in his own court.[123] Concealment of treasure trove and usury were the subjects of a trial heard by the justiciar Ralph Basset in the country court of Huntingdon in 1116.[124] The defendant, a Saxon named Bricstan, was convicted and imprisoned, but he was later released after the saints supposedly visited his cell.

As noted above, in 1124 Ralph Basset hanged forty-four thieves in Leicestershire. The next year, in the words of the Battle abbey chronicler, Roger, "who was then administering the royal laws throughout England," sent a minister named John Belet and an ecclesiastic called William of Ely as his deputies to make a survey of the momentarily fatherless abbey of Battle; but the men were not a credit to their mission, for they seriously depleted the defenseless monastery's rev-

121. Melville Madison Bigelow, *Placita Anglo-Normannica,* pp. 68–71; Douglas, *William the Conqueror,* p. 306; Lyon, *A Constitutional and Legal History of Medieval England,* p. 191; Raoul C. Van Caenegem, *Royal Writs in England From the Conquest to Glanville* (hereafter cited as Van Caenegem, *Royal Writs*), p. 28.

122. *Regesta,* 2, no. 969.   123. *Ibid.,* no. 975.

124. *Ibid.,* no. 1129; Orderic Vitalis, 3:123–124. In the same year at Brampton in Huntingdonshire the curia regis, which included Roger, Bishop Robert Bloet of Lincoln, Sheriff Hugh of Buckland, Gilbert and Walter of Gloucester, and Ralph Basset, dismissed a claim against the abbot of Peterborough (Stenton, *English Justice,* p. 62).

enues.[125] There was no legal or judicial issue at stake in this commission, but it does indicate the poor reputation earned by many of the justiciars.[126] A bit later, sometime between 1124 and 1130, King David of Scotland and Bishop Roger, whom a contemporary Ramsey writer called "the justiciar of all England," ordered a fact-finding jury of twelve men to decide a dispute about some land of Ramsey abbey.[127]

Gradually such specific commissions gave way to eyres, more regular judicial circuits through one or more counties. The controversial origins, regularity, and extent of such circuits have been examined by William Reedy, who traced the localized eyre back only to 1124 when Ralph Basset heard pleas in Leicester.[128] Truly conclusive evidence for the operation of itinerant justices can be found in the pipe roll of 1130, in which eleven different circuit justiciars can be identified in one or more counties, but the practice seems to have been a fairly recent development.[129] Justices heard pleas for the treasury and pleas pertaining directly to the crown.[130] Justice was inseparable from finance, however, and both motives directed the itinerant justiciars, who closely supervised the royal manors and took assessments in the shires as well as hearing pleas.[131]

The development of itinerant justice was a great achievement, and H. G. Richardson and G. O. Sayles have stressed

125. *Chronicon Monasterii de Bello,* ed. J. S. Brewer (hereafter cited as *Battle Chronicle*), p. 60; in 1130 Belet was sheriff of Berkshire.

126. *Gesta Stephani,* p. 16; see also the excerpt from the *Leges Henrici Primi* quoted in *Regesta,* 3:*xxvii.*

127. *Cartularium Monasterii de Rameseia,* ed. William Henry Hart and Ponsonby A. Lyons (hereafter cited as *Ramsey Cartulary*), 1:143; Van Caenegem, *Royal Writs,* p. 83.

128. Reedy, "General Eyre," pp. 688–724.

129. Morris, *The Medieval English Sheriff to 1300,* pp. 101–102; for a different view, see Van Caenegem, *Royal Writs,* p. 28. Stenton, *English Justice,* p. 65, says that the general eyre was a fact before 1130, for which Ralph Basset deserved most credit.

130. *Pipe Roll,* pp. 18, 19, 26, 78, 91, 92, 113, 134.

131. *Ibid.,* pp. 24, 131, 133; Richard Fitz Nigel, p. 47; Hoyt, *Royal Demesne,* p. 93.

the similarity of the system which began under Henry I to the eyres organized by Henry II after 1166.[132] Nevertheless, William Reedy noted that the eyres of the first Henry did not deliberately cover the whole country within any definite period, nor at stated intervals, nor had the returnable writ which later brought so many cases directly to the royal courts yet been perfected.[133] These limitations, while important, do not deny the establishment of general eyres under Henry I; they only explain that they were less fully developed than those of Henry Plantagenet. Although the paucity of records prohibits final distinctions among various types of justiciars and eyres, the extension of justice through this system was very significant. Authorship of the plan cannot be proved to belong to Bishop Roger, for certainly Ralph Basset made an important contribution, but the viceroy was at least in the best position to further its implementation.

Bishop Roger apparently never made any attempt to codify the laws of his time, and the Norman kings were not themselves great legislators. Henry's coronation charter and a few writs dealing with coinage and wreckage embody his legal enactments.[134] Nevertheless, an ambitious attempt to organize the law was made by an anonymous writer in the second decade of the century whose unfinished work is usually called the *Quadripartitus,* after its proposed fourfold division.[135] The first book contained Saxon laws translated into Latin, the second was to have added recent law, the third was to have explained pleas, and the fourth was to have treated theft. Only the first part appeared as planned; in it

132. Richardson and Sayles, *Governance of England,* pp. 173–188, 204–207, argue that regular eyres began as early as 1106, citing Roger's commission to act as justiciar and protect Abbotsbury's lands (*Regesta,* 2, no. 754). This seems, however, to be a very specific royal command, not evidence for a general eyre.

133. Reedy, "General Eyre," pp. 722–724.

134. Henry G. Richardson and George O. Sayles, *Law and Legislation from AEthelberht to Magna Carta,* pp. 31–39.

135. *Ibid.,* pp. 41–43. The text was edited by Felix Liebermann, *Quadripartitus, ein Englisches Rechtsbuch von 1114.*

the author's analysis exhibited little trace of legal training or procedure. An equally anonymous contemporary who was better acquainted with the local administration of justice composed a text called the *Leges Henrici*, which apparently was intended to serve as the third part of the earlier treatise.[136] It dealt with criminal law but omitted land law and itinerant justice and said nothing of the justiciar's court at the exchequer. It is thus highly unlikely that either man worked or wrote under Roger's direction; both probably served bishops or barons, rather than being royal clerks.[137]

Despite the undoubted improvements in justice and finance which Bishop Roger encouraged, his contemporaries were probably more impressed by his direct execution of the king's commands. Henry was a dynamic man who knew the most intimate details of his kingdom, and Roger was the perfect choice to effect his will; in the words of Richardson and Sayles; he was a "co-adjutor of genius." [138] Over fifteen hundred of the king's writs and charters have survived; most record gifts to religious houses, confirmations of land transactions, and commands for particular things. Although many were issued in Normandy, which Roger rarely visited, three hundred eighteen of these writs—roughly one in every five—involved the viceroy in one way or another. Although he traveled widely in England, his attestations were chiefly recorded at Westminster, Winchester, Windsor, and Woodstock. Administrative responsibilities occasionally required him to remain some distance from the royal court, but he still witnessed more gifts and confirmations than anyone else.

136. Richardson and Sayles, *Law and Legislation*, p. 43. William Stubbs, in *Lectures On English History*, ed. Arthur Hassall (London, 1906), pp. 143–166, argues that it was written between 1112 and 1118 as the unsystematic notes of a student from lectures on Anglo-Norman law.

137. Richardson and Sayles, *Laws and Legislation*, p. 45. Lady Stenton, in *English Justice*, p. 23, said that the author must have been a judge in the king's service.

138. Richardson and Sayles, *Law and Legislation*, p. 33.

Forty-four extant royal writs (including three forgeries) were supposedly sent to Roger during Henry's reign, sixteen of them before 1117. The overwhelming number concern Salisbury diocesan matters (twelve relate to the monastery of Abingdon, alone) or lands in Wiltshire, Dorset, or Berkshire. A few, however, were clearly the king's commands to his viceroy. Writs for young Matilda's aid in 1110 and for payments to the canons of Holy Trinity have already been mentioned. Other examples can be cited more briefly. In 1123 Roger was directed to give Archbishop William Corbeil of Canterbury seisin in all his archiepiscopal lands.[139] Six years later the viceroy was told to see that port officials allowed the goods and ships of St. Ouen of Rouen freedom from tolls.[140] A similar provision was ordered for the goods of the Montebourg monks.[141] These writs were sent from Normandy, and, in the last two instances, justices were given precedence over sheriffs. In 1132 Henry wrote to Roger in his capacity as exchequer official, ordering that the Cistercians of Rievaulx were to be freed from Danegeld.[142] The total of these commands to Roger as viceroy is not remarkable, but they do illustrate the range of his concerns.

I have found only thirty-one charters which Roger issued in his own name.[143] Like the royal writs, they are gifts, confirmations and orders; one is a personal charter; fifteen refer to strictly diocesan affairs; the other fifteen are viceregal directions carrying out the king's wishes, but even some of these seem to have been issued in his capacity as bishop as well as justiciar. Roger usually referred to himself simply as the bishop of Salisbury, but he may well have intended some commands to carry the force of several jurisdictions.

The establishment of Reading abbey illustrates one combination of Bishop Roger's civil and religious responsibilities. In the year 1120 the Channel wreck of the great and sup-

139. *Regesta*, 2, no. 1417 (no. *CLXXII*).   140. *Ibid.*, no. 1572.
141. *Ibid.*, no. 1682.   142. *Ibid.*, no. 1741.
143. See Appendix 2.

posedly unsinkable White Ship left Henry mourning for the loss of his only legitimate male heir, William. In grief he turned to religion and called upon the Cluniac monks to found a monastery at Reading, Berkshire, in Roger's diocese. Prior Peter and seven monks from Cluny joined several others from Lewes priory in Sussex, and together they began a house at Reading on June 18, 1121; the monastery was not actually part of the Cluniac system, but people often thought of it as such. On April 15, 1123, Hugh, the prior of Lewes, was chosen first abbot of Reading, and Peter returned to Cluny.[144] Thrifty Henry founded few important monasteries, but he lavished affection and wealth upon this abbey and chose it for his own final resting place.[145]

The properties and churches Henry gave for the abbey's endowment, although they included holdings of three ancient extinct abbeys, were not a convenient whole. Between 1121 and 1125 Bishop Roger therefore acted as the king's deputy in properly sorting out these gifts. Creating a monastery was a complex process, and it is not surprising that the royal foundation charter, a dubious document in its present form, dates from as late as 1125.[146] This charter breathed much of the spirit of the Gregorian reform movement, for it granted the abbey immunities from lay authorities who might want to requisition its possessions for external work,

144. Information on Reading's early days can be found in its annals in *Ungedruckte Anglo-Normannische Geschichtsquellen,* ed. Felix Liebermann, pp. 10–11. Its history can be read in Albert Way, "Contributions Towards the History of Reading Abbey;" Jamesion B. Hurry, *Reading Abbey;* and in Brian Kemp, "The Foundation of Reading Abbey and the Growth of Its Possessions and Privileges in England in the Twelfth Century." See also Kemp's *Reading Abbey,* and "The Monastic Dean of Leominster" (Leominster was a Reading priory in Herefordshire).

145. He and his daughter, Matilda, gave the abbey a precious relic thought to be the hand of Saint James the Apostle (*Regesta,* 2, no. 1448). The monastery was built slowly, however, and was not finally dedicated until 1164.

146. *Ibid.,* no. 1427; no. 1474 is a *so-called* portable version; see also Kemp, "The Foundation of Reading Abbey," pp. 400–405.

and it allowed the abbey custody of all its own goods during abbatical vacancies.[147] When assessing Bishop Roger's own contribution to the esablishment of this new monastery, it should be remembered that the king was in Normandy from 1123 to 1126; as the Saxon chronicler put it in 1123, Henry "committed all England to the care and government of Bishop Roger of Salisbury." [148]

One of his first tasks for Reading was to direct the process of bringing alienated churches and parts of manors back into the abbey's proper demesne. This necessitated some exchanges of land. One such instance involved the famed monastery and pilgrimage shrine of Mont St. Michel in Normandy, which received lands in Budleigh, Devonshire, in exchange for the churches of Wargrave and Cholsey in Berkshire, which were then granted to Reading. King Henry first notified his barons of this exchange, and copies of his writ were recorded in both the Reading and Mont St. Michel cartularies.[149] Immediately thereafter, in 1123, the Norman abbot wrote to tell Bishop Roger of the exchange and ask him to hasten the transfer of the Devon lands. He addressed Roger by a revealing title, "the reverend lord and father, Roger, by the grace of God, Bishop of Salisbury, vigorous administrator of the realm of England (*strenuo regni Anglie provisori*)." [150] Although Roger's reply is lost, copies of his charter confirming both the exchange and the grant of the Berkshire churches have been preserved in three Reading abbey cartularies.[151] It is noteworthy that in these agreements spiritualities were primarily regarded as sources of income and were easily exchanged for temporalities. Brian Kemp, who has written intensively about Reading abbey, has

147. Other immunities from tolls and taxes were also granted, Kemp, "The Foundation of Reading Abbey," p. 405.
148. *Anglo-Saxon Chronicle,* 2:190.   149. *Regesta,* 2, no. 1418.
150. British Museum Manuscripts, Egerton 3031, fo. 47; Harley 1708, fo. 195.
151. Charter 8.

pointed out that the abbot of Mont St. Michel profited from this exchange and that King Henry paid handsomely to consolidate Reading's holdings.[152]

In his charter Roger noted that Reading also received the manors of Cholsey and Thatcham. And, indeed, about this same time Henry ordered Roger to try to recover any Cholsey lands which might have left its demesne. He should gather an inquest of the hundred men to ascertain whether the sheriff of Berkshire or the reeve of Cholsey had alienated any properties.[153] Roger's dual responsibilities as bishop and viceroy were inextricably mixed in all these arrangements; he was executing Henry's directives and simultaneously supervising changes in his own diocese.

Shortly thereafter, probably in 1124, from Westminster Roger issued a formal general confirmation of Reading's many privileges.[154] He addressed himself to all the country's ecclesiastical and lay barons, using the extraordinary title *procurator of the realm of England under King Henry* (*Rogerius episcopus Saresberiensis sub domino nostro rege Henrico regni Anglie procurator*). Lady Doris Stenton, who first published this document, observed that it was definite evidence that the absent king had sent his writ to the justiciar, who then issued one in his own name ordering fulfillment of the king's commands. She also suggested that this procedure apparently did not satisfy the Reading monks, who seem to have created a royal grant of their own to be recorded in their cartulary.[155] There is also some doubt whether Roger's charter is wholly accurate as it stands, but it appears that it was at least based on an actual writ.[156] His

152. Kemp, "The Foundation of Reading Abbey," p. 214.
153. *Regesta*, 2, no. 1423 (no. *CLXXV*).   154. Charter 9.
155. Doris M. Stenton, "Roger of Salisbury, *Regni Anglie Procurator*," pp. 79–80. Herbert Losinga, *Epistolae,* letter 26, used the word *procurator* to describe Roger; and Orderic Vitalis, 4:107, used it to describe Ranulf Flambard. William of Malmesbury, *H.N.,* p. 3, used a form of the word to describe how Roger managed King Stephen's affairs: *procurationes eius administraret.*
156. Charter 9.

use of such a novel title at this time may be related to the fact that after the deaths of Queen Matilda and her son William there were not even nominal rivals to his authority. The new queen, Adeliza, never seems to have acted as regent, and even remote competitors like Count Robert of Meulan and Bishop Robert Bloet had died by 1124. Roger was now viceroy in name as well as in fact; he did, however, conclude his confirmation by indicating that it was issued by the king's own command.

Some brief time after the above declaration was promulgated, Roger sent an equally formal charter to the sheriff and lords of London, and, again using his title of procurator or viceroy, told them that by the king's order he had granted Reading abbey and its abbot Hugh a London minter named Edgar.[157] This moneyer would henceforth pay to the abbey the same dues other coiners paid to the king, a very generous privilege, indeed. Since Edgar was granted as an individual, he may have been a serf. The viceroy's earlier confirmation had said that there would be a minter at the abbey itself, but now he was moved to London. This raises the possibility that the great mutilation of coiners in the winter of 1124/1125 may have intervened and that the bishop felt he could better watch the coiner's work in London; pennies that Edgar struck in London later in the reign still exist.[158]

More than a decade afterward, sometime in the reign of King Stephen, Roger again turned to Reading matters and sent a brief, pointed writ to the archdeacon and clergy of Berkshire. Written at Winchester, it simply reads, "I forbid anyone to teach school at Reading without the agreement and good will of the abbot and convent." [159] A secular school must have preceded the monastic one, and evidently some secular clerk had been, or had remained, teaching there

157. Charter 10.
158. Brooke, *English Coins,* p. *clxxix* (Type *xv*).
159. Charter 22.

against the abbot's expressed intention. This certainly seems like a purely diocesan problem, but the form of the document is that of a chancery writ, and Roger's dual role of bishop and viceroy gave his orders additional strength.

However well Roger executed Henry's commands, it should not be assumed that he shared the king's enthusiasm for the new monastery. Actually, Reading received few important gifts except from members of the royal family. Roger's first charter to the abbey noted that he confirmed to its use the manor of Thatcham; what it did not indicate was that Roger himself held Thatcham church and apparently had no intention of parting with it, though it passed to Reading after his death.[160] Bishop Roger also held the church of Stanton Harcourt, Oxfordshire, and that too seems to have fallen to royal hands only after his death, and thereafter to Reading.[161] Since these churches did not descend to Roger's successor Bishop Jocelin, he must have held them as personal gifts and not as diocesan property.

Some of Roger's other viceregal writs may be mentioned more briefly. Between 1119 and 1129 he restored some commercial privileges to the monks of Bury Saint Edmunds.[162] He again closed with the phrase "by the king's writ (*per breve regis*), indicating that his own directions followed a royal command. In fact, the very wording of Roger's charter copies that of the king in this and some other writs; evidently the chancery did not evolve a separate viceregal style. About the same time, Roger issued a similarly authoritative

160. *Regesta,* 3, no. 698 (December 1139–1141). Ten years later Duke Henry of Normandy forbade Archdeacon Roger to take Thatcham church from the Reading monks (no. 705). This may well have been Roger of Berkshire, who may have been Bishop Roger's son, Roger the chancellor (see Appendix 3).

161. *Regesta,* 3, no. 697. Between 1130 and 1133 a royal writ notified Bishop Roger that a Reading monk, Ingelram Apostolicus, had given the abbey the land of Whitsbury (*Regesta,* 2, no. 1862); King Stephen later confirmed this (*Regesta,* 3, no. 685). For the complications of the grant, see Kemp, "The Foundation of Reading Abbey," p. 247.

162. Charter 13.

writ from Westminster informing all the barons of Kent that, by the king's order, he had granted the abbot of St. Augustine valuable hunting rights.[163] So too, the viceroy ordered that the Spalding monks could peacefully hold their lands and that the archbishop of York's men could have easements in the woods of the archbishopric.[164] Roger's purely episcopal writs and the viceregal writs he issued under Stephen will be discussed later. On the whole, however, the great work of administration was completed during Henry's reign.

Roger was very active in London, the greatest city of the realm, and he visited it often. In 1130 he was pardoned more than eight pounds for burgage payments, indicating his London estates must have been quite substantial.[165] On the other hand, his viceregal position apparently gave him no special responsibilities or powers in the city. Indeed, the burgers jealously guarded their communal government and the main innovation of Henry's reign as far as London was concerned seems to have been the establishment of a local justiciar who would protect royal interests in important pleas and in the profits of justice.[166] No outsider was to be justiciar over the men of London.[167]

One of the most interesting things about Roger's tenements and ecclesiastical benefices in London was that they were partially designed to serve his governmental interests. His greatest and most prestigious holding in London was the deanship of the collegiate church of St. Martin-le-Grand.[168] This wealthy college of secular canons whose bells

163. Charter 14.   164. Charters 16, 18.
165. See Chapter 3 for a discussion of Roger's land holdings. His pardons in the pipe roll of 1130 are listed in Appendix 4.
166. Frank M. Stenton, *Norman London,* p. 18.
167. *Regesta,* 2, no. 1645.
168. *Regesta,* 3, no. 259. There is a short history by Alfred John Kempe, *Historical Notes on the Collegiate Church of St. Martin-le-Grand.* The main post office now covers the site, and nothing of the church remains. For a brief site description and a plan, see M. B. Honeybourne, "The Sanctuary Boundaries and Environs of Westminster Abbey and the College of St. Martin-le-Grand."

rang out the curfew each night seems to have been built in the deserted palace of Edward the Confessor. It was one of the two churches in southern England—Westminster Abbey being the other—which could grant permanent sanctuary to fugitives; it also boasted one of the oldest schools in the kingdom. Roger may have resided at St. Martin's when he went to London, but more significant for his administrative work was the fact that he regularly used some of its nine prebends as benefices for government clerks.[169] St. Paul's cathedral chapter provided other prebends for official clerks, and Roger's own secular chapter at Salisbury also consistently supported and supplied clerks and chaplains for the royal bureaucracy.[170] Roger was thus both civil and ecclesiastical superior to many of the men who worked under him.

The bishop not only provided well for his clerks, but he also kept after the king to increase the endowments of St. Martin's, usually managing to secure a personal interest in such gifts himself. Sometime between 1108 and 1122 he asked the king to give the college the church of St. Botolph, Aldersgate, with its lands and possessions.[171] The original writ of

169. *Regesta*, 3:*xi–xv*, identified six such canons: Adam, Richard de Boulogne, his son Robert de Boulogne, Robert de Cornuvilla, Master Mannard, and Peter the Scribe. Bishop in *Scriptores Regis*, pp. 24–25, called this last canon Scriptor 14; he, or an imitator of his style, wrote many writs for Saint Martin's. Scriptor 11 also drafted documents for the college. Two other canons of the college, Hugh and Tiold, witnessed in 1137, see Norman Moore, *The History of St. Bartholomew's Hospital*, 2:27–33.

170. Everard of Calne held the prebend of Mora at Saint Paul's; Nigel of Ely (incorrectly, I think, equated with Nigel of Calne) held Chiswick; and a Wymund, who may have been Roger's appointee as prior of Saint Frideswide's, held Nesden; see Diana E. Greenway, *John Le Neve, Fasti Ecclesiae Anglicanae, 1066–1300* (hereafter cited as Greenway, *Fasti*), 1:61, 41, 63. Nigel of Calne held Calne prebend at Salisbury (*Regesta*, 2, nos. 1664, 1204, 1209, 1231, 1236). Other government officials and clerks—Everard of Calne, Geoffrey Rufus, Nigel of Ely, Roger the Poor, and Adelelm the treasurer—also held Sarum prebends and (save Geoffrey) archdeaconries. Since Everard and Nigel of Calne each had a nephew named William, they may have been brothers. William of Calne held Mora prebend in Saint Paul's after Everard (Gerenway, *Fasti*, 1:61; *Pipe Roll*, p. 18).

171. *Regesta*, 2, nos. 1106, 1107. This church came from a priest named Thurstan, who apparently became a canon of Saint Martin's.

Bishop Richard de Belmeis of London to William, the dean of Saint Paul's, ordering this at Roger's request still exists.[172] During the same period the viceroy also successfully petitioned for the church of Newport, Essex, to be given to the canons, but he first retained a life interest in it for himself.[173] The canons also held certain lands at Maldon, Essex, and rights to hold fugitives.[174] Rogers' own perquisites as dean included the soke, lands, and houses at Cripplegate, which were kept for him by one of his servants, a man named Griffin.[175] Three stalls at Newgate market also belonged to the dean and were held for Roger by another retainer, Peter Futnud, who may have been one of the canons.[176]

One of Bishop Roger's original charters, the only one on which his seal is preserved, mentioned lands at Ludgate which the powerful sheriff Hugh of Buckland once held of him.[177] Roger and Hugh were old allies who frequently acted together before the latter's death in 1116 or 1117; in fact, of the forty-three royal writs addressed to Roger by the king, eleven were sent jointly to Hugh, a man chroniclers sneered at for having been "raised from the dust" but who may have been a cleric, himself.[178] Roger's personal writ was

172. Westminster Abbey Manuscript 13478. William became dean in 1111, so this may narrow the date of the king's gift.

173. *Regesta*, 2, no. 1362. King Stephen confirmed this for the canons (*Regesta*, 3, nos. 537, 538).

174. *Regesta*, 3, nos. 552, 543.

175. *Ibid.*, no. 526. In 1100 or 1101 Henry I had returned Cripplegate to Saint Martin's. William Rufus had taken it because of discord between the canons and Count Eustace of Boulogne (*Regesta*, 2, no. 556).

176. *Regesta*, 3, nos. 526, 529. A royal writ sent to Roger before 1131 gave Peter, a clerk of Saint Martin's, land in Wilton (*Regesta*, 2, no. 1079). This must have been after 1121, since Bishop Jocelin noted that the gift came from Henry and Adeliza, see *Vetus Registrum Sarisberiense or Registrum S. Osmundi Episcopi*, ed. W. H. Rich Jones (hereafter cited as *Register of St. Osmund*), 1:337. Peter was still alive when his church was given to the prebend of Heytesbury between 1141 and 1147 (*Regesta*, 3, no. 793).

177. Charter 6.

178. *Regesta*, 2, nos. 613, 615, 703, 707, 722, 728, 730, 937, 956, 958, 959. Orderic Vitalis, 4:164, specifically listed Hugh as one of Henry's new men; also included were Ralph Basset and Geoffrey de Clinton.

probably issued shortly after Buckland's death but cannot be placed more precisely. It informed the barons, sheriffs, officials, and men of London that Roger granted Geoffrey the Constable some land at Ludgate which Hugh had purchased from Peter Futnud and held of Roger. The terms of service were specified exactly and remind one of exchequer payments, for an ounce of gold was demanded initially and annual rents thereafter, payable at Easter and Michaelmas. The charter was found among the ancient deeds of St. Martin's, and, although nothing in the text indicates it, the Ludgate property probably belonged to Roger in connection with his post as dean. Geoffrey seems to have been constable of Roger's castle at Kidwelly, a canon of St. Paul's cathedral, and a witness to an 1137 grant in favor of St. Bartholomew's hospital.[179]

Bishop Roger was a benefactor of St. Bartholomew's, Smithfield, an Austin priory and hospital erected in 1123 by Rahere, a former royal courtier.[180] Before 1137 the viceroy gave this worthy house the church of Saint Sepulchre with its possessions inside and outside the city.[181] Saint Sepulchre's, Saint Bartholomew's, and Saint Martin's were all close neighbors in Norman London. Roger was quite interested in Austin foundations, and, although he did not endow it per-

179. Charter 6.
180. The original account of the house was edited by Norman Moore, *The Book of the Foundation of St. Bartholomew's Church in London,* and translated from the Old English by E. A. Webb as *The Book of the Foundation of the Church of St. Bartholomew, London.* Each man also recorded its history: Norman Moore, *The History of St. Bartholomew's Hospital;* E. A. Webb, *The Records of St. Bartholomew's Priory and of the Church and Parish of St. Bartholomew the Great, West Smithfield.*
181. The actual grant seems lost, but the gift was mentioned in a charter of Henry III (*The Cartae Antiquae, Rolls 11–20,* ed. J. Conway Davies, no. 340. When Prior Rahere divided the hospital from the priory in 1137 and appointed Hagno master of the hospital, Saint Sepulchre's was part of his endowment (Webb, *Records,* 1:77); the charter is reproduced in Moore, *Hospital,* 1:25–26. Bishop Roger also witnessed a royal gift in 1133 (Moore, *Hospital,* 1:39–42 [not recorded in the *Regesta*]).

sonally, he did witness several grants in behalf of Queen Matilda's favorite London priory, Holy Trinity, whose canons also received the generous gift from the farm of Exeter mentioned some time ago.[182] The first prior, Norman, elected in 1108, had once studied at Laon.

All Roger's London dealings ultimately benefited churches, schools, hospitals, and his own clerks. Nevertheless, the bishop's generosity was not wholly altruistic, for he frequently obtained handsome perquisites for himself at the same time. For all its power, London was a tiny world, and many of its clergy served the government and its viceroy.

Before returning to Roger's other activities, it might be good to summarize this long chapter. His contemporaries agreed that the bishop of Salisbury was the king's principal minister of government, second only to the king in power and authority. Roger's strong personality and high positions impressed chroniclers even more than his concerte achievements did. Administrative intricacies seldom interested monastic writers, and therefore not all the viceroy's reforms can be fully detailed today. Nor can a definite causal link between his presence and the new procedures always be proved, but there is no reason to doubt his overriding influence. The bishop's changes seem to have been effected without substantial opposition, and until 1135 no great crisis endangered his control. Judged by the standards of the twelfth century, even the coinage reforms were moderately successful.

Roger's responsibilities included executing direct royal commands, administering and spreading royal justice, collecting, evaluating, and accounting the revenue, and, in general, acting as viceroy whether the king was in England or absent in Normandy, as was frequently the case. He was

182. *Regesta*, 2, nos. 897, 898, 906, 909, 915, 1261, 1514, 1529. For Roger's patronage of Austin houses, see Chapter 4. A royal writ of between 1114 and 1116 directed Roger to protect the London properties of Saint Peter's, Ghent (*Regesta*, 2, no. 1148; see also no. 730).

called justiciar, baron of the exchequer, second only to the
king, and administrator of the country. He even called
himself procurator on two occasions, but usually attested
simply as the bishop of Salisbury. I have most often called
him viceroy, but the title was unimportant; beginning at the
latest in 1109, his power was real. Duties were undefined, but
he was the king's confidant, troubleshooter, and executive.
A bishopric gave him status, but talent made him successful.
Although not necessarily original in his ideas, he molded
practices to his design and people to his use. His passion for
education was genuine, but also related to his government's
great need for literate servants.

By 1110 the exchequer had developed, and its abacuslike
board served to demonstrate and judge accounts. Tallies were
given as receipts, and debits and credits were recorded on
pipe rolls. Steps were continually taken to improve the
silver coinage, and payments to the exchequer were evaluated or assayed before being accepted. The new exchequer
acted as a court, and other forms of royal justice were made
readily available to the people through a circuit of itinerant
justices. Bureaucracy grew apace as clerical and lay ministers
loyally served the government and were completely dependent upon it for their rise in society. Royal writs sent to
Roger and writs issued in his own name corrected and confirmed all sorts of tenurial and fiscal transactions. Many of
these commands merged his viceregal and episcopal duties,
and justice and finance were rarely distinguishable.

Government was strong under Henry and Roger, but the
truth of it may be somewhat distorted by the available charter and chronicle evidence which necessarily concentrates
our view on the workings of the central authority. Even so,
it is difficult to estimate the effectiveness of that authority.
There is a long leap between devising good plans and having
them properly executed. Unfortunately, many of the personal
frustrations and political struggles which must have deep-

ened Roger's experience remain unknown, as does his attitude toward groups like the self-seeking barons, the aggres-
sive townsmen, and the so-called passive peasants. Some
subjects, like the minters, found ways to work around the
laws for a time. Others procrastinated or refused to comply
with royal instructions. Frequently the king had to issue
several writs dealing with the same problem, or he had to
threaten a heavy fine to secure agreement. Occasionally, he
and Roger ended their commands with phrases like, "see to
it, or I'll send someone else," as if they half expected the
recipient, who was sometimes one of their own justiciars, to
ignore the command.[183]

Despite such passive resistance, part of which may be
accounted for simply by the primitive system of communica-
tions, the exchequer was a great success. When King Henry
died in 1135 he left a treasure conservatively estimated at
more than one hundred thousand pounds of fine silver
pennies, plus innumerable gold and silver ornaments.[184]
Judged by the standards of the day, the value of the coin
alone was astronomical. If the annual exchequer yield
throughout the reign was similar to the sixty-six thousand
pounds recorded in 1130 (and that was only part of the royal
income), the amount which was saved each year to accumulate such a hoard was truly impressive. Government was
indeed profitable, and the king's chief minister should be
considered a financial wizard.

Although the viceroy's accomplishments delighted the
ruler, they did not make Roger popular with others, but
then, few of his contemporaries had any appreciation of
administrative technique or reform. A few writers, recording
only the most obvious traits of the new officials, complained
of their greed and lack of social background, but others said

183. *Regesta*, 2, nos. 1271, 1495, 1520, 1521, 1541, 1684, 1754,
1837, 1848, 1882, 1962. Roger's use of a similar phrase (Charter 24)
actually dates from 1138.

184. William of Malmesbury, *H.N.*, pp. 17, 25.

that the magistrates and justiciars were unjust.[185] Some of
these charges can be dismissed as mere objections to change
or outside interference, but others surely represent deeply
felt repeated grievances. At different times the king even admitted that his courts had not treated individuals fairly, but
the number of such instances is small, and the far greater
volume of judgements rendered and accepted indicate that
such cases were exceptional.[186] Nevertheless, in 1130 the
king had nightmares of angry farmers, soldiers, and clergy-
men threatening him.[187] Raising money for the government
and treating its subjects roughly apparently went hand in
hand. If Roger merits praise for the establishment of new
administrative and judicial procedures, he also deserves part
of the blame for not more closely controlling the venal conduct of some of his subordinates. While it is perhaps to his
credit that he undertook his viceregal duties very reluctantly,
his own record is not untainted for at his death he admitted
despoiling two religious houses of their properties "unjustly
and without judgement." [188] These were largely personal
matters, unconnected with his governmental conduct, and it
is probably more significant that no one, even after his death,
accused him of ever giving a dishonest judicial decision, or of
designing a system to oppress his people.

No great legislation, comprehensive national survey, or
ringing document of individual liberty appeared in this

185. Orderic Vitalis, 4:164; Richard of Hexham, *Historia,* p. 140;
Gesta Stephani, pp. 15–16; Adelard of Bath, *Natural Questions*
(quoted in Hollister, *Twelfth Century Renaissance,* p. 144); *Leges
Henrici Primi* (quoted in *Regesta,* 3:xxvii); *Battle Chronicle,* p. 60.
   186. *Regesta,* 2, for example, nos. 1193, 1416, 1541, 1566, 1853.
See also nos. 1610, 1637.
   187. John of Worcester, pp. 32–33; see also Chapter 5. John drew
a sketch of these dreams in his chronicle and reported that they
were told to him by Grimbald the royal physician. In the first illustration Henry lies asleep and three rustics armed with farm im-
plements and a long charter torment him. In the second four knights
in armor brandish their swords above him. In the last panel three
bishops and two monks hover about leaning on crosiers; one also
flourished a long charter roll.
   188. Charters 28–31.

reign, but many good, sound administrative practices did. From a rather formless mass of personal loyalties, Roger shaped a more impersonal system, which at least encouraged order and fair government. Although momentarily shaken by his disgrace in 1139 and by the consequent anarchy of Stephen's later reign, Roger's contributions nevertheless became the basis of the legal and financial apparatus of all succeeding English governments.

3

Shepherd of Salisbury

FOUR GREAT ROMAN ROADS led to Roger's town, and as he traveled to the exchequer or to the treasury or to the king's court, or made stately progress about his own diocese, he traversed fabled ground. King Arthur supposedly fought in the district, and ancient monuments like Stonehenge, Silbury Hill, Avebury, and the White Horse gave his lands an aura of history, mystery, and romance. His cathedral was not the graceful edifice now towering above the lowland marsh by the River Avon, for that exquisite church was erected early in the thirteenth century; a hundred years before, the diocese was ruled from the huge mound now called Old Sarum, a site about a mile and a half north of the present city of Salisbury.[1]

Only overgrown ditches, high earthen ramparts, and flint-outlined ruins remain of the original Salisbury, but it is still an extremely impressive place with commanding vistas of wide territories. Its great dry outer moat encloses an area of almost thirty acres and at its highest point it rises two hundred forty feet above the Avon. Early Iron Age men fortified the site with some of the oldest defenses in England, and later it knew Roman and Saxon garrisons. The con-

1. Hugh de S. Shortt wrote an excellent site guide, *Old Sarum,* which I have followed closely in parts of my discussion. For a brief but extremely fine analysis of the early history of the diocese, see Kathleen Edwards' report in VCH, Wiltshire, 3:156–164. See also VCH, Wiltshire, 5:51–57, for the later history of the borough. Visitors to the site should not miss the collections in the Salisbury and South Wiltshire Museum, which contain a reconstruction of Roger's cathedral, castle, and town, an exhibit of Old Sarum pottery and a selection of sculptural fragments from the old cathedral.

quering Normans dug a circular inner ditch and threw up a motte to carry their small wooden castle; this second hill was later enlarged to a height of sixty feet and evenutally supported a great stone keep. Thus Norman Salisbury was actually two ring mounds, one built upon the other. In the northwestern sector of the lower bailey stood the cathedral from whose transepts curved the town buildings, which are still largely unexcavated.

Despite its haunting surroundings, Old Sarum was a rather dreary spot. The cramped town growing beneath the royal castle was a dry, waterless bastion which seemed to catch every wind that blew; even today it is chilly and uncomfortable at the best of times. William of Malmesbury called it "a fortress rather than a city, situated on a high hill and surrounded by a massive wall." [2] The close proximity of the cathedral and the castle which overlooked it frequently made it difficult for the canons to conduct religious services in a reverent atmosphere. Later in the twelfth century the satirist, Peter of Blois, complained that the glare of the white chalk hurt men's eyes and, referring to the worsening relations between the canons and the castle garrison, he described the cathedral as "the ark of God set up in the temple of Baal." [3] In the 1220s the harassed clergy and townsmen descended to the surrounding plain, built a new cathedral, and gradually abandoned the hill; the castle remained in fitful use until the middle of the fifteenth century.[4]

From this ancient stronghold Roger ruled a diocese comprising Wiltshire, Berkshire, and Dorset, which had been created as recently as 1075, when Herman, bishop of Ramsbury and of Sherborne, had combined his two separate sees,

2. William of Malmesbury, *G.P.*, p. 183.

3. Peter of Blois, *Opera*, letter 104.

4. Old Sarum is now frequently remembered as the most famous of the "rotten boroughs" which sent representatives to Parliament, including the elder Pitt, until the reform of 1832. Edmund Burke is reputed to have said of Old Sarum, "They only know the streets by the color of the corn and their only produce is members of parliament."

and, in keeping with Archbishop Lanfranc's general reorganization of the English church, moved his cathedral seat to the larger town of Salisbury, or Sarum. Three years later, Herman died, having barely begun his splendid new church. He was succeeded by a former royal chancellor and close friend of the Conqueror, Bishop Osmund. About 1091 this gifted ecclesiastical administrator settled a chapter of secular canons in the rising cathedral, constituting them according to the Norman model, with a dean, precentor, chancellor, and treasurer as leading members. The cathedral clergy were intended to assist the bishop and to provide daily religious services in his church; the new Salisbury canons succeeded so well that they were soon noted for their musical skill and their devotion to learning.[5] Archdeacons were also created to help govern the diocese. To further his governance Osmund drew up regulations for his cathedral chapter and its liturgical services. Several kinds of ritual were then current in England, but he desired a uniform standard for his cathedral and the whole diocese; the reform proved popular and gradually spread to other dioceses. Bishop Roger must have later encouraged this, too, for similar regulations were instituted at Chichester cathedral about 1115, at Lichfield about 1139, and at Wells about 1140.[6] The new Salisbury cathedral was at last completed by Bishop Osmund in 1092, but five days after its consecration a storm tore off the roof and leveled parts of the walls; it was still unrestored at Osmund's death in 1099.

When the settlement of the investiture controversy finally enabled Bishop Roger to exercise his full episcopal functions, repair of his cathedral must have been one of his first concerns. Nevertheless, it is probable that his curial responsibilities prevented him from rebuilding as quickly as he had in-

5. William of Malmesbury, *G.P.*, p. 183.
6. Kathleen Edwards, *English Secular Cathedrals in the Middle Ages*, p. 141. See also Edmund Bishop, *Liturgica Historica*, p. 276–301.

tended, and indeed the precise date of the reconstruction is unclear. It proudly pierced the sky by at least 1125, however, for William of Malmesbury then claimed that Roger "built anew the church of Salisbury, and beautified it in such a manner that it yields to none in England but surpasses many, so that he had just cause to say, 'Lord, I have loved the glory of thy house.' " [7]

Choosing as his model the Conqueror's Abbaye-aux-Dames in Caen, the bishop redesigned Osmund's church by greatly expanding its choir and presbytery and adding a central tower, twin turrets and a porch to the imposing west front, and seventy-five-foot-wide transepts on the sides. The total length of the enlarged cathedral reached three hundred sixteen feet, not an exceptional size, but certainly filling all the limited available space. It was splendidly decorated, as were all of Roger's buildings. Green and white stones paved the nave and aisles, elaborately carved blue-black capitals adorned the columns and walls, and expensive red and green porphyry was imported from Italy to add even greater richness. Attractive sculptural fragments, now exhibited in the lapidarium on the site and in the Salisbury and South Wiltshire Museum, include a fine head of Christ and several lively cats. A large cloister graced the northeastern corner of the church, an innovation in its time since it was the earliest cloister in the country used for secular clergy processions; its location was also unusual, for most cloisters sought shelter on the southern sides of great churches. An adjoining crypt, still quite discernible, probably supported the chapter house and library.

The famous nineteenth-century historian Edward A. Freeman in a once widely quoted passage celebrated Roger's artistic genius by claiming that he introduced a new and

7. William of Malmesbury, *G.R.*, 2:483. M. W. Beresford and J. K. S. St. Joseph, *Medieval England: An Aerial Survey,* p. 185, date the refurbishment from 1125 to 1138, but William of Malmesbury's observation indicates that much was done before this time.

lighter architectural style into the country.[8] Unfortunately, this unsupported judgment cannot be confirmed, since little more than groundplans of his structures remain. Nevertheless, William of Malmesbury believed that all of Roger's buildings were of such extraordinary beauty and their stone courses so correctly laid that the joints escaped the eye and led men to imagine whole walls were composed of a single block each.[9]

In the inner bailey at Salisbury Roger also reconstructed the royal castle and made it into his personal headquarters. Normally the sheriff of Wiltshire would have resided and transacted business there, but apparently he lodged elsewhere. Unlike many Norman castles, this great keep was really a quadrangle of low buildings enclosing an open courtyard. A tower did rise in the northeast corner, but in many ways the complex was a palace rather than a castle, and it was ornamented accordingly. A ground-floor chapel dedicated to Saint Margaret was vaulted in three bays and carried another, dedicated to Saint Nicholas, on the floor above. The exterior was embellished with pilasters and roofed over with glazed tiles. Saint Margaret's foundations still survive, as do massive latrine pits in other parts of the castle, which bespeak a large, fairly elaborate household. Roger also strengthened the bailey with another wall. There was always some work in progress; the pipe roll of 1130, for example, recorded that Sheriff Warin disbursed forty shillings "for making a door in the cellar of the tower of Salisbury." [10] Most other buildings of the inner bailey seem to have been erected after Roger's time.

Like so many Normans, Roger had a veritable passion for building, and he indulged himself by raising castles and

8. Edward A. Freeman, *The History of the Norman Conquest of England*, 5:638–639. Roger A. Stalley has begun investigations of the bishop's artistic interests and has completed a Master's report, "The Patronage of Roger of Salisbury."

9. William of Malmesbury, *G.R.*, 2:483.

10. *Pipe Roll*, pp. 12–13.

churches throughout his diocese. William of Malmesbury critically noted how extravagantly Roger pursued this passion, "since he took a special pride in building, unsurpassed within the memory of our time, he erected magnificent buildings on his estates for the mere upkeep of which his successors will spend their efforts in vain; his own see he glorified beyond measure by wondrous adornments and buildings, without any sparing of expense." [11]

At the old episcopal seat of Sherborne, but somewhat apart from the abbey, Roger built a stone bastion whose interior groundplan was similar to that of Salisbury. In many ways Sherborne is the more interesting castle.[12] It was Roger's citadel, not a royal fortress. Large parts of the gatehouse, the curtain wall, the chapel, and the tower keep and its attendant rooms are still standing, and some of its elaborate plumbing has been uncovered. This was no mere motte and bailey arrangement, but a skillfully planned concentric castle. It was placed atop a limestone outcrop which commanded a main road and was practically surrounded by two branches of the River Yeo. In fact, Bishop Roger once wrote that the castle was situated on an island.[13] The outer defenses were finely made and very impressive. A dry rock-cut moat thirty feet deep was surmounted by a wall twenty-six feet high and seven feet thick. This curtain actually formed an

11. William of Malmesbury, *H.N.*, p. 38.
12. The Historical Monuments Commission report on Dorset, 1(1952):64–65, contains a brief examination of the castle, a groundplan and several photographs. C. E. A. Bean, F.S.A., excavated there for many years and James Gibb of the Sherborne School modeled a reconstruction for the new Sherborne Museum. The recent excavations of Peter R. Smith of the Inspectorate of Ancient Monuments seem to confirm that there was a castle at Sherborne before Roger's time. Joseph Fowler, *Medieval Sherborne,* is the best account of the town.
13. Charter 19. Fowler, *Medieval Sherborne,* pp. 6, 105, suggests that Roger gave up his residence near the abbey and selected a spot outside the town at Castleton because, like a true Norman, he wanted to live apart from his Saxon tenants. This is most unlikely. His grant of independence to Sherborne abbey and the natural strength of the new location were probably more decisive considerations.

octagon, with four long walls ending in sharp diagonals. There were small towers in these angles, a massive gateway in the southwestern corner, and another entrance in the north wall. Three and a half acres were sheltered within the walls.

Sherborne castle must have taken many years to build, and, although the date of its first construction is unknown, it may have been begun about 1122 when Roger surrendered control of the nearby monastery. The dominating tower keep was seventy feet high and may date from about 1130.[14] As at Salisbury, it was but one corner of a group of inner multi-storied buildings surrounding an open courtyard, a scheme which again provided for a comfortable, even luxurious, palace, rather than a mere fort. A great hall, chapels, and residence quarters formed other parts of the complex and a kitchen was apart from the quadrangle, off to one side. Warm, yellow stone from nearby Ham Hill in Somerset was used throughout, and several tastefully planned rooms had barrel vaults, some with chevron-patterned arched windows. Deeply carved wall ornaments shaped into beaked heads have also been found in the ruins. There were apparently three chapels: Saint Mary Magdalene's in the northeast corner just outside the castle wall was probably for the tenants; the keep itself housed a second chapel dedicated, appropriately for a military installation, to Saint Michael the Archangel; and evidently another was maintained in honor of Saint Probus.[15] While Salisbury castle appears to have been built somewhat earlier and has a more dramatic loca-tion, Sherborne castle seems to have been much more ex-pertly designed and magnificently executed.

A third tower was constructed in the very churchyard of Malmesbury abbey. Its historian, William, rightly com-plained that the castle was not a stone's throw from the

14. VCH, Dorset, 2:133, claimed the castle was erected in 1137, but that seems much too late.
15. Fowler, *Medieval Sherborne*, p. 107. On p. 119 he oddly sug-gests that the castle probably had few rooms.

monastic buildings (*vix iactu lapidis*);[16] indeed, it is literally a very short stone's throw from the west door of the present abbey to the Bell Hotel, which occupies the castle site and incorporates one of the castle walls. Although a burghal hidage fort previously exsted there, Roger's castle could not have been built before 1118 when he assumed control of the abbey.[17] It is not surprising that, like a warlord, the bishop was somewhat ruthless in securing desirable land. Doubtless reflecting the feelings of his brother monks, William charged, "anything bordering his property that suited his requirements, he extracted at once by prayer or price, otherwise by force."[18] The order of the bishop's methods is at least interesting.

On the rolling downs of bleak Salisbury Plain the bishop constructed his greatest castle, Devizes, on land belonging to his episcopal manors of Cannings and Potterne. Henry of Huntingdon called this mammoth fortress, which was surrounded by extensive earthworks, the most splendid castle in Europe.[19] The site was prehistoric, but very little is known about it. In 1113 a castle burned to the ground there; this was probably a wooden motte and bailey arrangement erected by Bishop Osmund. It was rapidly rebuilt in stone, and by 1121 part was fit enough for Bishop Roger to hold an ordination there.[20] Although it was thoroughly destroyed some centuries later and has not been systematically excavated, it is possible to gain some impression of the Norman appearance of Devizes, which seems to have followed a fairly traditional plan. A moat about thirty feet deep surrounded a mound built up to roughly the same height, and on this was placed a thick-walled, rather square keep, mea-

16. William of Malmesbury, *H.N.*, p. 25.
17. There is a short description of the castle remains in Henry Rees, "Malmesbury: Its Castle and Walls."
18. William of Malmesbury, *H.N.*, p. 25.
19. Henry of Huntingdon, p. 265.
20. "Annals of Winchester," in *Annales Monastici*, 2:44. Lincoln and London castles burned the same year. Gregory, bishop-elect of Dublin, was ordained there (Eadmer, *H.N.*, p. 298).

suring about seventy by eighty by ninety feet high. Large
sections of the thick outer walls were still standing in the
sixteenth century which even then impressed travelers with
their strength and costly appearance. Apparently some of the
rooms of this castle were also decorated with exceptional
charm.[21]

Duke Robert Curthose was imprisoned at Devizes from
1106 to 1126, with twelve loyal knights to stand his guard.[22]
Sanitary conditions being what they were in the twelfth
century, it is very likely that as Roger's prisoner he also
lodged in the bishop's other castles. Perhaps Curthose recalled his military experience in Normandy and the Holy
Land and used it to assist Roger in planning his castles.

Today Devizes, like Sherborne, is a most attractive town.
In Roger's time it was already a borough served by two
churches. Saint John's was directly beneath the castle and
was probably used by the garrison, and Saint Mary's may
have been for the townsmen. Saint John's is especially noted
for its fine Norman tower and its chancel with chevron-
patterned arches. Whether these churches were erected dur-

21. The present owner of the castle, Edward Mazewski Kemp,
graciously showed me the grounds and reconstructed buildings; the
area of the original main hall beneath the keep has been exposed.
He possesses fourteen extraordinary wooden corbel heads tentatively
identified as early twelfth-century work, which he believes may have
once decorated Roger's great hall. They are strikingly individual por-
traits (three wear crowns or wreaths) with sad, care-worn, mildly distorted features. John Leland (*Itinerary*, 5:82) praised the castle ruins
in the mid-sixteenth century. James Waylen, whose imaginative nineteenth-century painting of the Norman castle now graces the Devizes
town hall, wrote *Chronicles of Devizes*. Edward Stone, *Devizes Castle: Its History and Romance,* contains useful information and a
groundplan, but has errors and must be used with care. A more recent analysis is R. H. Cunnington, "Devizes Castle: A Suggested Reconstruction." Ralph B. Pugh is now preparing a history of Devizes.

22. Matthew Paris, *Historia Anglorum,* 1:206; Orderic Vitalis,
4:486. Apparenly Robert was briefly imprisoned at Wareham before
being moved to Devizes ("Annals of Winchester," in *Annales
Monastici,* 2:42). Matthew Paris, *Historia Anglorum,* 1:212–213,
3:180, told a fanciful tale of the duke's escape, recapture, and
blinding in 1109. See also David, *Robert Curthose,* pp. 178–189. See
Chapter 5 for the duke's removal from Roger's custody in 1126.

ing Roger's lifetime or shortly after his death is uncertain, and indeed there are many simliar churches with Norman features scattered throughout the diocese. Unfortunately, they are equally hard to date, but they do suggest that the whole diocese profited from Roger's enthusiastic construction.

Roger was as keenly interested in education as he was in architecture; and shortly after becoming bishop he decided to upgrade the educational institutions in his diocese. The monastic schools concentrated on the instruction of choir monks, but his learned cathedral chapter also supported a school administered by a canon, called the master of the schools (*archischola*), who managed the endowments, provided the books, and appointed and paid teachers.[23] Roger believed this school should have the best possible instructors, so he turned to the continent for a recognized scholar. Very early in his episcopate he made contact with Hildebert of Lavardin (c. 1056-1133), Bishop of Le Mans and one of the most famous poets of the age. One wonders when and how Roger came to know such a great literary figure. His original request is lost, but Hildebert's courteous reply congratulated Roger on his well merited election as bishop and his great zeal for learning. Agreeing to send his own precentor, Guy of Étampes, a man of great intelligence and character, Hildebert told Roger that in Guy he would find many masters.[24]

23. The monastic schools at Reading and Abingdon were among the oldest in the country. At Abingdon there was a grammar school at the Church of Saint Nicholas for boys not destined for the monastery (A. E. Preston, *The Church and Parish of Saint Nicholas, Abingdon*, pp. 272-277). A charter of Abbot Faritius was subscribed by a *Richardus pedagogus*, (*Abingdon Chronicle*, 2:123).

24. Hildebert of Lavardin, *Opera*, letter 22, col. 219. Dom Beaugendre, an editor of Hildebert's works, suggested that three of his poems (cols. 1420-1423, 1430) may have been dedicated to, or written about, Bishop Roger. One praised a bishop across the sea, another a prelate building his cathedral, and a third criticized a man who was both bishop and abbot. The circumstances fit Roger and the identification is possible, but there is nothing in any of the poems to connect them directly with him.

Guy, also called Grumar the Breton, seems to have studied under Anselm of Laon and to have written a gloss on grammar and dialectic.[25] He went to England early in the century and was made a canon of Salisbury cathedral, where he taught for a number of years until, at the latest, 1125 when he was elected bishop of Le Mans to succeed his friend Hildebert, who had become archbishop of Tours. Another schoolmaster, Alwinus, was mentioned in 1122.[26]

In 1113, while Guy was probably still at Sarum, a group of nine canons from Laon cathedral visited Roger's town seeking alms for repairing their own church, which had been destroyed in a communal riot the year before. Roger hospitably entertained them all, for his own nephews, Alexander and Nigel, had studied at Laon for a long time.[27] A Salisbury resident was cured through the canons' intercession. Later they visited nearby Wilton nunnery to venerate the relics of Bede and to pray at the grave of the poetess Muriel. While in the southwest, they caused a bit of trouble by expressing skepticism about the legends of King Arthur.

About ten years after the Laon canons' visit, the Sarum

25. Edwards, *English Secular Cathedrals,* p. 182. Unfortunately little is known about Guy's work at Salisbury. For these few details I am indebted to Dr. Eleanor Rathbone, who is studying English cathedrals and schools in the twelfth century. For more about Guy (d. 1136), see his biography in *Actus Pontificium Cenomannis,* Chapter 36, in *Vetera Analecta,* ed. Jean Mabillon (Paris, 1723), esp. p. 320. The twelfth-century library at Salisbury included the works of Saint Augustine, a collection of Pauline epistles, Isadore's *Maxims of the Learned,* the *Maxims of Hilary,* the *Diadem of Monks,* Rufinus, Jerome the Presbyter, and Anselm on parts of the New Testament. The Salisbury manuscripts of these works still survive (see William Dodsworth, *An Historical Account of the Episcopal See and Cathedral Church of Sarum, or Salisbury,* p. 22).

26. Charter 7. In December 1139 King Stephen gave the Sarum chapter some of Roger's churches for the work of the master of the schools (*Regesta,* 33, no. 789).

27. Herman of Tournai, *De Miraculis S. Mariae Laudunensis,* cols. 982–983. See also J. S. P. Tatlock, "The English Journey of the Laon Canons." For Muriel, see J. S. P. Tatlock, "Muriel, the Earliest English Poetess," PMLA, 48(1933):317–321.

students entertained another traveling group, this time, a band of monks from Savigny who were seeking prayers for their late abbot, Vitalis.[28] Such enrollments were usually, but not exclusively, sought from individuals and communities especially known to the deceased, and Savigny was in Avranches, Roger's home diocese. The Salisbury students composed a poem in praise of Vitalis as well as adding to the roll of prayers.

The most famous student to pass through Roger's schools was John of Salisbury, the great humanist and political theorist. Born about 1115, he studied at Sarum until 1135 when he left for the higher learning at the emerging university of Paris; John could have told us much about Roger. It is quite possible, for instance, that the bishop was his patron. John, however, wrote very little about his youth, and his one reference to the schools at Sarum was distinctly unflattering. As a young boy he was sent to a priest to learn the Psalter, but the tutor preferred to use his innocent students to help forecast the future. John was not adept at this activity, which he considered sacrilegious, and he found satisfaction in reporting that the teacher later repented and took refuge in a monastery.[29] Despite such an awkward beginning, John's later scholastic progress abroad may indicate generally good training at Salisbury.

Bishop Roger was fortunate that the responsibilities of his cathedral clergy were already fairly well established when he took up residence.[30] The dean was the presiding officer of the chapter, and no canon could leave the cathedral without his permission. Furthermore, whenever the bishop was absent, the dean assumed his administrative duties. Next in importance was the precentor, or cantor, who managed

28. Léopold Delisle, *Rouleaux Des Morts,* pp. 337–338. Vitalis died in 1122. In 1113 or 1114 the diocese had also signed a roll for Matilda, abbess of La Trinité de Caen, daughter of the Conqueror and sister of Henry I (*Ibid.,* p. 189).

29. Clement C. Webb, *John of Salisbury,* pp. 3–4.

30. *Register of St. Osmund,* 1:3–15.

the choir. The master of the schools, later called the chancellor, supervised the school, drafted episcopal letters, and kept the seal of the church, but it is doubtful that he had any highly organized staff to help him.[31] Finally there was the treasurer, who kept the ornaments, relics, and wealth of the church and furnished candles for its liturgical services.

In Saint Mary's Cathedral, Salisbury, as at other chapters of secular canons, each member was granted with his choir stall a prebend, or benefice, to support and maintain him in his work. Benefices varied widely in value, but were usually rents from lands within the diocese and tithes of individual churches. Later specific prebends would be assigned to particular officials, but these matters were still fluid in Roger's day. There was also a common fund which was divided among the resident canons, each of whom was expected to be present for part of the year, although regulations requiring definite residence periods were never very successful, especially when several canons were away on government service.

Bishop Roger seems to have taken an active interest in diocesan and chapter organization. Such matters certainly progressed well during his long episcopate, similar as they were in some ways to the administrative affairs that so absorbed him in government. He increased the number of prebends so significantly that Sarum soon housed one of the largest secular chapters in the country. From the original thirty-two canons instituted by Bishop Osmund, the number grew under Roger to near fifty-two, its eventual full complement.[32] Not all the new prebends were outright

31. Edwards, *English Secular Cathedrals,* pp. 181–183; C. R. Cheney, *English Bishops' Chanceries, 1100–1250,* pp. 39–45.

32. The creation of the prebends of Calne (1107–1116), Heytesbury (1101–1116), Hurstbourne (1107–1122), Shipton and Bricklesworth (1107–1116 from Arnulf the Falconer), and Rothfen (1107–1135) can all be noted in Henry's writs (*Regesta,* 2, nos. 1164, 753, 824, 1163, 1972); see also VCH, Wiltshire, 3:158–159.

gifts, however, and some entailed troublesome conditions. Bishop Ranulf Flambard of Durham, a notorious pluralist, retained a life interest in the prebend of Heytesbury.[33] Another one caused even greater difficulties. Arnulf the Falconer had been granted lands by the Conqueror for his faithful service, and in Bishop Osmund's time Arnulf obtained William Rufus's consent to give some of these lands to Sarum for a prebend for his own son. In about 1115 or 1116, he wished to create a second prebend for another son, Humphrey, but first he complained to the king that the cathedral chapter was not keeping the terms of the original grant.[34] Henry wrote to Roger, to the dean, and to the chapter at Salisbury, commanding them to observe the agreement properly, noting that the question had been thoroughly investigated in his own royal court and in the archbishop's court where they all had agreed to the conditions. Apparently the Sarum men had been quite reluctant to reach a settlement, for the king threatened to withdraw the churches back into his own hands if they did not abide by the covenant. Arnulf then gave churches for the second prebend, Henry notified his justiciars of it, and Bishop Roger issued a writ conceding Arnulf's rights of presentment to the prebends.[35]

These unwelcome, anti-Gregorian, lay rights came up again in 1122 when the royal collector, Serlo, gave tithes from some Devon churches for a prebend to be established for his son, Richard, and for his next of kin thereafter. Roger's formal and gracious charter records this gift.[36] About the same time, in a very unusual move which will be discussed shortly, Bishop Roger gave the prebend of Sherborne to the abbot of Sherborne abbey, thereby introducing a monk into a chapter of secular canons.[37]

The chapter's main concern was the cathedral, not the

33. *Regesta*, 2, no. 753.
34. *Register of St. Osmund*, 1:380 (omitted in the *Regesta*).
35. Charter 5. *Regesta*, 2, no. 1163, is Henry's confirmation.
36. Charter 7.   37. Charter 9.

whole diocese. To visit the parishes, inspect religious houses, gather rents from episcopal manors, and collect Peter's Pence, Bishop Roger relied upon four archdeacons, two for Wiltshire and one each for Berkshire and Dorset. These archdeacons had prebends to support them in their work and thus were members of the chapter like other canons. A third group of officials, both laymen and clerks, constituted Bishop Roger's personal household (*familia*). Included were a steward (*dapifer*), a butler (*pincerna*), a constable, and several chaplains. The steward was an important mesne tenant and usually supervised the bishop's estates; a knight named Osmund served in this capacity from before 1114 until after Roger's death in 1139.[38]

Much of the main work of local parish organization and church construction was also undertaken during the first half of the century. Roger's role cannot be detailed, but evidently he sought what help he could from prominent laymen. For example, sometime after 1122 a Geoffrey of Saint Martin gave tithes to the cathedral on the condition that a curate would say mass in his chapel three days a week when he and his wife were there and one day each week when they were away.[39]

Salisbury was quite a wealthy diocese, and Roger obviously enjoyed the pleasures its resources offered him. His building program alone would have bankrupted many a lesser see. Some estimate of his holdings can be obtained from the one extant pipe roll. In 1129/1130 Danegeld was collected at a rate of two shillings for each hide of land.[40] Since Roger was pardoned £147 5s. 1d., he must have held approximately 1482½ hides.[41] Thus he seems to have been a greater landowner than the king's nephew, Stephen of

38. Charters 4, 19, 26, 27, 30. Osmund was pardoned thirty shillings for Danegeld in 1130 (*Pipe Roll*, p. 23).

39. *Register of St. Osmund*, 1:215; the editor incorrectly dated this at 1098.

40. Henry of Huntingdon, p. 258.

41. See Appendix 4 for his pipe roll pardons.

Blois, who held 1,339 English hides, and his holdings compared favorably with the 1,565 hides controlled by Earl Robert of Gloucester. One of the great justices of the realm, Richard Basset, held only 176 hides in eleven counties.[42] Of course, not all Roger's lands were personal holdings; most were held as diocesan ordinary of Salisbury, and, as would be expected, the overwhelming number of hides were located in his diocese, with more than half in Wiltshire, alone.

Burgage payments were also recordeed in 1130. Although these pardons cannot be converted into hidal measurements, they do show some proportional distribution of tenements in different towns. Roger's pardon for Salisbury itself was only fifteen shillings, but it was not much of a town, and the cathedral would not be counted in this total. Pardons of more than six pounds in Winchester and more than eight pounds in London indicate the extensive and valuable properties he enjoyed in the seats of government.[43] Other very small pardons were recorded for Oxford and towns in Gloucestershire and Staffordshire. To these pipe roll entries must be added Roger's other ecclesiastical possessions; he was a pluralist on a grand scale, holding several prebends in his own chapter and various other benefices scattered throughout the country.[44]

42. Patterson, "Robert of Gloucester," p. 994; Davis, *King Stephen,* p. 14; Southern, "Place of Henry I," p. 135. Only demesne lands of barons were recorded, and overseas possessions were naturally omitted. Ultimately, therefore, Stephen and Robert probably held a great deal more than Roger.

43. Roger was pardoned thirty-seven shillings' worth of land in Winchester in the "Winton Domesday" (1112–1115) (*Domesday Book,* 5:535).

44. Only the prebend of Cannings was mentioned by name (Charter 26). Roger was abbot of Sherborne (until 1122), and Malmesbury (after 1118), controlled Abbotsbury (sometime after 1106) and Middleton (for five years), and held the deanry of Saint Martin-le-Grand, London, and probably the deanry of Wolverhampton in Worcester (Charter 28). In connection with Sherborne he briefly held Horton and Kidwelly priories and the church of Saint Mary Magdalene, Sherborne; with Saint Martin's he held Saint Botolph's, London,

One might have thought Roger would have shown a
deep, continuing interest in Normandy, but apparently
his concern for it was relatively minor. He rarely visited
it, for his position as viceroy usually required him to remain in England.[45] Nevertheless, he is said to have had extensive Norman possessions, at least at Valognes, St. Mar-
couf, Warevilla, and Popevilla.[46] Archbishop Hugh of
Rouen, abbot of Reading until his elevation in 1129, noted
that Roger held the church of Amanvilla at farm from the
nuns of Saint Amand of Rouen and that he gave them continual trouble about it. Hugh claimed that he frequently
communicated with Roger on this account.[47] The details of
this quarrel are lost, but the bishop did significantly aid
another Norman monastery, the convent and leper hospital
of Saint Giles of Pont Audemer. His letter reflects the mixture of generosity, self-interest, and drive for proper administration which characterized so many of his acts.
Writing as "Roger by divine permission humble minister of
Salisbury," acknowledging this congregation's modest resources and great charity to all wayfarers, and asking prayers

---

and Newport and Maldon churches in Essex. In Oxford he held the
churches of Headington, Saint Mary Magdalene, Saint Michael's,
and All Saints, in connection with the priory of Saint Frideswide
(Charters 12, 30, 31). His life interests in the endowments of Cirencester abbey included the churches of Frome in Somerset, Avebury
in Wilts, and Shrivenham, Cookham, and Bray in Berks (Charter
27). In Oxford he also held Stanton Harcourt church and in Berkshire, Thatcham church, both of which passed to Reading abbey after
his death. He held the prebend of Langford in the Lincoln cathedral
chapter and Langford church in Oxfordshire (*Registrum Antiquissimum*, nos. 139, 179). The churches of Littleton, Hants, and Lavington, Wilts, were his (Charter 30) and probably the chaplaincy
of Pevensey (*Regesta*, 2, no. 1360).

45. For Roger's trips abroad, see Chapter 5, Note 11.
46. Haskins, *Norman Institutions,* p. 136; John Horace Round,
*Calendar of Documents Preserved in France Illustrative of the His-
tory of Great Britain and Ireland,* I, *918–1206,* no. 909. In 1142
Archbishop Hugh of Rouen reported that King Stephen had given
Roger's holdings to a convent of canons regular just erected at St.
Lo, Coutances.
47. Round, *Calendar,* no. 99. This was written between 1154 and
1164.

for himself and for the church of Sarum, he gave them the greater tithes of the church of Sturminster, Dorset.[48] The smaller tithes were reserved for the support of a priest who would personally serve the religious needs of Sturminster. Roger closed by saying that he did this freely, at no man's urging, but because he kept God alone before his eyes. The wording of the charter suggests that the viceroy might have personally observed the congregation's work. Saint Giles was founded between 1129 and 1135 by Count Waleran of Meulan, who later bitterly opposed Roger and helped bring about his ruin.[49] Perhaps the bishop's gift was an unsuccessful attempt to maintain good relations with the count, or, to give Roger the benefit of his own phrasing, perhaps it was a generous freewill offering which he did not wish misinterpreted as an effort to curry the count's favor.

Roger's intentions regarding Salisbury were less ambiguous, and he used his influence to obtain many valuable gifts for his cathedral and chapter. Only Abbot Faritius of Abingdon in the period between 1100 and 1117 and Abbot Hugh of the new royal foundation at Reading between 1122 and 1129 seemed equally fortunate in winning the king's favors. The archbishops of Canterbury and York received fewer gifts than their high positions might have warranted. The church of Salisbury received tithes from the New Forest and all the forests in the diocese, and its canons were exempted from all customs and tolls in markets and fairs in England.[50] Tithes of more than twenty churches

48. Charter 21.

49. The town of Sturminster in Dorset belonged to Waleran's twin, Robert (*Regesta*, 2, nos. 843, 1918). For more on Waleran and St. Giles, see August Le Prévost, *Memoires et Notes de M. August Le Prévost Pour Servir à l'Histoire de Département de l'Eure*, 2:549.

50. *Register of St. Osmund*, 1:200–206; *Regesta*, 2, nos. 1162, 1273, 1972; *Charters and Documents Illustrating the History of the Cathedral, City, and Diocese of Salisbury in the Twelfth and Thirteenth Centuries*, ed. W. Rich Jones and W. Dunn Macray (hereafter cited as *Sarum Documents*), p. 4, no. 111.

were given to the cathedral of Saint Mary, and the bishop
and his church also gained the very lucrative privilege of
holding a seven-day fair at the feast of the Nativity of the
Blessed Virgin (September 8)—three days before the feast,
the feast, and three days afterward.[51] Queen Matilda granted
the cathedral all her own rights in the tolls of the Salisbury
market, which later in 1130 amounted to forty shillings.[52]
Private individuals gave other gifts, and exchanges were arranged whereby distant lands were traded for possessions
within the diocese.[53]

As the chapter grew large and wealthy, it became increasingly independent of the bishop. This was common
in the first half of the twelfth century to most English
cathedrals, secular or monastic. The growing feudalization
of life and the frequent absences of curial bishops from
their sees diminished the intimate and paternal relations
that had prevailed in earlier centuries between bishops and
their cathedral clergy. Then, too, the tendency of English
kings to keep bishoprics vacant for years and to seize their
revenues often caused chapters untold financial hardships.
Dividing the possessions of the bishop from those of his
chapter seemed to offer a solution to this problem. Even
the regulations of Bishop Osmund foresaw this, for they
provided that canons would be instituted by the bishop,
but would receive their benefices from the dean with the
consent of the chapter.[54]

The process of dividing diocesan holdings can be illus-

51. *Regesta*, 2, nos. 753, 824, 1164, 1291, 1972; *Register of St.
Osmund*, 1:202, 208. See also VCH, Wiltshire, 3:158–159.

52. *Regesta*, 2, no. 1199; *Pipe Roll*, pp. 12–13.

53. *Register of St. Osmund*, 1:202–203, 205, 349; *Reegsta*, 2, nos.
1716 (a gift of Croc the huntsman), 1360 (Roger exchanges the
chapel of Pevensey with Prior Hugh of Lewes who gives him the
lands of Hervey of Wilton in Netheravon; Stephen confirmed this
more than twenty-five years later, *Regesta*, 3, no. 450).

54. *Register of St. Osmund*, 1:5. This might be a thirteenth-
century interpolation.

trated at Salisbury under Bishop Roger. Between 1107 and
1116 King Henry gave the canons the tithes and under-
wood of the New Forest, but at the same time he also gave
Roger and his successors hunting tithes there.[55] Clearly, a
division of revenues was intended. On the other hand,
there are also examples where the bishop and his chapter
worked together to strengthen their holdings.[56] By a simple
expedient, Roger prevented a complete separation of bishop
and chapter like that at other cathedrals. Many chapters
permitted only canons to attend chapter meetings, thereby
excluding the bishops, but at Sarum the bishop reserved a
special prebend for himself and thus attended chapter meetings, if not by episcopal, at least by prebendal right.[57]

Medieval prebends had many uses. Not only did they
support choir members and cathedral officials, they also
provided handsome livings for relatives and retainers. Many
bishops even collected prebends to augment their own in-
comes. Bishop Roger was such an acknowledged pluralist.[58]
He also practiced nepotism on a grand scale, but differed
from other prelates in that he was able to appoint the same
relatives to both governmental and ecclesiastical positions.
Many of these men later became bishops. To cite just a few
cases: Roger's nephews, Alexander and Nigel, each held
Salisbury prebends and archdeaconries; Alexander became
bishop of Lincoln in 1123; Nigel was a royal treasurer and
later was bishop of Ely after 1133. Everard was a chancery
clerk who held a Sarum prebend and an archdeaconry
there and became bishop of Norwich in 1121. Geoffrey
Rufus was a royal chancellor, a Salisbury canon, and the
bishop of Durham after 1133. Roger's own son, Roger the

55. *Regesta*, 2, no. 1162. In the *Pipe Roll* (p. 13) Roger was pardoned for the farm of Wilton from which his canons received an
eleven-shilling grant.
56. Charter 7; *Regesta*, 2, no. 1372.
57. *Sarum Documents*, p. 5, no. 4; *Register of St. Osmund*, 2:220.
58. See Note 44.

Poor, was a royal chancellor and probably a Salisbury arch-deacon; his probable brother, Adelelm, was a royal trea-surer, archdeacon of Dorset, and dean of Lincoln.[59]

Building castles, schools, and churches, and enlarging, organizing, and bestowing chapter holdings were but parts of the bishop's duties. Roger also visited parishes, conferred sacraments, and held synods to discuss moral and theologi-cal issues. On great liturgical feasts he offered solemn masses in the cathedral and preached to the canons or to the assembled faithful. It was a demanding schedule, so in order to devote needed time to his governmental obligations Bishop Roger frequently deputized his canons and arch-deacons to perform the routine chores of his episcopacy. In 1129/1130 one such fairly typical diocesan meeting was held in the church of Hill Deverel under the presidency of Adelelm, archdeacon of Dorset, at which it was decided that the church belonged to the prebend of Heytesbury. Elyas Giffard, the donor of the church, wrote to Bishop Roger confirming this judgment.[60]

Although he relied heavily on such subordinates, Bishop Roger was considered a very conscientious bishop. William of Malmesbury reported that he had a fixed policy of setting aside mornings for church affairs and devoting afternoons to governmental problems.[61] This may be a charming over-simplification, but more likely it represents a genuine effort Roger continually made to balance his heavy responsibilities. In addition to all the other concerns, particular attention was always given to one obligation—his regulation of the monasteries within his diocese.

Anglo-Norman monasticism came to its full and glorious maturity in the early decades of the twelfth century. En-couraged by the peace and prosperity promoted by the gov-

59. See Appendix 3.
60. *Register of St. Osmund,* 1:349–351. See *Regesta,* 2, nos. 1201, 1302, and *Bath Cartularies,* pp. 49–51, for a Bath dispute in 1121 in which Archdeacon Joel of Salisbury acted as Roger's deputy.
61. William of Malmesbury, *G.R.,* 2:484.

ernment of Henry and Roger, the number of monks increased, treasure accumulated, libraries multiplied, and great new buildings arose.[62] The organization of English monasticism was fairly clear. Although most monks followed the rule of Benedict, their abbeys were completely autonomous from each other and not related to fraternal congregations like Cluny. English abbeys usually averaged fifty to sixty black-robed monks, most of whom were drawn from the class of wholly free landowners. Times were changing, however, although few men yet realized that this period which witnessed the origins of the universities and the coming of new religious orders like the white-robed Cistercians would also see the end of the Benedictine centuries and the gradual decline of the paramount influence of the Black Monks.[63] A straw in the wind was the increasing rivalry between secular and religious clergy, part of which was reflected in Roger's life and in the opinions of monastic chroniclers who wrote about him.

By dominating abbatical elections, the king effectively controlled the monasteries of his realm. Abbots, like bishops, were, after all, great barons and lords of immense fiefs as well as ghostly fathers to their communities. Between 1100 and 1140 an abbot was generally "elected" in the royal presence by a small delegation of monks who voted for the candidate proposed by the king and his council. This was hardly in the Gregorian tradition, but it was the accepted practice. Except for a few exempt houses, spiritual supervision of monasteries fell to the local bishops, and it was not unusual for them to attempt to control the temporal affairs of the houses as well. In the second half of the cen-

62. Orderic Vitalis, 4:91–92, 115; David Knowles, *The Monastic Order in England, 943–1216*, pp. 423–425, 711; David Knowles and R. Neville Hadcock, *Medieval Religious Houses: England and Wales*, pp. 356–364.
63. Prestwick, "War and Finance in the Anglo-Norman State;" Norman F. Cantor, "The Crisis of Western Monasticism, 1050–1130."

tury appeals to Rome for exemption from episcopal regulation dramatically multiplied, but till then a strong bishop
like Roger of Salisbury could frequently do as he wished,
provided he did not counter the king's intentions.

The diocese of Salisbury contained several venerable
monasteries. Malmesbury and Abingdon were prominent
houses, and Henry's own foundation was at Reading. There
were wealthy nunneries at Shaftesbury and Wilton and
lesser abbeys at Horton, Sherborne, Cerne, Abbotsbury, and
Milton. Since monastic chroniclers tended to record extraordinary events rather than the routine of life, the information
detailing Roger's relations with the monasteries of his diocese is very uneven and more often than not consists of
complaints about what these writers considered to be his
exploitation of their houses.

The great historian of English monasticism Dom David
Knowles has depicted Roger as a villian who greedily
snatched helpless abbeys into his clutches.[64] Donald Nicholl
called him a notorious opponent of the monks.[65] Certainly
some of Roger's contemporaries shared these views. The
author of the *Gesta Stephani* declared that Roger removed
the abbots of Malmesbury and Abbotsbury and made those
houses his handmaids; supposedly they were not restored to
their ancient splendor until after his death.[66] The monk
who completed Florence of Worcester's chronicle maintained that Roger stripped those same abbeys of their honors
and privileges.[67] William of Malmesbury said that King
Henry lavished "whole abbeys of monks" on the bishop, offering these details:

[Roger] was conscious of his power and abused God's indulgence somewhat more persistently than befitted such a
man. Finally, as the poet says of a rich man that he "Pulls

64. Knowles, *Monastic Order in England,* pp. 273, 614.
65. Nicholl, *Thurstan Archbishop of York,* pp. 183, 187.
66. *Gesta Stephani,* p. 65.
67. John of Worcester, p. 59; Florence of Worcester (Continuator's part), 2:122.

down and builds, exchanges square for round," so Roger tried to turn abbeys into a bishopric, the property of a bishopric into an abbey. Two most ancient monasteries, those of Malmesbury and Abbotsbury, he attached to the bishopric as far as lay in his power; the priory of Sherborne, which belongs directly to the bishop of Salisbury, he turned into an abbey, suppressing the abbey of Horton, on that account, and adding it to Sherborne.[68]

Obviously, Roger's concern for monasticism was not devoid of a large measure of self-interest, but a closer examination of his activity makes it seem inappropriate to attribute to him any consistent monastic policy.

Sherborne abbey had once been the seat of a diocese, and it had a proud heritage stretching back to the sixth century. More recently, Stephen Harding, the founder of the Cistercian order, and Cardinal Robert Pullen, had studied there.[69] When Bishop Herman had moved his cathedral to Sarum about 1075, Sherborne monastery, which had been the cathedral chapter, declined in importance and became a mere priory directly under the bishop's control. Its fortunes rebounded under Bishop Roger, who built one of his tremendous castles up the road, planted a vineyard, stocked a fishpond, and generally became attentive to the needs of the monks there by increasing their possessions and dependent houses.

In 1114 Roger was in Wales as part of Henry's summer campaign, and on July 19, with the king's consent, he gave Sherborne priory land at Kidwelly.[70] Noting that he had

68. William of Malmesbury, *H.N.*, pp. 37–39.

69. Pullen evidently studied at Laon and became an archdeacon of Exeter before lecturing on the Bible at Oxford between 1133 and 1138. Henry I offered him a bishopric, which he refused. Several of his relatives were at Sherborne; he later aided the monks when they quarreled with Bishop Jocelin. See F. Courtney, *Cardinal Robert Pullen*, in *Analecta Gregoriana*, LXIV(1954):4; British Museum Additional Manuscript 46487, fo. 70v.; John of Hexham, *Historia*, p. 319; "Annals of Oseney," in *Annales Monastici*, 4:19.

70. Charter 4. He may have also accompanied Henry's 1121 campaign, as he was with the king at Hereford that summer (*Regesta*, 2, no. 1294).

paced off the boundaries of his donation himself, the bishop had a large part of his household witness his formal charter, including his brother Humphrey, Osmund the steward, Edmund the custodian of Kidwelly Castle, and Alwin a priest of the borough. Two days later he consecrated a nearby cemetery and confirmed the gifts it received from the area's Norman, French, and Flemish settlers.

Roger had apparently been marcher lord of this part of southern Wales since about 1106.[71] His early timber castle with earthen ramparts was built on the spot where the Lesser Gwendraeth falls into the sea and guards the road to Carmarthen.[72] In the shadow of the castle the borough of Kidwelly had sprung up, and Roger was reported to have urged Flemings to settle there as early as 1108.[73] This was all part of the government's policy to pacify Wales through colonization. Across the river he dedicated a church to the Virgin Mary and planted a tiny priory of about three monks, which was made a dependent cell of Sherborne.[74]

Surprisingly, Roger did not hold the lordship of Kidwelly until his death, as it was transferred to Maurice of London some time before 1135.[75] John Beeler has declared that the

71. John E. Lloyd, *A History of Wales,* 2:429–430. I have not found any contemporary evidence for Roger's reception of this responsibility, but it seems accurate, as Hywel ap Gronw was slaughtered in 1106.

72. Practically nothing remains of the Norman castle. For a description, see Cyril Fox and C. A. Ralegh Radford, "Kidwelly Castle, Carmarthenshire: Including a Survey of the Polychrome Pottery Found There and Elsewhere in Britain."

73. Davies, *Episcopal Acts,* 1:113–114. Here again, although there is abundant contemporary evidence for the Flemish immigration in the early decades of the twelfth century, I have been unable to make a precise connection with Roger himself, but it seems obvious that he must have encouraged the men to come, since they settled so extensively in his domain.

74. For a discussion of its location and fragmentary remains see John E. Lloyd, *A History of Carmarthenshire,* 1:138–139, 355.

75. Lloyd, *A History of Wales,* 1:429–430. William Dugdale, *Monasticon Anglicanum,* 4:65, suggests that a Richard Fitz William intervened beween Roger and Maurice. That seems unlikely, but after 1122 this Richard and Maurice both made gifts to Sherborne

castle and lordship had passed to Maurice by 1116, but in 1130 one of Roger's men was killed thereabouts.[76] The great Welsh authority J. E. Lloyd suggested that Roger may have parted with the lordship but retained the castle.[77] Indeed, his constable, Geoffrey, was still there fighting in 1136.[78] On the other hand, Kidwelly priory remained dependent upon Sherborne right up to the dissolution of the monasteries under Henry VIII.

Sherborne gained another house under Roger, but this time it was not a tiny new foundation like Kidwelly, but the abbey of Horton, which dated from 1050. About twenty miles south of Sherborne, Horton was an unimportant monastery on the Dorset coast which later probably never held more than five monks. In July 1122 the king declared that, by the advice of his council and with the consent of Bishop Roger, he had decided to unite his abbey of Horton with the priory of Sherborne.[79] Considering the inconvenience of the abbey's location and its small endowment, he hoped that, instead of two weak houses, one strong convent would now rise to serve the Lord. This is precisely the type of streamlining which appealed to Roger's orderly administrative instincts. Although the action offended some monastic chroniclers, it is difficult to appreciate their reasoning, for a house as poor as Horton could not even conduct proper choir services.

(Dugdale, *Monasticon Anglicanum,* 4:65). Maurice was the son of William of London, a witness of Roger's grant in 1114 (Charter 4).

76. John Beeler, *Warfare in England, 1066–1189,* p. 226. The men of Carmarthenshire owed the exchequer forty shillings for the man's death (*Pipe Roll,* p. 90). It was a violent age; in 1130 alone Roger was pardoned fines for eleven other murders (*Pipe Roll,* pp. 15, 20, 21, 74). Bishop Bernard of St. David's apparently held the honor of Carmarthen in 1130 (*Regesta,* 2, no. 1649).

77. Lloyd, *A History of Wales,* 1:470.

78. Gerard of Wales, *Opera,* 6:79. For more on Geoffrey, see Charter 6.

79. *Regesta,* 2, no. 1325; Knowles and Hadcock, *Medieval Religious Houses,* p. 68. The date was given in British Museum Manuscript, Cotton Faustina A II, fo. 25v; see also "Annals of Margan," in *Annales Monastici,* 1:10.

Roger ruled Sherborne for twenty years, protecting and supporting the monks and increasing their endowments. Naturally he acted through a prior, but ultimately he was in control. Then in 1122, following the union of Horton and Sherborne, he brought the latter house to the status of a fully independent abbey; Prior Thurstan became first abbot of its fifty monks.[80] This act alone belies the criticism that he was a consistent opponent of monks. It is something of a moot point whether Roger or Thurstan was responsible for the reconstruction of St. Mary's Abbey. Suffice it to say that they must have worked in harmony, and the result is compatible with the beauty and splendor of Roger's other buildings. Here, too, they used the warm, mellow Ham stone quarried near Montacute in Somerset and built with strong, clean lines. Large stretches of their Romanesque walls remain, as do the great columns of the crossing.[81] There were extensive renovations in later centuries, and today the glory of the abbey is its extensive fan vaulting. The Norman monastic buildings were largely destroyed, but traces of them can be found in the present Sherborne School.

Roger took very positive steps to increase the new abbey's endowments, and shortly after 1122 he gave the cathedral prebend of Sherborne to the monastery. This was an extraordinary provision, for it meant that a Benedictine

80. For the number of monks, see Knowles and Hadcock, *Medieval Religious Houses,* p. 77. In 1122 or 1123 ten monks, including Edwin the prior, attested the mortuary roll of Vitalis of Savigny; several of the names are definitely Saxon (Delisle, *Rouleaux Des Morts,* p. 326). Knowles, *Monastic Order in England,* p. 133, argues that Sherborne became independent of Roger in 1109 when Ely became a diocese. I do not see the connection (the information Knowles cites as William of Malmesbury, *G.P.,* p. 175, seems rather to be in Liebermann, *Ungedruckte Anglo-Normannische Geschichtsquellen,* p. 23).

81. The so-called Bishop Roger's Chapel, now used as a choir vestry, is primarily a thirteenth-century addition, but it does preserve Norman walls on its southern and western sides. James F. Gibb's excavations have uncovered extensive foundations of the old Saxon church and monastery.

abbot would have a canon's stall in a chapter of secular
clergy.[82] When Bishop Osmund created thirty-two stalls at
Sarum, he appropriated the tithes of Sherborne to support
one such prebend. The first occupant was most likely Hubbald, a very learned man and a stammerer; he was also an
archdeacon of the diocese and, therefore probably appointed
a vicar to perform his ecclesiastical duties in the parish of
Sherborne. Reportedly, Hubbald was cured of terrible pains
through the intercession of Saint Aldhelm of Malmesbury,
whose relics had been taken to Salisbury.[83] After the archdeacon's death Roger gave the benefice to Abbot Thurstan.

Some years later there was an investigation about this gift,
during which a Sherborne monk named Robert (who had
become prior of Breamore) told what he remembered.[84] It
seems that when Bishop Roger invested Thurstan with a
copy of the canons' rule and a loaf of bread—the traditional
symbols of membership in the chapter community—the
other canons objected strongly. Robert reported that they
murmured against the bishop as much as they dared,
arguing that he was making a canon of a monk. Later
there were complaints that the abbot often missed chapter
meetings and choir duties. The fact that Robert had been
appointed his deputy for these responsibilities, thus becoming the first vicar choral to serve at Salisbury, and fulfilled them for many years apparently made no difference.
Moreover, instead of appointing a secular clerk as vicar for
the ministry of Sherborne itself, the abbot chose the sacrist
of his own monastery for that parish work. Worst of all,
Bishop Roger had conferred the prebend jointly on the abbot and the monastery so that there would never be a
vacancy in the prebend, whereas normally when a canon
died at Salisbury the revenues from his former prebend re-

82. Fowler, *Medieval Sherborne*, p. 99. For a somewhat similar
procedure at York, see Nicholl, *Thurstan Archbishop of York*, pp.
116–117, 123–130.
83. William of Malmesbury, *G.P.*, p. 429.
84. *Sarum Documents*, pp. 16–17.

verted to the common fund of all the chapter members for the next year.[85]

Roger's unprecendented support for Sherborne abbey came in the midst of increasing antagonism between monks and secular clerics across the country.[86] It is therefore interesting that just about then the cantor of Roger's own cathedral, Canon Godwin, was urging moderation and reconciliation in the regular-secular disputes. Both monks and canons lived according to a rule, he wrote, and their differences were really very unimportant.[87] Monks, regular canons, secular canons, and clerics were all members of one body, the universal church. Different members had different functions, and thus their lives varied in minor details. Secular canons like himself, for example, should certainly not be called irregular because they had possessions. Such property was not wasted on vain things, but was spent for their work and ecclesiastical needs. One wonders whether Godwin's patient, reasonable meditation expressed his bishop's thoughts; their positions seem very similar.

Moderate or not, Roger was a strong man and easily suppressed criticism of his actions. His successors were not so fortunate, and the Sherborne prebend troubled the abbey and the chapter for many years.[88] When Sherborne became an abbey, Roger also gave it the nine manors he and his episcopal predecessors had held in fee for it as titular abbots. This meant that the monks became tenants-in-chief of the king and owed regular knight service.

85. *Register of St. Osmund,* 1:17–18.   86. See Chapter 4.

87. *Meditaciones Godwini Cantoris Salesberie, ad Rainilvam Reculsam,* Bodleian Manuscript, Digby 96, esp. fos. 20–24. He witnessed one of Roger's charters in 1122, Charter 7; also see Edwards, *English Secular Cathedrals,* p. 7; Hope Emily Allen, "On the Author of the Ancren Riwle," pp. 639–649, 666–669.

88. After the monks agreed to contribute to the common fund during abbatial vacancies, the chapter even admitted a few other abbeys to its confraternity. See Fowler, *Medieval Sherborne,* pp. 95–103; *Register of St. Osmund,* 1:249–250; *Sarum Documents,* pp. 48–51; VCH, Wiltshire, 3:160.

Some time after 1129 Roger made over to the abbey several more valuable gifts, some for Nicholas the sacrist and others for the abbey as a whole.[89] Included were Saint Swithun's fair (July 13–17) as King Henry had given it to him, the church of Saint Mary Magdalene and fishing rights in the stewponds, a mill adjoining Saint Andrew's chapel as compensation for two other mills swamped by the previous pond, a small endowment to repair books, venison for the abbey guests, and another plot of land near the old episcopal palace to substitute for a portion of the monks' graveyard which had been taken to make a road. These gifts were presented to the abbey on the occasion of the dedication of the church of Saint Mary Magdalene and were thereafter formalized in Roger's charter. Erecting buildings, tearing down mills, making roads, planning ponds, and exchanging properties, all were happening at Sherborne as they were throughout Roger's diocese. The viceroy must have also put up a deer park in the area to provide venison. His passages describing fishing rights are written with such gusto that one suspects he may have been an angler himself.

If Sherborne prospered under Roger, Abbotsbury did not. This tiny coastal abbey, founded in 1044 and still a center of Saxon traditions, was so poor that it had not subdivided its land, but supported its one knight on its demesne. In 1106 the king had ordered his justiciars, Bishop Roger and Sheriff Alfred of Lincoln, to protect it; if anyone harmed the abbot, he incurred a ten-pound fine.[90] Nevertheless, Roger later deposed the abbot himself and made the abbey "his handmaid instead of a mistress." [91] Evidence of Roger's spoliation is found in a complaint made during the reign of Henry II by an abbot who contended that he could not fulfill his military obligations because Roger had given away two

89. Charter 19.   90. *Regesta*, 2, no. 754.
91. *Gesta Stephani*, p. 65.

hides of Abbotsbury's land (*contradicente conventu ecclesie*) to a certain Nicholas de Meriet for the marriage of his grand-daughter.[92]

Another Dorset house, Milton, or Middleton, also a center of Saxon ideals, was in Roger's hands for five years. King Henry had asked him to hold it after the death of an abbot, and Roger converted two tenements held by rents into knight fees—good feudal practice, but one which deprived the abbey of needed revenues.[93] These abbeys never obtained satisfaction during the bishop's lifetime, and such minor incidents show how completely small monasteries could fall under a strong prelate's control.

Malmesbury abbey, the popular shrine of Saint Aldhelm, had prospered under Abbot Geoffrey (1081–1105), the tutor of William the historian, and under Abbot Edulf (1105–1118), but it had had a long record of conflict with its diocesan bishops. In 1055 Bishop Herman had tried to move his episcopal seat there, and, although he had Edward the Confessor's support, Earl Godwin had intervened and Malmesbury had remained independent.[94] Years later, Hubert Walter, then bishop of Salisbury, unsuccessfully tried much the same thing.[95] It is surprising that, except for periods at Glastonbury, although William lived and wrote at Malmesbury throughout Roger's episcopate, he tells hardly anything about his own abbey's relations with the viceroy. Even after Roger's death William remained strangely circumspect and uninformative.

Roger was more adroit than his predecessors in dealing with Malmesbury. About 1108 he helped obtain a larger

92. *Red Book of the Exchequer,* 1:211; see also VCH, Dorset, 2:10. Stoke Antram was the land in question.

93. *Red Book of the Exchequer,* 1:210; see also VCH, Dorset, 2:59. The knights were Robert de Monasteriis and William Fitz Walter.

94. William of Malmesbury, *G.P.,* pp. 182–183, 420.

95. Knowles, *Monastic Order in England,* p. 324.

fair for the monks, and at another time he gave them land to augment their guest house.[96] Then, for some unknown reason, in 1118 he deposed Abbot Edulf and took over the abbey himself. One reporter said he acted without cause, while another wrote only that he usurped the vacant abbey by royal power and held it for many years.[97] The term *royal power* may refer to his viceregal authority. William, who should have been most fully informed, merely said that Roger attached the abbey to his bishopric as much as possible. He really seemed more annoyed about Roger's building a castle right next to the abbey.[98] Even though he had the queen's support, Edulf had roused Archbishop Anselm's displeasure, and Roger may have shared the primate's feelings and waited to act till after Matilda's death in 1118.[99] Apparently the pope understood Roger's motives, for in 1126 Honorius II confirmed his possession of Horton, Abbotsbury, and Malmesbury.[100] Alexander of Lincoln was in Rome that year and undoubtedly obtained this bull for his uncle.[101]

Five years later, in 1131, King Henry "restored" Malmesbury to Saint Mary's Cathedral and to Roger, its bishop,

96. *Regesta*, 2, no. 971; *Registrum Malmesburiense*, ed. J. S. Brewer and Charles Trice Martin (hereafter cited as *Malmesbury Register*), 2:63.

97. "Annals of Winchester," in *Annales Monastici*, 2:45; British Museum Manuscript, Cotton Vitellius, A X, fos. 59v.–60. In one place Knowles gave the date 1125, and in another, 1117 (*Monastic Order in England*, pp. 273, 180).

98. William of Malmesbury, *H.N.*, pp. 25, 38–39. Roger's occupation is not mentioned in William's other works, although there may be a veiled reference in *G.P.*, p. 175, where he said that oppression continued "up till our own times"; see also *Gesta Stephani*, p. 65.

99. Anselm, *Opera Omnia*, 5:326–328, letters 384, 385. Edulf had tried to gain Anselm's favor with a present.

100. *Papsturkunden in England*, ed. Walther Holtzmann, 2:141–142, no. 7.

101. Henry of Huntingdon, pp. 246–247. Alexander also obtained papal confirmation of his own privileges (*Registrum Antiquissimum*, 1:193, no. 248).

as a demesne abbey (*ut dominum suum et sedem pro-
priam*).[102] This does not mean that Roger had lost control
of the abbey, rather that he seems to have been strengthen-
ing his hold over it. Probably referring to Herman's abortive
move, the king observed that Malmesbury had once been
an episcopal seat in Wiltshire. He did not press the point,
but declared that the monastic order would be preserved
there and that the abbey would remain under the bishop's
direction. In 1139 Roger received additional papal support
when Pope Innocent II sent him a blanket confirmation of
all his holdings.[103]

The *Gesta Stephani* claimed that Malmesbury abbey was
restored to its ancient glory only after Roger's death.[104] It
is an interesting judgment. After his protection was withdrawn in 1139, a freebooter named Robert Fitz Hubert
seized Malmesbury tower, burned the village, and molested
the monks. Fitz Hubert was a bit of a sadist who enjoyed
staking out his prisoners naked in the sun, smearing them
with honey, and leaving them to the flies and insects. Luck-
ily, he was soon killed by one of his own kind. When the
monks did eventually elect an abbot, they chose a certain
John who supposedly freed them from their past slavery,
as William of Malmesbury put it.[105] John's election was
promptly canceled by Henry of Winchester, the papal
legate, who accused the monks of simony for having bribed
King Stephen to grant them a free election. This rather
comic affair offers a clue to the chief offense Roger supposedly gave Malmesbury. He did not persecute monasteries,
but he did wound Black Monk pride by depriving some of
their abbeys of their cherished independence.

Roger's relations with Abingdon abbey were quite different. Although this wealthy abbey was situated in Berk-

102. *Regesta*, 2, no. 1715; *Sarum Documents*, p. 6, no. 6.
103. Holtzmann, *Papsturkunden in England*, 2:160–161, no. 20.
Alexander and Nigel also received confirmations.
104. *Gesta Stephani*, p. 65.
105. William of Malmesbury, *H.N.*, pp. 36, 40–44.

shire, he never attempted to control it, perhaps because it was such an early favorite of the king. Abbot Faritius (1105–1117), that talented physician who so frequently sought royal justice, obtained many valuable privileges for his house, most in writs executed by Bishop Roger.[106] Faritius and Roger exchanged lands, too. In 1114 the abbot was almost elected archbishop of Canterbury, but that time Roger opposed him.[107] Between 1114 and 1117 a nasty quarrel broke out between Faritius and his eighty monks about monies to be spent in the refectory. Oddly enough, this case was not directly referred to Roger as diocesan bishop, but instead the king appointed a royal commission, consisting of Ralph, the new archbishop of Canterbury, Bishop Roger, and Sheriff Hugh of Buckland, to settle the problem.[108] It must have been one of Faritius's last appearances, for shortly thereafter he gathered his monks about him, ordered word to be sent to Bishop Roger and Abbot Edulf of Malmesbury, and died.[109]

The king's favoritism passed with Faritius, and he kept Abingdon in his own hands for the next four years, taking two-thirds of its revenues.[110] Then in 1121 Abbot Vincent (d. 1130) was elected in the royal presence, and Roger, who had probably urged his selection, escorted him in ceremonial to his abbey.[111] During Vincent's tenure, possibly in 1127, the king claimed that the abbey was exercising illegal privileges and seized it once again as forfeit.[112] Armed with his charters, the abbot rushed to court, where Henry ordered Roger to read them aloud; then, apparently satisfied, he re-

106. *Regesta,* 2, nos. 937, 956, 959, are examples.

107. See Chapter 4.

108. *Abingdon Chronicle,* 2:146–149.

109. *Ibid.,* pp. 289–290. The abbey housed about eighty monks at this time (Knowles and Hadcock, *Medieval Religious Houses,* p. 58).

110. Knowles, *Monastic Order in England,* p. 613.

111. *Abingdon Chronicle,* 2:161.

112. *Ibid.,* pp. 163–164, 278; *Regesta,* 2, no. 1477; VCH, Berkshire, 3:52. The hundred of Hormer and the market of Abingdon were in dispute.

stored the abbey's prerogatives. Nevertheless, poor Vincent still had to pay three hundred marks for undisputed title to his claims; in order to pay the debt he was forced to melt down some of the gold work above the high altar of his abbey. Justice was indeed great profit.

Roger's dual role as viceroy and bishop came up again and again in cases like this. At other times he punished some men who had stolen Abingdon's hay and even issued a writ ordering one of its churches to perform its services under pain of interdict.[113] In 1130 he consecrated Ingulf as its new abbot.[114] In every case Roger's relations with this house seem scrupulously correct. This was also true of Henry's new foundation at Reading, which seems to have replaced Abingdon as Henry's favorite charity.[115] In the 1120s Roger acted hand in glove with the monarch to establish this house, significantly, as justiciar and not as diocesan bishop—this was another monastery which was to remain strictly under royal control.

Little can be said of Roger's supervision of other Salisbury monasteries. He did confirm gifts to and from churches and houses in the diocese, but as routine episcopal activity.[116] The nunneries of Shaftesbury and Wilton do not appear to have objected to his guidance, and their silence, while a dangerous argument, is an eloquent denial that he had any consistent policy of exploiting rich houses. Roger seems to

113. *Abingdon Chronicle*, 2:84, 121, 134, 160; *Regesta*, 2, no. 1800; Charter 3.

114. John of Worcester, p. 30; Florence of Worcester (Continuator's part), 2:92.

115. For Roger and Reading, see Chapter 2.

116. For example, Charter 2, where Roger confirms gifts to Tewkesbury abbey. I have not uncovered anything significant about Roger's relations with the nunneries Shaftesbury (Dorset) and Wilton (Wiltshire, very close to Sarum), the abbeys Cerne (Dorset) and Amesbury (Wiltshire), or the priories Loders (Dorset), Holme (a Cluniac house in Dorset), Wallingford (Berkshire), and Hurley (Berkshire). Cerne was a rather disreputable abbey whose abbot was deposed in 1102, but matters reached a head after Roger's death (*Foliot Charters*, pp. 507–509).

have treated problems individually as they arose, aiding some monasteries and using others. His episcopal colleagues, men like Herbert Losinga of Norwich, Henry of Winchester, and Alexander of Lincoln, all tried to control abbeys; [117] Roger was different only in that the chroniclers, already in awe of his governmental status, seem to have remembered only his oppression of their houses. Actually, they had more cause to bless than to bewail his interest.

To his high ecclesiastical position Roger brought the same talents which characterized him as a statesman. As an administrator, he mastered the details of efficient government, knew the value and necessity of properly delegating authority, and had the strength of purpose to prune away lifeless and outdated institutions. As a politician, he understood the paramount role of finance, was adaptable in all his policies, and was able to influence Henry to support his plans. As a bishop, he translated his organizational genius, love of order, and ambition for power and display to the use of the churches and monasteries of his diocese. At all times his powers and responsibilities intermingled. His objectives were equally complex. The union and conflict of his positions can be seen better as the focus of his episcopal activity shifts from his own diocese to the general ecclesiastical issues of the whole kingdom.

117. Knowles, *Monastic Order in England,* pp. 274–275, 586.

4

Canons, Monks, and Bishops, 1107–1135

BISHOP ROGER was a very busy man, skillfully balancing diocesan responsibilities and governmental duties, but he seems to have been somewhat less interested in his role as a member of the English hierarchy. The upheavals of the investiture controversy had passed with the settlement of 1107, but other religious disputes remained. No one issue was of overriding importance, and no one man, not even the energetic bishop of Salisbury, was dominant in the episcopacy. The inspiration and glory of the First Crusade, the wonders of increasing education, the appearance of new religious orders, and the phenomenal growth of monastic houses lifted men's spirits, but the significance of these changes was sometimes lost amidst a welter of ecclesiastical politics, clerical rivalries, charges of prejudice, and annoying problems of precedence and protocol.

Scattered details surviving from the period between 1107 and 1135 limit definition of Roger's national ecclesiastical policy, but there is no reason to believe he took a consistent stand on all issues throughout the generation. It has already been suggested that his governmental and diocesan activity exhibits a high degree of creative pragmatism, and, although Austin canons and archiepiscopal elections to Canterbury particularly interested him, his relations with the larger English church show much the same approach. A pragmatist tends to be moderate and tolerant, more interested in how issues affect things than in the issues themselves; although strong in principles, he is still not afraid to change his mind.

Surely this was Roger's experience at Salisbury, Winchester, and Westminster, and it probably did not desert him in church synods and in discussions of theological, moral, and ecclesiastical issues.

One cause he championed throughout his life, however, was that of the Austin canons. The good years from 1100 to 1140 meant prosperity not only for the Benedictine monks, but also for the regular, or black, Austin canons. It was their golden age of expansion, and forty-three houses were planted during the reign of Henry I alone, several of which were materially assisted by Bishop Roger, including St. Bartholomew's and Holy Trinity in London.[1] The viceroy went off to see the rustic priory of Llanthony in Wales, where he was so impressed by the canons' strict obedience that he urged the court to support it. According to Gerald of Wales, who called the viceroy "the principal ruler of the kingdom under the king" (*principalem regni tunc sub rege rectorem*), Roger told the curia that the whole royal treasury could not purchase a cloister equal to Llanthony.[2] This allusion to the mountains which surrounded the priory on every side was a nice light touch; either he was briefly inspired to poetry, or he was teasing his solemn audience.

Roger manifested a somewhat similar humor in 1121 when he aided Merton priory in Surrey, a recent Austin foundation of one of his governmental colleagues, Gilbert

1. John C. Dickinson, *The Origins of the Austin Canons and Their Introduction into England* (hereafter cited as Dickinson, *Austin Canons*), pp. 131–139.

2. Gerald of Wales, *Opera*, 6:39. This was written in 1191 and Gerald rather enigmatically said of Roger that it was a virtue to love virtue, even in another man, and a proof of innate goodness to detest vices formerly unavoided. The bishop's visit was undated but may have been between 1122 and 1131 when the learned Laon graduate Robert of Bethune was prior. George Roberts in "Llanthony Priory, Monmouthshire," speculated that Roger may have helped build the priory. The Llanthony canons, less enamored of their site, moved to Gloucester about 1136 and thereafter the foundations were known as Llanthony Prima and Llanthony Secunda; see Dugdale, *Monasticon Anglicanum,* 6:127–136; Lloyd, *A History of Wales,* 2:445–446.

the great sheriff of Surrey, Cambridge, and Huntingdon. For some time Gilbert had sought a royal charter confirming Merton's rights and endowments, but, despite the offer of a handsome monetary gift, the king put off the sheriff's petition. Henry frequently insulted and mistreated his sheriffs and, although he seems to have liked Gilbert, he was probably holding out for even more money. On the other hand, the liberties contained in Gilbert's proposed charter were apparently so far ranging that some legal advocates at the court claimed they were afraid to show it to the king. Gilbert and Robert, the prior of the house, also dreaded that Henry might nullify the whole charter when it was read to him. The sheriff therefore skillfully courted Bishop Roger's favor and asked him to discuss the document's contents with the king. The bishop sympathized with the priory's plight and when in the ensuing conference at Winchester Henry complained that the text reserved no jurisdiction to himself and that there was no provision for service to him, Roger lightly replied, "You reserve everything to yourself all the better when you give freely to God." Henry's first wife had patronized Merton and the king was in a religious mood after Prince William's untimely death so his viceroy's gentle smiling plea was partially successful and the liberties were apparently confirmed without further argument. Gilbert was still required to pay the king one hundred pounds of silver and six marks of gold, however, and the royal charter specifically stated that the church would technically remain in the king's hand. Roger made a special notation at the end of the charter that he had confirmed it himself. A few years later, Gilbert flattered the treasury collectors into somewhat easing his debt.[3]

3. College of Arms Manuscript 28, fos. 6–8; Marvin L. Colker, "Latin Texts Concerning Gilbert, Founder of Merton Priory," *Studia Monastica* 12 (1970 fasc. 2):243–244, 256; *Regesta,* 2, no. 1301; Dickinson, *Austin Canons,* pp. 117, 128. This charter was also witnessed by an Archdeacon Alexander; perhaps this was Roger's nephew. The Merton Annalist places these events in 1121, but there

The Salisbury clergy were represented at Merton for Serlo, a former dean of the Sarum cathedral chapter, joined the new foundation. In 1130 this Serlo was chosen first prior of a new Austin monastery at Cirencester in Gloucestershire. Bishop Roger granted this house some splendid endowments, but he retained a life interest in all his gifts.[4]

Cirencester received Roger's encouragement to establish a daughter house in his own diocese, and in 1139 Bradenstoke priory was founded in Wiltshire.[5] Most of all, however, the bishop was associated with the canons of Saint Frideswide's, Oxford.

Now Christ Church, Oxford, Saint Frideswide's priory was originally settled by secular canons in the early eleventh century, but they were replaced much later by more strictly observant regular canons from Holy Trinity, Aldgate.[6] In 1111 Bishop Roger exchanged some of his own lands for Abingdon abbey holdings near Saint Frideswide's, since the abbey was unwilling to build a house there; King Henry ratified the transfer between 1113 and 1116.[7] The date the

---

is a possibility (depending upon when one places Robert of Gloucester's reception of his earldom) that the charter may not have been issued until the summer of 1122. Round, *Geoffrey de Mandeville*, p. 433, thought the charter was spurious.

4. *The Cartulary of Cirencester Abbey, Gloucestershire*, ed. C. D. Ross (hereafter cited as *Cirencester Cartulary*), 1:21, 24–25; Charter 27.

5. British Museum Manuscript, Stowe 925, fo. 34; *Cirencester Cartulary*, 1:144; VCH, Wiltshire, 3:276–278. The endowment lands were given by Walter 'le Eurus,' father of Patrick first earl of Salisbury, shortly before June 1139 in the presence of Bishop Roger.

6. *The Cartulary of the Monastery of St. Frideswide at Oxford*, ed. Spencer Rogert Wigram (hereafter cited as *St. Frideswide Cartulary*), 1:9. There were about thirteen canons there in the early twelfth century (Knowles and Hadcock, *Medieval Religious Houses*, p. 149).

7. *Regesta*, 2, no. 1128; Dickinson, *Austin Canons*, p. 114; Dugdale, *Monasticon Anglicanum*, 2:133–134, 143–145. The antiquarian Anthony Wood noted that the Abingdon monks had given Bishop Roger the land, but added, "though, as tis thought, he rather took it away from them." Apparently he was not fully aware of previous land transaction; see Anthony Wood, *Survey of the Antiquities of the City of Oxford Composed in 1661–1666*, 2:147–149.

black canons were installed and the priory erected is indefinite because years would elapse between the original commitment, the permanent habitation of the house, and the official blessing by the diocesan bishop. Saint Frideswide's does not seem to have been formally completed until 1122, and then it was the king who was given credit for founding the house, although the bishop seems to have been its real patron. The first prior, Guimund, a former royal chaplain well known for his learning, was an independent person who, according to one story, once simulated illiteracy with the complaint that King Henry seemed to prefer such men for clerical advancement.[8] Several of his successors were also learned men, and the priory is connected with the remote origins of Oxford University.

The viceroy's subsequent relations with these canons were rather ambiguous. In the 1120s the monastery received several royal gifts, including a seven-day fair at the feast of the Translation of Saint Benedict (July 10), some of which were given in the new reforming spirit, free of any lay demands or burdens.[9] Two of Roger's own viceregal writs further protected the canons' property, including the manor, the tithes, and the hundred court of Headington, which the bishop himself had once held for the canons.[10] Between 1131 and 1135 the king again granted the canons the fair and all the customs with which Bishop Roger ever held it.[11] Then on his deathbed the bishop restored to the priory whatever he had taken away from it, including the fair of Benedict.[12] These confusing transactions are not easy to sort out, but apparently Roger gave the priory some things, held others in trust for it, and kept yet others back which at various times he returned to it, regained for himself, and returned once more. Despite this, he was in excellent company in supporting the Austin canons, for saintly Arch-

8. William of Malmesbury, *G.P.,* pp. 315–316.
9. *Regesta,* 2, nos. 1342–1345.   10. Charters 12, 17.
11. *Regesta,* 2, no. 1957.   12. Charters 29, 30, 31.

bishop Anselm had vigorously encouraged them as a means of spreading church reform.

After the settlement of the investiture controversy, Archbishop Anselm also firmly supported the king and worried chiefly about maintainting the customs and privileges of Canterbury. In 1108, for example, there was a dispute about where the new abbot of Saint Augustine's should be consecrated.[13] Abbot Hugh, formerly a monk of Bec, claimed it for his new abbey; Anselm disagreed. The king sent a delegation of abbots and bishops, Roger among them, to induce the archbishop to relent, but he remained adamant. Henry, who was not very interested in such matters, finally told him to consecrate Hugh wherever he wanted. Henry also failed to help Anselm obtain the submission to Canterbury of Thomas, the newly elected archbishop of York. Anselm wrote to all the bishops, declaring that he would not consecrate Thomas until he had professed obedience to Canterbury, but the question was still unsolved when Anselm died on April 21, 1109.

Unusual splendor graced the Whitsuntide court following the primate's death. Rejoicing in the passing of his former opponent, whom Hugh the Chantor claimed Henry never loved after 1107, the king raised the issue of Thomas's consecration at his council.[14] The bishops were anxiously debating the import of Anselm's letter when his old enemy, Robert Count of Meulan and Earl of Leicester, burst in upon their deliberations and gruffly demanded to know who among them would now dare support the mandate of a dead man.[15] Oddly enough, the bishops, including the shrewd lord of Salisbury, all held firm. It was a difficult decision, for the count had tried to make it appear that they were flouting the king's will. Fortunately, a compromise was worked out in which Thomas made a vague submission to the vacant

13. Eadmer, *H.N.*, pp. 188–190.
14. *Ibid.*, pp. 199–211; Hugh the Chantor, *The History of the Church of York, 1066–1127*, pp. 13–33.
15. Eadmer, *H.N.*, pp. 207–208.

chair of Canterbury and was at last consecrated on June 27, 1109.

Roger's ecclesiastical relations with most bishops were fairly standard. He met with them in councils, joined them in dedicating great churches, and helped consecrate new colleagues, participating in at least six of the latter functions during his episcopate.[16] All were united in a common faith and a common service to the king. His relations with William Giffard bishop of Winchester (1100–1129), an early supporter of the Austin Canons and Roger's nearest episcopal neighbor, were fairly typical. Winchester cathedral and other houses in that diocese had possessions in the Salisbury diocese which Roger agreed to watch over.[17] In 1108, for example, a royal writ informed Bishops William and Roger and the sheriff of Wiltshire that the king had restored to the monks of Winchester some Wiltshire lands which had been alienated from them when his father had made provision for William Escudet, his cook.[18] Four royal writs directed Roger to make arrangements for the Wiltshire possessions of the nuns of Romsey, a prominent Hampshire house.[19] Two of Bishop Giffard's own writs were witnessed by Roger and his friend, Bishop Bernard of Saint David's together, including one in which William admitted unjustly despoiling the monks of Saint Peter's.[20]

The composition of the English episcopate about that time

16. See Appendix 1.

17. *Cartulary of Winchester Cathedral*, ed. A. W. Goodman, p. 5, no. 8. Also see *Regesta*, 2, no. 745.

18. *Regesta*, 2, no. 884. See *Winchester Cartulary*, p. 100, no. 220, for Bishop Giffard's later (1111–1114) writ to the same effect. He noted he had consulted with the queen, Bishops Roger, Robert of Lincoln, Richard of London, and Ranulf of Durham, and other men including, Nigel of Calne, Ralph Basset, and Hugh of Buckland, before restoring the land.

19. *Regesta*, 2, nos. 811, 874, 883; *Regesta*, 3, no. 722. Two of these (nos. 874, 883) concerned similar alienations of land to Willian Escudet.

20. *Winchester Cartulary*, pp. 1–2, nos. 1, 2. For similar confessions by Roger see Charters 28, 29, 30, 31. For one by Bishop Ranulf Flambard of Durham in 1128 see *Durham Episcopal Charters*, ed. H. S. Offler, pp. 112–113.

is quite interesting.[21] Although the Norman kings patronized monasticism, they usually chose their bishops from among their curial servants. When Roger was consecrated in 1107, the four other bishops anointed with him also had served in the royal chapel or chancery. In fact, of the nine bishops elected between 1100 and Anselm's death in 1109 only one, Ralph of Rochester, was a monk, and Rochester was a peculiar bishopric uniquely dependent upon the archbishop of Canterbury. It has been suggested that Henry may have favored curialists in order to offset Anselm's reform policies.[22] Indeed, after his death the proportion of curial bishops fell somewhat; eight new bishops came from the court; five were former cathedral dignitaries, although many curialists were also canons and archdeacons, too; and five were monks. Over the long haul the number of monastic bishops remained fairly constant throughout the reigns of Henry and Stephen.[23] The monks thought they were losing ground, however, and their situation was highlighted by the fact that most of the monastic cathedral chapters were ruled by secular bishops, whereas only the chapters of York, Lincoln, Salisbury, Exeter, Chichester, Hereford, and London were staffed by secular canons.

The simple distinction between secular and regular clergy ought not be overemphasized, for the English church was not a static thing, nor were there always clear-cut differences of opinion. The king had his interests and the churchmen theirs, but frequently the two coincided. There was no solid clerical block, either. Black monks, white monks, regular canons, secular canons, ordinary diocesan clergy, the monastic hierarchy, and the secular hierarchy, all had slightly different and sometimes contrasting interests. Denis Bethell, for example, has recently detected significant divisions within

21. For recent studies of this episcopate see Everett U. Crosby, "The Organization of the English Episcopate under Henry I;" Martin Brett, "The Organization of the English Secular Church in the Reign of Henry I."

22. Cantor, *Lay Investiture*, pp. 291–292.

23. Knowles, *Monastic Order In England*, pp. 709–710.

the black monks, themselves, between such ancient and conservative houses as Canterbury, Malmesbury, Peterborough, Bury, and Worcester, which stressed Saxon traditions, local privileges, and feudal ideals, and the more progressive houses like the Cluniac foundations and Cluniac-inspired Reading abbey, which followed the newer directions of the Gregorian and Cluniac reforms.[24] He has also demonstrated that the monks were not as important in the episcopate before 1100 as was once thought and that the decade of the 1120s was actually a positive renaissance for them in England. It is noteworthy that the monastic chroniclers and historians came almost exclusively from the more reactionary group of houses. I myself suspect that Roger's black monk foundation at Sherborne sought a path somewhere between the two factions.

After Anselm's death, King Henry kept the see of Canterbury vacant for five years, excusing the delay by declaring that such an important decision required much careful thought, especially as he wished to appoint a primate equal to Lanfranc and Anselm, the choices of his predecessors.[25] Meanwhile, following the notorious example of his brother William Rufus, the king appropriated the archiepiscopal revenues, although he did leave those of the monastic chapter at Christ Church in peace. This, by the way, is a good example of the utility of dividing the revenues and possessions of the bishop from those of his chapter. Ralph d'Escures, Bishop of Rochester, administered the diocese while Henry pretended to search for a new primate.[26]

Pope Paschal II kept admonishing Henry to fill the vacancy, and the bishops of England and the monks of Canterbury kept pleading for a new religious superior. Finally, in 1114 the king decided to make his selection and called a great council to meet at Windsor on April 26. A Canter-

24. Denis Bethell, "English Black Monks and Episcopal Elections in the 1120's."
25. William of Malmesbury, *G.P.*, p. 125.
26. Eadmer, *H.N.*, pp. 221.

bury election differed in several respects from the election of a bishop like Roger. For one thing, Canterbury cathedral possessed a monastic chapter rather than a secular chapter as at Sarum. A long line of monks had occupied its chair, and it was a jealously guarded tradition that a monk should always be archbishop. The actual elective power of the chapter was in considerable doubt, however, for the bishops of the country claimed that the selection of an archbishop was so important that they should participate; and, in fact, the bishops had clearly taken the initiative in the 1093 election of Anselm. The real decision was to be made by the king, but, after the Gregorian decrees against lay interference in free episcopal elections, he had to move more discreetly.

Contrary to the precedents set by his brother and father, Henry did not look to the Norman abbey of Bec for his archbishop, but preferred instead Faritius, Abbot of Abingdon. A native of Arezzo, Faritius may have studied at the famous medical school at Salerno. His skill was highly valued and well rewarded in England. He had even assisted Queen Matilda in her first confinement. Henry was prepared to support Faritius's candidacy vigorously, but he also wanted the approval of the prelates and barons of his curia regis.

Bishop Ralph of Rochester and a delegation of Canterbury monks went to the council in 1114 uncertain of why they had been called. On the road to Windsor someone from the curia told them that Abbot Faritius was to be their new archbishop and they were enthusiastic about the choice. The chronicler Eadmer, a member of the chapter delegation and thus an eyewitness to these events, agreed with the aspirations of his brother monks. When he saw the abbot of Abingdon at the council, he concluded that his election was practically assured.[27]

Some of the bishops and lay magnates did not favor Faritius's candidacy, however, and, led by Bishops Roger of Salisbury and Robert Bloet of the powerful see of Lincoln,

27. *Ibid.,* pp. 222-223.

they proposed that a secular cleric or a priest from the curia, rather than a monk, should be chosen as archbishop. These two claimed that they opposed Abbot Faritius because it was unseemly that a man who had examined the urine of females should become episcopal ruler of England.[28] Such objections to the abbot's medical practice are clearly fatuous, but the bishops may have feared having another Italian well acquainted with Gregorian decrees, especially with Faritius's reputation as a vigorous reformer. There was even a nationalistic tinge to their objection, as they observed that a worthy archbishop could certainly be found among the many good Norman clerks. It is extremely unlikely that Roger opposed Faritius on personal grounds, for they had already cooperated on several occasions and Roger had frequently championed Abingdon's rights.

The Canterbury monks tried to stand their ground, crying that a monk had always ruled their house and always should, but Bishop Ralph of Rochester was quietly put forward as a compromise candidate. A former abbot of Saint Martin's, Seéz, and a friend and disciple of the great Anselm, Ralph was technically a monk but had ceased to live according to the rule of Benedict. He proved acceptable to the king, who withdrew support from Abbot Faritius; Ralph was enthroned on May 17, 1114. Pope Paschal, who was disturbed that he had translated himself from one see to another without papal approval, only confirmed the election after receiving further proofs of Ralph's character.[29]

This whole dispute was something of a surprise. Evidently, the king had not consulted Roger privately beforehand, or else the bishop had felt so strongly about the election that he was willing to oppose Henry in public. No one attained his real objective. The king backed down rather quickly, but he

28. *Abingdon Chronicle,* 2:287. Bethell, "Episcopal Elections," p. 675, very critically, and rather unfairly, called this a "characteristically coarse joke," of Bishop Roger. For Faritius reputation as a reformer see, William of Malmesbury, *G.P.,* pp. 126–127.

29. Cantor, *Lay Investiture,* pp. 303–309.

never was one to fight costly battles for uncertain results. It cannot be determined whether Bishops Roger and Robert Bloet really wanted a secular clerk or whether this was merely one of their arguments to prevent a high Gregorian from becoming their superior. In either case, they must have been quite confident to disagree with the king so directly, but events proved them correct and their arguments swayed the rest of the council. Oddly enough, the king now appears to have been more sympathetic toward a reformer than anyone else.

The monastic chroniclers did not consider this election a major assault on their order, and the Abingdon abbey chronicler, who noted the events without censure, was the only writer to mention Bishop Roger's role.[30] William of Malmesbury and Eadmer of Canterbury both discussed the episcopal desire to overturn Canterbury's age-old tradition, but neither connected it with a wider struggle.[31] Bishop Ralph and Bishop Herbert Losinga were the only monks then in the episcopate, but when Herbert was asked by an abbot to write a treatise defending the monastic vocation, he refused, declaring in a very sensible way that both monks and seculars were priests and therefore shared the same dignity.[32]

In more trivial things Roger was not always able to enforce his views, either. In 1121 King Henry was a fifty-one-year-old widower with the Empress Matilda as his only legitimate heir, so he decided to marry again. His wedding to Adeliza of Louvain was to take place on January 24, 1121, at Windsor Castle. Because Windsor lay within the jurisdiction of the diocese of Salisbury, Roger claimed the right to officiate. Although the archbishop's speech was still impaired from a stroke he had suffered two years before and even though Roger had officiated at the funeral of Queen Matilda in 1118,

30. *Abingdon Chronicle,* 2:287; this writer said Faritius was actually elected, but this must be a mistake.

31. By 1125, however, Eadmer was seeing a general attack on the monastic order, see Note 55.

32. Herbert Losinga, *Epistolae,* letters 59, 60.

the other bishops supported Ralph's contention that the king and queen were his special parishioners and that only he or his delegate could perform their marriage. Ralph selected the bishop of Winchester, who performed the ceremony as the deputy of Canterbury.[33] It was an insignificant check in Roger's career, but it does indicate how jealously bishops guarded their real or supposed rights. Later there was an embarrassing scene when the king appeared wearing his crown and Archbishop Ralph demanded to know who but himself could place the diadem on the royal head. Henry did not seem to think it important, but Ralph rather clumsily recrowned him.[34]

About eighteen months later on October 22, 1122, after a rather undistinguished episcopate of eight and a half years, Ralph of Canterbury died. Less than five months later, King Henry acted with surprising speed to assemble his court at Gloucester for Candlemas Day, the feast of the Purification, February 2, 1123. Remembering the troubles of 1114, he urged his counsellors to choose for themselves whomsoever they wished to be archbishop, for he would approve their choice.[35]

Unwilling any longer to bear the rule of a monastic primate, the bishops petitioned for the right to choose a clerk, and the king assented. The Peterborough chronicler who reported this election declared that the choice of a secular clerk had been planned long before by Bishop Roger and his old ally Bishop Robert Bloet.[36] But in January 1123 Bishop Bloet, who had been in recent disfavor at the court, fell from his horse at Woodstock and died in the arms of the king and Bishop Roger.[37] Thus, if there was a predetermined

33. William of Malmesbury, *G.P.,* p. 132; Eadmer, *H.N.,* p. 292. Adeliza was a patron of poets and may have spent much of her time near Salisbury on lands given her by the king; Urban T. Holmes, "The Anglo-Norman Rhymed Chronicle."

34. William of Malmesbury, *G.P.,* p. 132; Eadmer, *H.N.,* p. 292.

35. *Anglo-Saxon Chronicle,* 2:188.   36. *Ibid.*

37. *Ibid.;* Symeon of Durham, 2:268; Henry of Huntingdon, pp. 299–300.

policy—and some of the following events make it seem unlikely—Roger was left to execute it alone.

The Saxon chronicler explained that the bishops wanted a secular archbishop "because they never loved the monastic rule but were always against the monks and their rule." [38] Why a Peterborough monk should feel this way is unknown, but in Roger's case it is plainly not true. I have already proposed that he seems to have had a pragmatic monastic policy; and, in fact, in these early years of the second decade of the twelfth century he was busily engaged in raising Sherborne priory to the status of a full abbey independent of himself, in assisting the canons of Saint Frideswide's, and in carrying out Henry's instructions for Reading abbey. Nevertheless, he did oppose the election of a monk. It is conceivable that he wished the office for himself, but that is doubtful in view of his many responsibilities as viceroy, and the absence of evidence of such an ambition. It is also doubtful that he still feared the accession of a zealous reforming archbishop. Certainly he was anxious to advance his own kind, the secular clergy, but it is also possible that Roger may have had reform ideas of his own, believing, for example, that monks belonged in their monasteries and not in seats of power throughout the kingdom.[39]

By royal command a delegation of Canterbury monks traveled all the way to Gloucester to elect their spiritual leader. Intent that he should be a monk, their prior offered the names of several monastic candidates, but the bishops cried out that they would not accept a monk as long as equally fit secular clerks were available.[40] The chapter countered with the old arguments that from the days of Saint Augustine of Canterbury only monks had ruled as archbishops and there seemed no valid reason to set aside this venerable tradition. Falling on their knees, the monks then begged

38. *Anglo-Saxon Chronicle,* 2:188.
39. For a somewhat similar view see Note 78.
40. Symeon of Durham, 2:268; Orderic Vitalis, 4:431–432.

Henry not to abandon their ancient heritage, but this only served to strengthen the opposition of the bishops.

Desperate, the monks next unsuccessfully asked for a recess to consult their whole convent and Bishop Ernulf of Rochester, who had looked after their welfare since Archbishop Ralph's death. Ernulf was the only monk then in the episcopate, but he had been too ill to come to Gloucester. If a somewhat later writer Gervase of Canterbury is to be believed, the bishops overreacted, declaring that the monks ought to be expelled from the church for being contemptuous. "The king is master," they reportedly said, "and it does not become you to oppose his will in any respect." [41] These words sound out of character for the bishops, who did not always follow the king themselves, and they also remind one of Robert of Meulan's high-handed manner back in 1109. In any event, the monks did obtain a two-day delay.

Time purchased very little, for when the council reconvened the names of four nonmonastic clerics were offered to the Canterbury monks with the understanding that one of them should be elected archbishop. The defeated chapter chose William of Corbeil, prior of the Augustinian monastery of Chick, or Saint Osyth, in Essex, whom they preferred because he at least was an Austin canon and a friend of the great Anselm. [42] William had been at Laon before 1117, but opinion about him varied. Symeon of Durham praised him, but Henry of Huntingdon said that he would not list his virtues, as they did not exist. [43] Evidently he had been suggested by Bishop Richard of London, but he was not well

41. Gervase of Canterbury, *Opera,* 2:379–380.
42. *Ibid.;* Symeon of Durham, 2:269; the *Anglo-Saxon Chronicle,* 2:189, said the monks and laymen refused to accept William until the papal legate made it clear he would not annul the election.
43. Symeon of Durham 2:269; Henry of Huntingdon, p. 314. Cecily Clark, *The Peterborough Chronicle,* p. 86, said that in a passage William of Malmesbury later omitted from his text he surmised Archbishop William disappointed many of the seculars who elected him by proving too frugal and ascetic for their more liberal tastes.

known to the king, who asked Archbishop Thurstan of York and Athelwold, Prior of Nostel, about him.[44]

Shortly after the election, a papal legate, Henry, the abbot of Saint Jean d'Angély, arrived from Rome to collect Peter's pence. He told the king, a distant relative, that it was not right that a clerk should be set above monks, but Henry ignored the criticism because, as the Saxon chronicler noted, of his high regard for the bishop of Salisbury.[45]

Archbishop Thurstan of York offered to consecrate William of Corbeil, but the archbishop-elect demanded that Thurstan consecrate him as Primate of All England, which Thurstan refused to do.[46] William was therefore consecrated by his own suffragan bishops, Roger among them, on February 25, 1123.[47] The two archbishops then set out separately for Rome, William to seek his pallium and Thurstan to affirm his right to consecrate Canterbury; the reform programs had ended the days when kings would have decided such questions for themselves. Thurstan arrived first and convinced the Roman curia that William had been elected against the will of the chapter. Four charges were leveled against him: he had been elected in the royal court, a place for blood judgments, not episcopal elections; he had been chosen more by the bishops than by the monks; York had not been allowed to consecrate him; and he himself was not a monk.[48]

Although William's replies are lost, his mission was successful, and probably not because he bribed the curia, as the hostile Peterborough writer claimed.[49] More likely, Pope Calixtus II (1119–1124) willingly approved the election as a favor to Henry's son-in-law, Emperor Henry V. Calixtus

44. Bethell, "Episcopal Elections," p. 677; Hugh the Chantor, *History of the Church of York*, pp. 108–109.

45. *Anglo-Saxon Chronicle*, 2:189.

46. Denis Bethell, "William of Corbeil and the Canterbury-York Dispute."

47. *Anglo-Saxon Chronicle*, 2:189; Symeon of Durham, 2:269.

48. Hugh the Chantor, *History of the Church of York*, p. 112.

49. *Anglo-Saxon Chronicle*, 2:189.

and Henry had recently concluded the long struggle over investitures in the empire by their concordat at Worms in September 1122.[50] The Calixtinum allowed episcopal elections to be held in the imperial presence. Moreover, if the election were disputed, the emperor should support the opinion of the more mature members of the episcopate. Henry of England must have known all these details, and he could certainly claim that he had listened to the advice of his bishops. Thus the pope readily confirmed the English king's new archbishop as a demonstration of good faith in his own promises, and a purely insular dispute was thereby affected by international complications. Furthermore, criticism of the black monks was not confined to England. During the Lateran Council at Easter 1123, canons were promulgated which restrained the monks' activities beyond their cloister walls. They were forbidden to give public penances, for example, and were to obtain holy oils and ordinations only from their diocesan bishops.[51]

In this election the balance of power shifted somewhat. The king's role was remarkably passive, and the lay barons supported the monks against the curial bishops. Perhaps the nobles were beginning to resent the increasing preponderance of secular bishops in the civil government. Nevertheless, the monks and magnates lost because, as the Peterborough annalist put it, "the bishop of Salisbury was strong and controlled all England and was against them with all his power and ability."[52] The reference to Roger's viceregal authority is significant; in a basic policy decision like this, his opinion as bishop was reinforced by his prestige as justiciar.

Descriptions of two Canterbury elections do little justice to sixteen years of Roger's work in the hierarchy of England, but they recall the range of his concerns and the complexity of his motives. His uncanny ability to profit from all events

50. K. Leyser, "England and the Empire in the Early Twelfth Century."
51. Nicholl, *Thurstan Archbishop of York*, p. 182.
52. *Anglo-Saxon Chronicle*, 2:190.

was further demonstrated at Easter 1123, when he arranged that his nephew Alexander should receive the immense see of Lincoln. The Peterborough writer who criticized so much of Roger's activity at this period commented stiffly that Alexander was elected entirely for the love of Roger.[53] The same unknown author observed that in June, before crossing to Normandy, King Henry "committed all England to the care and government of Bishop Roger of Salisbury." The king was no sooner back in Rouen than he wrote to instruct his viceroy to allow William Corbeil seisin of his Canterbury demesne.[54]

The debate about the place of the monastic clergy continued after the Canterbury elections. Cantor Godwin at Salisbury urged moderation, but in 1125 Eadmer of Canterbury passionately, but unsuccessfully, wrote urging the monks of the Worcester cathedral chapter to elect a monk as their new bishop.[55]

In 1125 another papal legate, Cardinal John of Crema, arrived in England with great flourish and promptly called a church council at London. Following the ordinances Calixtus II had promulgated at the Lateran Council, John and the English hierarchy passed strict decrees against priestly incontinence and ordered that marriages of the clergy were to be dissolved.[56] Such decrees had been passed at every synod during the reign, but clerical marriage and concubinage were long in dying; Bishop Roger seemed as immune to the orders as other clerks.

Cardinal or not, John was little credit to his mission. A haughty man, he insisted on receiving handsome presents

53. *Ibid.* Bishop Roger was a canon of Lincoln cathedral and held the church of Langford, Oxford, and Alexander founded a hospital at Newark for the souls of himself, his king, and his uncle; *Registrum Antiquissimum,* 1, nos. 139, 179; 2, no. 346; 3, no. 920.

54. *Regesta,* 2, no. 1417 (no. *CLXXII*).

55. Bethell, "Episcopal Elections," pp. 681–686. For Godwin see Chapter 3, Note 87.

56. *Anglo-Saxon Chronicle,* 2:191–192; Gervase of Canterbury, *Opera,* 2:381–382.

from churches and monasteries where he spent the night. On Easter Sunday he even humiliated Archbishop William Corbeil by appearing in full regalia to celebrate Mass in his place. Years later, Gervase of Canterbury moaned that the liberty of England had been violated on that occasion and attributed the dishonor to the fact that, although a good man, the archbishop was not a monk. Monks, he claimed, had never been subject to Roman legates.[57] This was nonsense, but the old monastic defensiveness lingered on in some houses. The contemporary Henry of Huntingdon, who was the son of one priest and father of another, told a scurrilous tale about the cardinal's being caught in bed with a prostitute.[58] There is no need to believe his story, but it does show the strong feelings aroused by the campaign to enforce clerical celibacy.

William Corbeil, accompanied by such lords spiritual as Alexander of Lincoln and Abbot Thurstan of Sherborne, left England on John's heels. They beseeched the pope, then Honorius II, to clarify the position of legate in England, and the pontiff neatly solved that problem and the persistent Canterbury-York rivalry by making the archbishop of Canterbury his permanent legate.[59] Although the precise primacy of the respective British sees was not yet settled, Canterbury automatically became superior because it was held by a papal legate. In 1127 Archbishop William held his own first legatine council, at which clerical celibacy was again one of

57. Gervase of Canterbury, *Opera,* 2:381–382.

58. Henry of Huntingdon, pp. 245–246. Another writer repeated the same tale, but switched the principal role to Bishop Ranulf Flambard, "Annals of Winchester," in *Annales Monastici,* 2:47–48. For Henry's father, Nicholas, see *Liber Eliensis,* ed. E. O. Blake, p. 276. For his son, Adam, to whom Henry sent a note about the Huntingdon song school, see *The Cartulary of Huntingdon,* ed. W. M. Noble, pp. 257–258. For Henry's grandson Aristotle, who died about 1157, see Charles Clay, "Master Aristotle," EHR, 76(1961):303–307.

59. Hugh the Chantor, *History of the Church of York,* p. 123. William of Malmesbury, *H.N.,* p. 11, gave the year as 1131, but this must be an error.

the main items on the agenda.[60] Bishop Roger, his nephew Alexander, and most other members of the hierarchy attended.

It was just about this time that the only uniquely English contribution to medieval theology, the belief in the Immaculate Conception of the Virgin Mary, was discussed.[61] Since certain monastic writers were the prime movers in the campaign for the widespread aceptance of this belief, their struggle included some elements of the wider secular-monastic conflict. Bishop Roger's part in these events is not completely clear, but it seems unlikely that he was deeply interested or thoroughly versed in these varieties of theological speculation.

The Saxons had celebrated the feast of the legendary miraculous conception of Mary by Saint Anne, but their Norman conquerors had dropped that December eighth commemoration from the liturgical calendar.[62] Nevertheless, great monasteries like Malmesbury, Evesham, and Canterbury remained centers of Anglo-Saxon culture and kept the tradition alive. William of Malmesbury, in fact, collected and wrote stories of the Virgin's many miracles.[63] The first great

60. John of Worcester, pp. 23–25; Florence of Worcester (Continuator's part), 2:85–86.

61. For accounts of the doctrine and the devotion, see Edmund Bishop, *Liturgica Historica,* pp. 238–259; A. W. Burridge, "L'Immaculée Conception dans la théologie de l'Angleterre médiévale;" S. J. P. van Dijk, "The Origins of the Latin Feast of the Conception of the Blessed Virgin Mary" (hereafter cited as van Dijk, "Origins"); Mirella Levi d'Ancona, *The Iconography of the Immaculate Conception in the Middle Ages and Early Renaissance.* Briefer explanations are found in Knowles, *Monastic Order in England,* pp. 510–513; Richard W. Southern, *The Making of the Middle Ages,* pp. 251–257.

62. David Knowles, book review of Richard W. Southern's *Saint Anselm and His Biographer,* EHR, 79(1964):788.

63. Richard W. Southern, "The English Origins of the Virgin's Miracles." William of Malmesbury's fifty-three miracle tales composed about 1138–1143 were edited by Peter N. Carter, "An Edition of William of Malmesbury's Treatise on the Miracles of the Virgin

Western collection of such Marian miracle tales was assembled by Anselm, Abbot of Bury Saint Edmund's from 1121 to 1148, a nephew of the great Archbishop Anselm. He had spent many years in Italy, where he had become acquainted with the Eastern church's celebration of the feast of the sinless conception of Mary and its doctrinal implications. When he carried these ideas back to England in the third decade of the century, they were eagerly welcomed by monks throughout the country who revered the old traditions. About 1125 at Canterbury, Eadmer, the biographer and friend of Saint Anselm, wrote a treatise, "The Conception of the Virgin Mary," which, while defending the feast, moved the discussion from the realm of liturgy to the higher plane of theology.[64]

Abbot Anselm, a none-too-stable character, found a fervent defender of the feast in another English monk, Osbert of Clare, the somewhat disreputable prior of Westminster.[65] It is from a letter of Osbert to Abbot Anselm that Bishop Roger's own part in the discussion of the feast is learned. Osbert said the feast was celebrated in many places and asked about the Roman authority for its commemoration. In passing, he bragged about an apparently recent experience he had had in celebrating it:

When the festival of that day was being celebrated by us in the Church of God, some followers of Satan denounced the thing as ridiculous and unheard of. In their envy and spite they got hold of two bishops who happened to be in the neighbourhood, Roger and Bernard, and roused their indignation at this new-fangled celebration. These bishops

---

Mary." For the Evesham writer, Prior Dominic, see J. C. Jennings, "The Origins of the 'Elements Series' of the Miracles of the Virgin."

64. Southern, *Saint Anselm and His Biographer,* pp. 290–296; van Dijk, "Origins," p. 437, erroneously believed this was written after 1129 and around 1140.

65. Southern, *Saint Anselm and His Biographer,* p. 10; R. H. C. Davis, "The Monks of St. Edmund, 1021–1148;" Pierre Chaplais, "The Original Charters of Herbert and Gervase, Abbots of Westminster, 1121–1157."

saying that the feast was forbidden in a council declared it must be put an end to as an untenable tradition. We, however, persisted in the services of the day which we had begun, and completed the glorious festival with triumphant delight. Then my rivals and those who bite like dogs in envy at the good things of other people, who are always trying to get their own follies approved, and bring into disrepute the words and deeds of the religious . . . shooting at me the arrows of a pestilent tongue, declared that a festival could not be maintained whose origination lacked the authority of the Roman church.[66]

Osbert defended the feast himself and urged Anselm to seek aid from learned men like Gilbert the Universal, the bishop of London, and Abbot Hugh of Reading, who observed the feast in his abbey at the king's request.[67]

In the autumn of 1129 Archbishop William Corbeil, acting as papal legate, summoned the bishops of England and Wales to a council in London. Thurstan of York, Alexander of Lincoln, Everard of Norwich, Gilbert of London, Roger of Salisbury, Bernard of Saint David's, and many other prelates attended; in fact, it was one of the largest ecclesiastical gatherings of the century. Henry of Huntingdon called the bishops "the pillars of the state and bright beams of sanctity at that time." [68] Most of the discussions again concerned clerical celibacy, but the Immaculate Conception was also debated and the celebration of its feast approved.[69] The influence of the king may have been decisive, for he was much in evidence at this council.

66. Osbert of Clare, *Letters,* no. 7.   67. *Ibid.*
68. Henry of Huntingdon, p. 251.
69. "Winchcombe Annals, 1049–1181," ed. R. R. Darlington, p. 125. There is some confusion as to the precise date of the council. The *Anglo-Saxon Chronicle,* 2:194, placed it Monday to Friday, September 30 to October 4; Henry of Huntingdon said it started on August 1. Both Knowles, *Monastic Order in England,* p. 512, and van Dijk, "Origins," p. 435, mistakenly recorded that it was presided over by the papal legate, John of Crema, who had held the council of 1127; van Dijk also oddly dated it September 30 to October 19. The Winchcombe Annals recorded the first celebration of the feast at its own house in 1126.

Osbert's letter was probably written shortly before the council.[70] Although momentarily exiled from his own monastery at Westminster, he was probably still in the London area when he celebrated the feast. It would be extremely helpful if it could be determined where and when Roger and Bernard were asked to intervene. Since their action seems more understandable during a vacancy in the London episcopate and since they may both have been in Normandy in December 1128, the most likely date appears to be December 8, 1127.[71]

Roger's part, as described by Osbert, is both puzzling and contradictory. The monk gives the impression that his celebration was interrupted, but it is more probable that his opponents protested to the bishops after the ceremony was concluded. It is highly unlikely that Osbert would have dared defy a direct command of the two prelates, one of whom was also the all-powerful viceroy of the kingdom. Oddly enough, however, Osbert made no special note of Roger's position.

Most curious is the bishops' rationale for opposing the feast. Osbert did not label them opponents and even admitted they had to be stirred up against the celebration. When they did declare it should be terminated as an untenable tradition, they cited a prohibition against the celebration in a church

70. Since Gilbert was consecrated on January 22, 1128 and Hugh was elected archbishop of Rouen before July 15, 1129, Osbert's letter can be placed between these dates. Hugh had been summoned to join the Roman curia as early as April 1128 but the king resisted such a transfer; the abbot was there in May–June 1129, however, and with Roger in Rouen in June–July 1129; Holtzmann, *Papsturkunden in England*, 2:162–164, nos. 21, 22; *Regesta*, 2, no. 1575. Van Dijk, "Origins," p. 434, believed the letter was written after the London council, but, if this were so, Osbert would surely have mentioned the council which upheld his cause, and also have given Hugh his new title.

71. *Regesta*, 2, no. 1575. It is equally difficult to place Bishop Bernard, but he may have been in Normandy in 1127 and in 1129, see nos. 1547, 1569, 1578, 1581, 1596. Knowles, Bishop, and Williamson, the editor of Osbert's letters, all suggested 1127 for the encounter.

council.[72] Such a previous discussion of the dogma, or feast, is unknown, and the prelates were probably simply recalling that Lanfranc had dropped the feast from the calendar.[73] Yet even this is strange. Although not theologians of note, Roger and Bernard were both unusually well informed men. It was Roger's business to know all the affairs of the kingdom, and Bishop Bernard, a former chaplain of the queen who still frequently attended court, had been to Roman councils in 1119 and 1123.[74] Surely each would have been familiar with the spread of Marian devotions and theology, even if not deeply interested themselves. Although the feast was not observed at Roger's cathedral of Saint Mary, he would certainly have known of any novelties in the liturgy of Reading abbey, especially if performed at the king's express command. If the Salisbury canons opposed the devotion, Roger might have accepted their view, but their opposition is nowhere evident, nor does it appear that Roger's objects were part of any antimonastic bias.

His response resembles his viceregal methods more than

72. As van Dijk indicates, the Latin, *qui hanc festivitatem prohibitam dicentes in consilio affirmaverunt,* is somewhat ambiguous. It can mean, "saying that the feast was forbidden in a council, they (the bishops) declared," or, "saying that the feast was forbidden, they declared in a council," or, "saying in a council that the feast was forbidden, they declared." The difference between the last two versions is not material, but clearly there are two interpretations. Either the bishops spoke of a previous council as an authority for opposing the feast (the usual interpretation), or they themselves spoke out in a council against it (Fr. van Dijk's view). The latter seems improbable as the date of Osbert's letter prevents such statements from having been made in the London council of 1129. It is conceivable, but nowhere recorded, that this could have been said at the council of 1127. None of this, of course, explains why the bishops opposed the feast.

73. Anselm of Canterbury had also opposed the idea of the Immaculate Conception, although the feast's celebration was not an issue in his day, Southern, *Saint Anselm and His Biographer,* pp. 290–296.

74. Lloyd, *A History of Wales,* p. 453. He was also in Rome in April 1129, *Book of Llan-Dav,* ed. J. G. Evans and John Rhys, pp. 30, 53–54.

anything else, for his order was essentially a directive for-
bidding further action until an inquiry had been made or
until a definite decision was reached. In short, too much
ought not be made of this incident, which was reported by
one unreliable witness prone to exaggeration and obviously
prejudiced. Even such staunch defenders of the Immaculate
Conception as Eadmer and William of Malmesbury never
related Roger or Bernard to their discussions.[75] The London
council of 1129 did resolve the issue in favor of the feast, but
no contemporary chronicler thought it worthwhile to record
the deliberations, and the decision was only barely mentioned in the annals of one house.[76]

This legatine council did attract attention for other reasons,
however, and doubtless Roger also was more interested in its
demand that all archdeacons and priests leave their wives by
Saint Andrew's Day (November 30) or be deprived of their
churches. After decreeing this, the simple archbishop and his
colleagues then asked the king to enforce their mandate, and
Henry promptly complied by placing a fine on priests who
would not leave their wives.[77] In effect, he licensed clerical
incontinence and derived profit from his technical support
of the church. Roger and his own Matilda of Ramsbury must
have enjoyed the humor of the monarch's righteous posture;
they certainly saw their own advantage in his edict.

Over the years the debate between the monks and the rest
of the clergy turned into pamphleteering. About 1132 Thurstan, the respected archbishop of York, entered the lists by
asking precisely what the status of monks was within the
church. His question was addressed to a well known scholar,
Theobald of Étampes, who was then teaching in the college

75. Van Dijk, "Origins," p. 441, suggests that Roger's opposition
to the feast continued until his death. I find absolutely no evidence
for such a view, and, in any case, it is based upon a misdating of
Eadmer's treatise; see Note 64. About 1137 Osbert wrote another,
more cautious letter about the Conception (van Dijk, pp. 437–439);
it adds nothing to our knowledge of earlier events.

76. "Winchcombe Annals," p. 125; see Note 69.

77. *Anglo-Saxon Chronicle,* 2:195.

of Saint George-in-the-Castle in Oxford, and who may have been associated with Saint Frideswide's priory.[78] Theobald had once challenged Faritius of Abingdon on the necessity of baptism by water and he had also defended the right of priests' sons to be ordained. Roger probably knew him well and most likely agreed with him on the last point, but their manner of debate was quite different. Theobald's reply to Thurstan was a severe condemnation of monastic privilege and involvement in the secular world. It was probably a much more strident answer than Thurstan had anticipated, and it called forth an angry, rambling counterargument from an anonymous, possibly Canterbury, monk. The monastic correspondent heaped scorn on Theobald's reference to the penury of secular clerks with unmistakable sarcasm, asking, "Oh penury! What about York? What about London? What about Salisbury? What about Lincoln?" The point was well made, but so, some thought, was Theobald's call for a true monastic withdrawal from the world.

In 1132, in yet another monastic quarrel, Roger found himself once again differing with the king on ecclesiastical policy, but this time his viewpoint prevailed. In 1127 Henry had given the abbey of Peterborough to his Cluniac nephew, Henry, the abbot of Saint Jean d'Angély at Poitou, a notorious pluralist and the papal legate who had condemned Roger's position in the Canterbury election of 1123. Expelled from his continental monastery and now rapidly wasting the resources of his new abbey, he was likened to a drone in a hive by the Peterborough chronicler.[79] In 1130 Abbot Henry began conniving with Abbot Peter the Venerable of Cluny to downgrade Peterborough abbey to the status of a priory and

78. Nicholl, *Thurstan Archbishop of York*, pp. 187–191. The complete text of Theobald's letter and the monk's long reply were analyzed and published by Raymonde Foreville and Jean Leclerq, "Un Débat Sur Le Sacerdoce Des Moines Au XIIe Siècle."

79. *Anglo-Saxon Chronicle*, 1127–1132, 2:192–197. For more on Abbot Henry see Cecily Clark, "The Ecclesiastical Adventurer: Henry of Saint Jean d'Angély."

subject it to Cluny. Since the king greatly admired Cluny and wished to support his relative in any case, Bishops Roger and Alexander had considerable difficulty two years later in persuading him to dismiss his worthless nephew.[80] Bishop Alexander was the local diocesan and probably initiated the action, which Roger then supported. The viceroy gained no personal benefit from his stand, not even the good will of the abbey historian, but apparently he believed the independence and integrity of the monastery important enough to risk offending the king.

Naturally, Bishop Roger was not always the champion of good causes, nor did he and Henry usually differ about ecclesiastical issues. Another clerical squabble between 1123 and 1133 may be more typical. A son of the previous bishop of Bath had seized some cathedral properties at Wells and refused to return them to the canons despite the efforts of Geoffrey, the new bishop. Henry and Roger supported the rebellious archdeacon.[81]

In 1133, as in 1123, Roger found profit in taking an independent position. Despite the disagreement about Peterborough, on May 28, 1133, the king still gave Roger's nephew Nigel, who was already royal treasurer, the vacant see of Ely. Typical of Henry's practice and Roger's ambivalence, the election was forced upon the monks of the Ely chapter. At about the same time another government official and Sarum canon, Geoffrey Rufus, the royal chancellor, was given the diocese of Durham. They were consecrated to-

80. *Anglo-Saxon Chronicle,* 2:195. Another Peterborough writer gave additional details about Abbot Henry and also affirmed the part Bishops Roger and Alexander played in preserving the abbey's independence, *The Chronicle of Hugh Candidus,* ed. William T. Mellows, pp. 99–104. Bethell, "Episcopal Elections," p. 693, theorized that Roger's opposition to Cluny, and his conjectured opposition to Peter's Pence, may have been financial, as he did not wish great sums of money to leave England. About 1132, or shortly thereafter, Bishop Alexander and the abbot of Peterborough quarrelled about the pleas and customs of the parish church of Peterborough. Alexander was victorious in this dispute, *Regesta,* 2, no. 1911.

81. *Ecclesiastical Documents,* ed. Joseph Hunter, p. 23.

gether at Lambeth on October 1, 1133, and, although Roger was not specifically mentioned, he was probably a coconsecrator.[82] Nigel did not remain in his new diocese very long, but, like his uncle, quickly returned to his duties at the exchequer. Unlike Roger, however, Nigel was not a very good bishop in his early years, for his deputy at Ely was a married clerk named Ranulf of Salisbury who severely oppressed the cathedral monks, whom Nigel did not protect quickly.[83]

If there is any consistency in Bishop Roger's ecclesiastical positions, it is certainly not that he was the notorious opponent of the monks some have thought. Rather, he seems to have been more like an old-style pre-Gregorian reformer: Monasteries were to be patronized and their standards maintained, but monks were to keep to their cloisters. If wealthy abbeys, or even tiny priories, provided opportunities for occasional episcopal aggrandizement, this did not affect his underlying concern for them or his belief in their value.

In some ways Roger was positively opposed to the new reforms sweeping the church. He was not celibate, and he did practice nepotism. He hedged on lay investiture and opposed completely free episcopal elections. His views on simony and theocratic monarchy are unknown, but he certainly did not champion their abolition. On the other hand, he did not share the king's belief in simply using men— monks or seculars—to his own advantage. Roger served Henry, and served him faithfully, but he did not encourage his cavalier exploitation of the church, and he could show surprising independence when he thought an issue was vital. It was no easy task, but Roger did try to hold his spiritual allegiance apart from his curial interests.

82. *Liber Eliensis,* pp. 283–284. About 1134 Bishop Roger gave the church of Ely a great cope; *Ibid.,* p. 294. For Geoffrey see *Regesta,* 2:ix–x.
83. *Liber Eliensis,* pp. 284–299; also see Chapter 5 for a conspiracy at Ely in 1137.

Power, Tension, and Division,
1126–1139

Bishop Roger's creative energy and mastery of administrative detail continued unabated throughout Henry's reign, but beginning in 1126 the king's attention, and hence the viceroy's work, shifted somewhat to more dynastic concerns. At this time Roger was at the height of his powers as a man and as a viceroy, and yet he had already accomplished a great part of his life's work. A loosely organized government was becoming more systematic and it easily bore the lengthy absences of its king. Efficient procedures were rejuvenating an antiquated legal routine, and a royal economy threatened by the the greed of its own minters and hampered by its rudimentary methods of accounting had been largely reformed. The church in the diocese of Salisbury and throughout the country received Roger's careful attention and flowered in the order and prosperity of his rule.

Unfortunately, things were not equally well in the king's family. Since the wreck of the White Ship Henry had been without a legitimate male heir and it gradually became evident that Queen Adeliza was not going to provide one. The king was in his late fifties and he believed that however ably Roger might act as caretaker of the realm, in the final analysis the strength of the country was its monarch. All kings worry about preserving their dynasty and Henry was insistent that an heir of his body should follow him in possessing the lands of the English kings and Norman dukes. Bastards abounded, but he thought only of his one surviving legitimate offspring, the Empress Matilda, whose husband Henry

V of Germany had died in May 1125. Despite Matilda's intense desire to remain in the empire where she was loved and honored, and despite Henry's own realization that his lay and ecclesiastical barons did not want a woman as sovereign, the king summoned his daughter to his side. Together they returned to England in September 1126.[1] Henry was worn out from three years amidst the never ending strife of Normandy, and Matilda was apprehensive about facing the half-forgotten, and supposedly hostile, barons of her homeland. It was an unpromising start for Henry's ambitious plans for the royal succession.

To the English the Empress Matilda appeared a haughty, scheming woman, and she evidently distrusted Roger from the very beginning, probably thinking he was one of the barons who objected to being ruled by a woman.[2] Immediately after her return, acting in concert with her kinsman King David of Scotland, she somehow persuaded her father to transfer the long-forgotten captive, Duke Robert Curthose of Normandy, from Roger's faithful custody to that of her own half-brother Henry's favorite natural son, Earl Robert of Gloucester.[3] As the Conqueror's eldest son Duke Robert and his heirs had a much better claim to England's throne than Matilda, and indeed back in 1101 King Henry had sworn that if he died without a male heir his brother should inherit his crown.[4] Ever since the defeat at Tinchebrai, Bishop Roger had kept the duke in close but honorable confinement at Devizes castle, but now the royal prisoner was made to exchange the Salisbury Plain for Bristol castle and later for distant, lonely Cardiff. Duke Robert's son, William Clito, whom Henry had neglected to imprison like his

1. This was not her first visit to England since her marriage. Roger had attested a writ (possibly spurious) with her in 1114–1116; *Regesta*, 2, no. 1174.

2. For estimates of her character see *Gesta Stephani*, pp. 59, 82; William of Malmesbury, *H.N.*, pp. *xv*, 56–58.

3. *Anglo-Saxon Chronicle*, 2:192.

4. Henry of Huntingdon, p. 233.

father, had long actively claimed Normandy and was supported in his efforts to regain it by the clever French king, Louis VI. Rebellions by Clito's friends had threatened Henry's control of the duchy and compelled him to campaign abroad.

King Henry pondered the succession problem for some months. His Christmas court at Windsor passed without event, and it was not until he moved to London to celebrate the Feast of the Circumcision January 1, 1127, that he decided to act. Then he harangued his vassals with a long address detailing the tragedy of his son's death and stressing that only Matilda now had a legal and hereditary claim to succeed him. Passing over Duke Robert and William Clito, Henry emphasized his daughter's royal descent from both her parents. He, his brother, and his father had been kings, and Matilda's late mother was an heir of the Saxon line which stretched back to Egbert of Wessex. The king then demanded that his barons swear to accept the Empress Matilda as their lady, if he should die without a male heir.[5]

At Henry's request, Bishop Roger then stepped forward, and, as William of Newburgh phrased it, "like a prudent man and second only to the king," he carefully explained the significance of the oath.[6] Roger was the type of man who could on some occasions exert remarkable independence and then on others trim his sails to the shifting winds of policy and circumstance. So it was in 1127, but it must have been a grim moment even for him. Matilda had already demonstrated that she distrusted him, and, indeed, the prospect of such a woman on the throne could hold little attraction for a man with his passion for order, efficiency, peace, and justice.

Roger urged the assembled lords to swear to support the Empress Matilda, and reluctantly they did, having little

5. William of Malmesbury, *H.N.*, pp. 3–4. 'Lady' was a technical term used by a female ruler until her coronation. For the date of the oath see John Horace Round, *Geoffrey de Mandeville: A Study in Anarchy*, pp. 30–32.
6. William of Newburgh, 1:23, 26–29.

choice. Archbishop William took the oath first, followed next by Bishop Roger, who then administered the formula to the rest of the hierarchy and to the lay barons at the court.[7] King David of Scotland, himself a possible heir through his mother, swore first for the laity. Robert Earl of Gloucester and Stephen Count of Mortain and Boulogne, the king's nephew, competed for the honor of next swearing for the empress, and Stephen won. This oath did not actually elect Matilda queen, but it was similar to the pledge given at Salisbury in 1116 when the barons had sworn allegiance to the late Prince William.

In May 1127, only five months after the barons had sworn their great oath, Henry secretly betrothed his daughter to Geoffrey Plantagenet, the son of Count Fulk of Anjou, the future king of Jerusalem.[8] When they were married the following June, she was twenty-five and he was fourteen. Roger had arranged for the barons to renew their pledge in London on April 29, 1128, but William of Malmesbury reported that, when news of the wedding became public some months later, men openly asserted that they would not keep their oaths after Henry's death.[9] Marriage of their proposed sovereign to any foreigner was bound to anger the proud Anglo-Normans, but an Angevin was particularly odious because of the ancient feuds between Anjou and Normandy. Henry claimed he chose Geoffrey partly to secure aid against William Clito, who had become count of Flanders after the shocking murder of Charles the Good. With the vast resources of his new fief and the strong backing of the French king, Clito was expected to press deeply into Normandy. Worse yet, Flanders itself was vital to the English economy.

7. *Ibid.;* Henry of Huntingdon, p. 265; William of Malmesbury, *H.N.,* p. 5, merely noted that the archbishops and other prelates swore the oath.

8. Henry of Huntingdon, p. 247.

9. William of Malmesbury, *H.N.,* p. 5; *Anglo-Saxon Chronicle,* 2:193. John of Worcester, p. 27, mentioned the oath of 1128 and stated that Anselm of Bury unsuccessfully tried to obtain exemptions from it for abbots.

Fortunately for Henry and Matilda, Clito was slain in July
1128 in another Flemish uprising. Six years later his father,
Duke Robert Curthose, then nearly eighty, quietly died in
a Welsh prison after enduring twenty-eight years of cap-
tivity.[10]

Bishop Roger may have made two quick trips to Normandy in these years, one in late August 1127, and the other
in early July, 1129.[11] His purposes are unknown, but they

10. William of Malmesbury, *H.N.,* p. 2; Henry of Huntingdon,
p. 247; *Gesta Stephani,* p. 7. Orderic Vitalis, 4:486, claimed that the
night Clito died old Robert Curthose awoke in his cell crying, "Alas,
my son is dead." He was apparently mistaken in thinking the duke
was still at Devizes.

11. The whole issue of Roger's visits to Normandy is a confusing
problem. Indeed, there is the distinct possibility that since he was
viceroy he never left the island kingdom at all. Some slight indica-
tions argue otherwise, however. He had extensive Norman possessions (see Chapter 3, Notes 45-49), issued a charter to a Norman
leper hospital in words which suggest he had observed their work
(Charter 21), and witnessed one royal charter at Rouen (*Regesta,* 2,
no. 1576) and maybe two others somewhere in Normandy (nos.
1575, 1915). The Rouen charter (no. 1576) was tentatively dated by
the *Regesta* editors to 1129, but Ralph Basset was also a witness
and, if Lady Stenton (*English Justice,* p. 60) is correct, Ralph died
in 1127. Another subscriber, Geoffrey chancellor, became chancellor
in 1123 thereby making terminal dates of 1123-1127. King Henry
was in Normandy early June 1123-September 11, 1126 and August
26, 1127-July 15, 1129. But in 1123 the Saxon chronicler noted the
king intrusted his realm to Bishop Roger, the viceroy was engaged
in Reading Abbey affairs between 1123 and 1125, and Ralph Basset
hung men in Leicester in December 1124. Thus the times Roger
and Ralph could have been in Normandy, for even a quick trip,
seem limited to 1125-1126 or late summer 1127. This charter (no.
1576) does have strikingly similar witnesses to writs issued in August 1127 (nos. 1499-1501) and may have been issued then. No.
1575 lacks a place of issue, but seems likely to have been sent from
Normandy as it concerns Norman affairs and three ducal bishops
witnessed it, including Archbishop Hugh of Rouen whose predecessor died on November 28, 1128. Another witness, Nigel de Albini,
died on November 21, 1129. Thus this charter seems clearly datable
to 1129 (West, *Justiciarship in England,* p. 23, for some reason gave
1130, however). Hugh was in Rome in May and June and Henry
returned to England July 15, so this text and Roger's presence in
Normandy, if he actually attested it there, seem narrowed to early
July 1129. If Ralph Basset died as late as 1129, perhaps both writs

may have been connected with Matilda's engagement and marriage, for only quite important business would have taken him away from his viceregal duties. By July 15, 1129, Roger and Henry were back in England preparing for such things as the London synod which issued decrees about celibacy and approved the feast of the Immaculate Conception. Chance distribution of evidence may be deceptive, but the third decade of the century seems to have been an especially active time in Roger's life, when his governmental, diocesan, and general ecclesiastical work were prodigious.

The decade of the 1130s, on the other hand, brought tension, division, and tragedy. In 1130 there seems to have been a major shake-up of government personnel. Geoffrey de Clinton was charged with treason at the Easter court, and, although acquitted, he lost some of his powers. Then at Michaelmas several other sheriffs, apparently unconnected with Geoffrey, were dismissed.[12] Was there really widespread corruption, and, if so, why had Roger not prevented it? Contemporary writers, who surely represented only a very specialized segment of national opinion, from time to time complained about the low quality of government officials and their lack of social background, about lay interference in the church, about poor coins and high prices, and about the greed and dishonesty of some judges; even King Henry dreamed

---

do date from that year as the *Regesta* editors suggest. Another much later writ (no. 1915) was issued at Falaise between 1133 and 1135, but only one of its two cartulary copies contain Roger's attestation, and most likely this was an error in transcription. There is a very remote possibility that a writ of about 1125 bearing Roger's witness may have been issued in Normandy (no. 1428). Thus, Roger conceivably could have been in Normandy in 1125, 1126, August 1127, and July 1129, but actually only the last two dates seem possible, and even they are tenuous. If Roger did go to Normandy at any time, the unanswered question appears—who ruled England while he and the king were away?

12. Orderic Vitalis, 3:403–404; Henry of Huntingdon, p. 252. See also Southern, "The Place of Henry I in English History," pp. 201–206; Stenton, *English Feudalism*, p. 218.

about peasants, knights, and clerics who felt they were mis-treated.[13] On the other hand, revenues poured into the exche-quer, disputes clogged the courts, and there was peace in the realm. The existence of possible mismanagement in 1130 may thus be less significant than the fact that steps were taken to eliminate it. Then too, the nervous king may have deliberately exaggerated his charges against certain sheriffs in order to dismiss individuals whom he thought might oppose his plan for Matilda's succession.

The troubles of 1130 could hardly be called a crisis, and Henry left them in August and sailed to Normandy. About the same time the following year, after a particularly rough crossing of the Channel, he returned to England, and then on September 8, 1131, the sixty-three year old king presided over a great council at Northampton, where he once more forced his barons to renew their oaths to Matilda.[14] It was at this well-attended royal council that the king supposedly "re-stored" Malmesbury abbey to the bishop and church of Salis-bury; this was probably a normal reconfirmation of Roger's holding, but it may have been conditional upon his further support for Matilda's succession.[15] The early 1130s were rather unproductive compared with the event-filled 1120s,

13. Orderic Vitalis, 4:164; Richard of Hexham, *Historia*, p. 140; *Gesta Stephani*, pp. 15–16; Adelard of Bath, *Natural Questions* (quoted in Hollister, *Twelfth Century Renaissance*, p. 144); *Leges Henrici Primi* (quoted in *Regesta*, 3:xxvii); *Battle Chronicle*, p. 60. John of Worcester, pp. 32–33, said Grimbald the royal physician told him about the three dreams which bothered Henry in Normandy in 1130. John also drew sketches of these dreams in his chronicle. About 1130 the king also visited the Somerset hermit, Wulfric of Hasel-bury. One of the royal courtiers accused Wulfric of tampering with the coinage, and the anchorite caused him to lose his speech; John of Ford, *Wulfric of Haselbury*, pp. 63–65, 116.

14. John of Worcester, p. 33, said Henry was so frightened by the Channel storm that he vowed to remit Danegeld for seven years and to make a pilgrimage to St. Edmund's shrine, if it abated. Round, *Geoffrey de Mandeville*, p. 31, doubted the authenticity of this oath in 1131. Matilda always stressed the oath of 1127, but it seems to have been repeated; see William of Malmesbury, *H.N.*, p. 10; John of Worcester, pp. 27, 34; *Regesta*, 2, nos. 1712–1716.

15. *Regesta*, 2, no. 1715.

but in 1132 the bishop intervened to assist Peterborough abbey, and a year later his nephew Nigel was granted Ely monastery and diocese.[16]

Despite the bad omens of an eclipse of the sun and a serious earthquake, in August 1133 King Henry left England for the last time. He died at Lyons-la-Foret December 1, 1135, after having gorged himself on a meal of lampreys.[17] Henry of Huntingdon offered one elegy, which Thomas Forrester rather freely translated in the nineteenth century:

> Hark! how unnumber'd tongues lament
> Henry, the wide world's ornament.
> Olympus echoes back the groan,
> And gods themselves his fate bemoan.
> Imperial Jove from his right hand
> Might take the sceptre of command
> Mercury borrow winged words,
> Mars share with him the clash of swords,
> Alcides' strength, Minerva's wit,
> Apollo's wisdom, him befit:
> Form'd like the Deities to shine,
> He shared their attributes divine.
> England, his cradle and his throne,
> Mourns, in his glory lost, her own.[18]

To the very end this stocky little man who was such a cruel, demanding, successful king remains an enigmatic personality, and classical allusions do nothing to unravel his mysteries. King Henry I was a ruler of considerable expertise in his own right, but it is doubtful that he would have been as great a monarch if he had not had at his side a counselor who

16. See Chapter 4.

17. Henry of Huntingdon, p. 254. In 1133 Wulfric of Haselbury had prophesied his death and had promised salvation because of his gifts to Reading abbey. Later Wulfric even saluted Stephen as the next king; John of Ford, pp. 116–117.

18. Henry of Huntingdon, p. 254; Thomas Forrester, *The Chronicle of Henry of Huntingdon,* p. 260. Orderic Vitalis, 4:238–239, and John of Hexham, *Historia,* p. 286, also offered favorable judgments on Henry's reign; see also Southern, "Place of Henry I," p. 155.

possessed the strength to effect his commands, the imagination to give substance to his government, and the independence to oppose some of his more avaricious designs. Henry and Roger stand together in history as they ruled together in life, complementary figures who jointly brought to fruition the greatness of Anglo-Norman England.

Disorders of all types broke out following the news of Henry's death, or so the chroniclers reported.[19] Too much should not be made of these disturbances, for the interregnum lasted less than a month, and the transfer of power was at first remarkably smooth. Nevertheless, the disruptions were a foretaste of what was to come, and they make us wonder about the actual depth of Roger's control of the country. His position as viceroy and regent was purely personal and had no real validity after the king's death, but men must still have looked to him to maintain order and justice.

After Henry's death, Roger apparently made straight for Winchester, rightly judging that the next claimant to England's throne would follow the practice of William Rufus and Henry himself by first marching there to demand the wealth accumulated by the former king. Henry's treasure was enormous—according to one account, more than one hundred thousand pounds of silver pennies and innumerable gold and silver vessels and ornaments.[20] Roger and the treasury chamberlain, William de Pont de l'Arche, commanded the soldiers guarding this vast hoard, but Henry of Blois, bishop of Winchester and abbot of Glastonbury, tried to bribe the chamberlain to surrender the money to him. William refused, and he and Roger prudently decided to await the first claimant to ride up the Winchester road.[21]

To her great misfortune, the Empress Matilda did not return to England immediately after her father's death but

19. *Gesta Stephani,* pp. 1–2; Orderic Vitalis, 5:54.
20. William of Malmesbury, *H.N.,* pp. 17, 25.
21. *Gesta Stephani,* p. 5; Richardson and Sayles, *Governance of Medieval England,* p. 222.

rather wasted valuable time in occupying Norman castles.[22] Her cousin Stephen of Blois acted with much greater dispatch. Braving a rough Channel and avoiding Robert of Gloucester's men at Dover and Canterbury, he landed in the teeth of a storm and headed straight for the seats of power, London and Winchester. Stephen had lived in England since 1113, and the London burghers joyously received him, shouting that he was the one man to restore peace, and elected him their king by a special privilege they claimed.[23] Stephen, who was already known as a courageous soldier, enhanced his popularity by immediately capturing and punishing some minor brigands who were terrorizing the countryside beyond the city walls.

Stephen then galloped over to Winchester, where Bishop Roger and William the chamberlain accepted his claim to the royal silver. Exactly what happened is a bit unclear. Robert of Torigni, a supporter of Matilda, wrote from Normandy that Roger "gave Stephen the crown and aided him to the utmost of his power." [24] Henry of Huntingdon, a friend of the viceroy's nephew Alexander, declared that Roger did all he could to raise Stephen to the throne and helped him more than anyone else at the beginning of the reign.[25] On the other hand, William of Malmesbury emphasized the role of his former patron, Henry of Winchester, claiming that Stephen brought Roger and William to his side, but that he would not have succeeded without Bishop Henry's cooperation.[26] According to this account, the bishop

22. William of Malmesbury, *H.N.*, p. 15, also wondered why she delayed crossing.

23. *Ibid.; Gesta Stephani*, pp. 3–5; Gervase of Canterbury, *Opera,* 1:94; Orderic Vitalis, 5:110; Davis, *King Stephen*, pp. 13–17. For a discussion of the precedents and later attempts to exert this claim see, May McKisack, "London and the Succession to the Crown during the Middle Ages."

24. Robert of Torigni, *Chronicle,* 4:127. Also see the "Annals of Waverly," in *Annales Monastici*, 2:225, where Roger is called "Roger the Great."

25. Henry of Huntingdon, pp. 256, 265.

26. William of Malmesbury, *H.N.*, p. 15.

of Winchester helped his brother, Stephen of Blois, because he believed that he would be upright in ecclesiastical affairs. Robert of Bath, the probable episcopal author of the very partisan pro-Stephen *Gesta Stephani,* offered no lofty motives for Bishop Henry's action, but merely observed that the whole enterprise depended upon him.[27] It is easy to see why these reports vary somewhat. All were written from second-hand knowledge, and there must have been many hurried conferences among Roger, Henry, William, and Stephen. The intriguing—and unanswered—question is how much of this was planned long in advance? One thing certain is that Roger's support was crucial, for if he and the administration he headed had decided to oppose Stephen and support their oath to Matilda, there would have been civil war.

Three weeks after King Henry's death—Henry of Huntingdon called it the twinkling of an eye—Stephen was quietly crowned at Westminster.[28] Archbishop William Corbeil of Canterbury, Bishop Roger, and Bishop Henry were the only prelates at the ceremony. No abbots and few nobles attended, and Roger apparently did not even have time to summon his episcopal nephews.[29] The absence of so many magnates indicated not only Stephen's haste, but also the barons' uncertainty.

Before the ceremony Archbishop William questioned whether he could rightly crown Stephen, recalling the embarrassing fact that Stephen, he himself, and all the other prelates and nobles had already sworn to support Matilda. Stephen's men tried to counter his scruples by charging that King Henry had forced his subjects to take the oath and that any oath taken under compulsion was invalid. Reminding him that the Londoners had already accepted Stephen, they

27. *Gesta Stephani,* p. 5.
28. *Ibid.,* p. 8; William of Malmesbury, *H.N.,* p. 13; Henry of Huntingdon, p. 256. See the *Anglo-Saxon Chronicle,* 2:309 (Plummers' edition) for the varying dates of his coronation.
29. Bishop Nigel may have still been in Normandy; he was there earlier in the year, *Regesta,* 2, nos. 1908, 1909.

further contended that only Stephen's resolute and soldierly qualities could stamp out those who were ruining the kingdom. Hugh Bigod and others even told the credulous archbishop that on his deathbed King Henry had repented of his demands and had released his barons from their oath. William of Malmesbury refused to believe this story, but these arguments were later advanced in Rome to support Stephen's cause.[30]

Bishop Roger said that he had his own good justification for breaking his oath to Matilda. William of Malmesbury stated that he often heard Roger say that he had been released from his promise because he had sworn only on the condition that the king should not give his daughter in marriage to anyone outside the country without first consulting him and the other chief men of the kingdom. The viceroy bitterly complained that no one had recommended the Angevin marriage and that only Robert of Gloucester, Brian Fitz Count, and the bishop of Lisieux had been aware of it. This explanation did not sound very convincing to William, however, and he added his own evaluation of it, "I would not say this as accepting the word of a man who knew how to adapt himself to any occasion according as the wheel of fortune turned; I, merely, like a faithful historian add to my narrative whatever was thought by people in my part of the country." [31] It was a hard judgement on Roger's veracity, but there seems to be no way to prove who was right, or whether Roger was indeed able to impose such a condition on his oath in 1127. It was a logical condition, but Henry rarely let others dictate terms to him. Roger certainly felt that he should have been consulted about the marriage and was furious that he was not. Actually, he ought to have known

30. William of Malmesbury, *H.N.*, pp. 6–7, 13; Gervase of Canterbury, *Opera*, 1:94; John of Salisbury, *Memoirs of the Papal Court*, p. 84. The *Liber Eliensis*, p. 285, added, "*Pro quo iuramento Rogerus episcopus Seresberiensis, ad cuius nutum pendebat totum regni negotium, et ceteri primates eum susceperunt.*"
31. William of Malmesbury, *H.N.*, p. 13.

better. Although kings may trust their ministers in governmental administration, they usually feel no need to consult
their official servants about what they regard as personal and
dynastic matters. The renewal of the oath in 1131 should
have made all these qualifications meaningless, but there is
some wavering doubt as to whether this later oath was in
fact ever administered.[32] Matilda herself always referred to
the first council in 1127.

A nobler excuse for Bishop Roger and Archbishop William is that they believed they were furthering the best
interests of the church. William of Newburgh stated that
the morals of the late king and some of his policies had offended the bishops, and they felt that a monarch created by
their favor might avoid such crimes.[33] There is considerable
merit to this late analysis. Few magnates wanted Empress
Matilda as their ruler, but they did not flock to Stephen of
Blois, either. It was rather the church, guided by the episcopal lords of Canterbury, Salisbury, and Winchester, that
provided the greatest support for his throne. At the coronation Archbishop William demanded that Stephen publicly
acknowledge his debt to the church by swearing that he
would restore and maintain its freedom. His brother, Bishop
Henry, stood as guarantor that the new king would respect
this oath. It was a great deal to expect from a man who had
already broken one oath, but all the principal figures at the
coronation were guilty of the same offense. At the coronation
Mass the kiss of peace was forgotten and not offered to the
people, a bad omen which men remembered in the years to
come.[34] About a week after the ceremonies on January 4,

32. See Note 14.
33. William of Newburgh, 1:26-29. Newburgh also castigated
Roger for being faithless to Matilda, saying his deeds were never
consistent with his dignity, p. 37. In a rather strange evaluation,
he called Stephen God's avenger against Roger for his perjury to
the empress.
34. William of Malmesbury, *H.N.*, pp. 14-15; John of Hexham,
Historia, p. 287. Gervase of Canterbury, *Opera*, 2:72, claimed the
host disappeared from the archbishop's hands.

1136, King Henry's body was quietly laid to rest in Reading abbey, with Bishop Roger as one of the few prelates in attendance.[35]

Stephen was a more appealing individual than his Norman predecessors. Courteous and kind, he was resolute in active pursuits and had a deserved reputation for prowess in battle. In less martial matters, however, he leaned heavily on his advisers, was particularly susceptible to flattery, and was inclined to promise more than he could deliver. Where King Henry had managed other men, Stephen was sometimes manipulated by his subordinates.[36] Initially, the new king made few changes in the conduct of royal affairs, and the chronicle writers reported that he entrusted Bishop Roger with the whole government of his kingdom.[37] He also handsomely rewarded the bishop for his part in bringing him to power. Roger was given the borough of Malmesbury, a very lucrative gratuity which could be added to the abbey and castle he already possessed there. His illegitimate son, Roger the Pauper, was made royal chancellor, and Roger the Pauper's probable brother, Adelelm, archdeacon of Dorset, was made royal treasurer.[38]

Stephen had won his crown through the intervention of the bishops, but Matilda also looked to the church to vindicate her claims. After learning of Stephen's usurpation of the

35. *Regesta,* 3, no. 386. Apparently the only other bishops present were William of Canterbury and Henry of Winchester.

36. For estimates of his character see, William of Malmesbury, *H.N.,* pp. 17–20; *Gesta Stephani,* pp. 14–16; Henry of Huntingdon, pp. 256–258, 283; Christina of Markyate, pp. 169–171. Also see Note 18, Chapter 6.

37. For example, Orderic Vitalis, 5:63.

38. William of Malmesbury, *H.N.,* pp. 38–39. For more on these men see Appendix 3. West, *Justiciarship in England,* p. 24, said that part of Roger's power rested on his family's control of government offices, but this would only have been true after Nigel became treasurer in 1125 or 1126, and in the very early years of Stephen's reign. In 1136 Stephen also rewarded Roger with lands at West Lavington, Wiltshire; *Regesta,* 3, no. 786. This made the bishop the principal landowner in that area; the tithes of the church of Lavington had already been made a prebend of his cathedral.

throne, she immediately appealed to Rome, but, armed with Henry's treasures, the new king's supporters were able to convince the papal curia that the oath to the empress had been forced upon the barons and that Henry had repudiated it on his deathbed. Innocent II dismissed the case without a decision, in effect, confirming the coronation. Shortly thereafter, the pope wrote to Stephen praising the order and justice which King Henry had provided and deploring the troubles which had arisen after his death. Innocent then recognized the new king and urged him to reestablish the good government of the past reign.[39]

Stephen received the papal confirmation in high spirits and held his first Easter court at Westminster was a magnificence long missed in the days of thrifty King Henry. Bishop Roger and most of the other prelates were there in full episcopal splendor, and the lay barons turned out in great force, with the notable exception of Robert of Gloucester.[40] Innocent's letter had absolved the uneasy conscience of England, and most lords gratefully turned from dynastic struggles to their own affairs. The matter never really rested, however, and time and time again Stephen would be plagued by reminders of his perjured oath to Matilda.

At London the archbishop convoked a synod which Stephen attended in state. It was a great public event, and the chronicler even noted how the common people milled about the sides of the great hall and pushed at one another to see the lords and hear the proceedings.[41] Believing the opportunity was ripe and the king agreeable, the bishops seem to have overplayed their hand. They exaggerated their past difficulties, claiming that under Henry, "a second Pharaoh,"

39. John of Salisbury, *Memoirs,* pp. 84 ff.; Richard of Hexham, *Historia,* pp. 147–150; Round, *Geoffrey de Mandeville,* pp. 250–262.

40. Round, *Geoffrey de Mandeville,* pp. 18–20; 262–266; Henry of Huntingdon, p. 259, placed the court at London. Robert B. Patterson, "Stephen's Shaftesbury Charter: Another Case Against William of Malmesbury," believes Stephen and Gloucester met before Easter 1136, not afterward.

41. *Gesta Stephani,* pp. 16–18.

the church had been "prostrate and downtrodden": [42] He had practiced simony, extorted gifts from them, and involved them in costly litigation. Ecclesiastical lands had been confiscated and converted to his own or some favorite's use. His moral life had been disgraceful, nor had he encouraged morality in his subjects. Anyone who had protested against these conditions was immediately persecuted and could regain royal favor only by purchase. There was truth in all these tales, none of which the bishops had dared to make public in Henry's lifetime, but they offered a very incomplete picture of the reign, as the bishops probably knew. Roger must have felt rather awkward during these criticisms, for he had executed many of the policies. On the other hand, he had been one of the very few to protest any of Henry's actions to his face. Stephen made no comment on the proceedings, but merely listened to the charges and then blandly promised that he would restore the freedom of the church.

To a point the king kept his word, and at Oxford in April 1136 he again formally recognized his debt to the church by issuing an expanded version of his coronation oath, which was devoted almost exclusively to the needs of the church. [43] Times had changed. Thirty-five years before, King Henry had addressed his coronation charter chiefly to the lay lords. Stephen forbade simony, reaffirmed the principle of separate clerical justice, confirmed the possessions of his prelates, and agreed not to demand revenues of vacant sees. Other kings had made similar promises; it was the emphasis which was novel, for the king was obviously playing for clerical support. Archbishop William, Henry of Winchester, Roger of Salisbury, Alexander of Lincoln, and Nigel of Ely led the list of witnesses in that order; a subtle change in precedence had occurred as Bishop Henry moved quietly ahead of the aging justiciar. The Norman bishops of Rouen, Evreux, and Avranches also signed; they would always support Stephen, even after their duchy was effectively under the control of

42. *Ibid.*   43. William of Malmesbury, *H.N.*, pp. 18–20.

Geoffrey of Anjou. Self-interest motivated Robert of Gloucester's signature, for he had decided to support the king as long as Stephen respected his position and privileges.[44] King David of Scotland and Roger the chancellor also witnessed this great charter, an original copy of which was deposited in Roger's cathedral and is still preserved in the Salisbury cathedral muniment room.

Thinking he had secured the loyalty of his barons, Stephen set out for Normandy after Whitsuntide, May 10, 1136, but, while he was awaiting a favorable Channel wind, a messenger brought news that Roger of Salisbury had just died.[45] Rumors were everywhere that year, including some recounting Stephen's death.[46] The report about Bishop Roger so stirred the king that he immediately postponed his voyage and rode for Salisbury, where he found Roger in health and in control of affairs. It is possible that the bishop had been quite sick, and it is interesting that the king indefinitely postponed his journey even after learning that Roger was well. After all, Salisbury is not that far from Portsmouth, and the king could have easily resumed his travels. It is also interesting that Roger had been at Salisbury, and not at London or Winchester or even at Portsmouth with the departing king. In any event, Stephen's visit was probably one of the occasions when he was heard to say of Roger, "By the birth of God! I would give him half England if he asked for it, until his time shall pass; he will grow tired of asking before I do of giving." [47] These were fine sentiments, more than Henry ever uttered, and Roger must have been pleased, but he was also shrewd enough to mark the difference between a man of words and a man of deeds.

44. *Ibid.,* pp. 17–18; *Gesta Stephani,* p. 8; Patterson, "Robert of Gloucester."

45. Orderic Vitalis, 5:63. For some unexplained reason, Appleby, *Stephen's Reign,* pp. 34–40, makes this event follow, rather than precede, the summer seige of Exeter Castle.

46. Henry of Huntingdon, p. 259.

47. William of Malmesbury, *H.N.,* p. 39.

In the summer of 1136 Roger accompanied Stephen to the siege of Exeter.[48] Its castellan, Baldwin de Redvers, had served Roger's administration well and had been amply rewarded by King Henry, but he had delayed paying homage to Stephen, so the new king had refused to confirm his holdings. Consequently, Baldwin raised the flag of revolt, and Stephen quickly marched against him with a very impressive baronial and mercenary army. Robert of Gloucester was part of that force, and he and his friends eventually persuaded the king to let Baldwin's men go free. R. H. C. Davis, the recent biographer of King Stephen, sees this as the first major mistake of the new reign, for the king "had shown everyone that though his army might be large, part of it was half-hearted; and that his own determination could be shaken." [49]

At the beginning of Lent 1137 Stephen sailed to Normandy to try to free his duchy from Geoffrey and Matilda and bring it under his own control. This time Roger went with him to Portsmouth, but he did not cross the Channel.[50]

While the king campaigned on the Continent, the bishop tried to rule the kingdom. Baronial discontent made government more difficult than before, but the chroniclers thought Roger was just as powerful under Stephen as he had been under Henry.[51] Although there was no letup in the intensity of his work, charter evidence indicates a slight decline in his total activity. During Henry's thirty-five-year reign, Roger had been involved in 320 of the more than 1,500 extant royal writs. During the first four years of Stephen's reign (1135–1139) he took part in 51 of about 440 transactions symbolized by royal writs issued in that period. Thus, he had been in-

48. *Regesta*, 3, nos. 572, 592.
49. Davis, *King Stephen*, p. 26. For the siege see *Gesta Stephani*, pp. 20–28.
50. Orderic Vitalis, 5:63, 83; William of Malmesbury, *H.N.*, p. 21; *Calendar of Charter Rolls, 1300–1325*, 8(1908):388. Alexander did go with Stephen ("Annals of Waverly," in *Annales Monastici*, 2:226).
51. Orderic Vitalis, 5:63; *Gesta Stephani*, p. 53.

volved in roughly one of every five Henrican writs, while under Stephen he was concerned with one of every nine. Forty-three of Henry's surviving writs were addressed in whole or in part to Roger; Stephen sent him six. In Henry's reign Roger traveled extensively throughout the realm and witnessed frequently at Westminster, Winchester, Windsor, and Woodstock, but under Stephen he apparently journeyed a bit less and witnessed principally at Westminster and Oxford. On the other hand, Stephen's writs cannot all be dated properly for these comparisons, while all of Henry's were issued during Roger's lifetime. Moreover, Henry was out of the kingdom for half his reign, whereas Stephen was away less than a fifth of the time Roger knew him as king.

The viceroy's writs still exhibited all their accustomed vigor. In 1138, for example, he wrote to the widow of one of his governmental colleagues:

Roger, Bishop of Salisbury, to Sibyl, the widow of Payn Fitz John. Greetings. On the part of the king, and on my own part, I order you to restore without delay all the properties which your husband acquired, the grass, the hay, and especially the vineyards of Mardon, and all his other things, as they were on the day the king granted them to Roger, the son of Miles of Gloucester, and to Cecilia, your eldest daughter. And let them hold them well and peacefully as the king ordered in his own writ. Witnessed by Roger the chancellor. At Malmesbury.[52]

Sibyl must have been quite a domineering woman and she held back these lands apparently claiming that her daughter should only receive her father's inherited lands; those which he had purchased should remain with her. Cecilia and Roger Fitz Miles, the children of two great itinerant justiciars, disagreed, and they evidently sought and won redress and Bishop Roger executed the royal decision. The extraordinary thing about this writ is the manner in which Roger coupled his name with the king's, thereby using a quasi-royal style

52. Charter 25.

and tone far stronger than any he had used under King Henry. Nevertheless, he still scorned employing any official title and referred to himself simply as the bishop of Salisbury.

The fact that the chancellor witnessed this writ suggests that some of his clerks were available to the justiciar when he needed them.[53] T. A. M. Bishop recently demonstrated that this particular directive was prepared by the same scribe who composed two of Stephen's later charters at Salisbury, and he has suggested that the clerk was probably one of Bishop Roger's chaplains whom the viceroy was employing in royal business.[54] Either suggestion is possible, and both remind us of the rather informal governmental structure which persisted despite all Roger's reforms and of the continuing mixture of secular and ecclesiastical functions and personnel.

Miles of Gloucester continued to worry about Payn Fitz John's property, and he approached Bishop Roger for another writ to be sent to the sheriff of Hereford requiring him to pay the alms Payn had given to the monks of Gloucester. If the sheriff neglected his duty, Roger's order said Miles would see to it himself.[55] On another occasion, Roger ordered the townsmen of Lincoln to grant his nephew, Bishop Alexander of Lincoln, twenty shillings' worth of land as a royal charter had provided. Twelve men of the city and twelve of the district were to be impaneled to award the

---

53. H. G. Richardson, *The Memoranda Roll for the Michaelmas Term of the First Year of the Reign of King John, 1199–1200,* p. *lxxxiii.* Also see Poole, *From Domesday Book to Magna Carta,* p. 136. West, *Justiciarship in England,* p. 19, incorrectly reported that none of Roger's viceregal writs bore an attestation, but four of those issued under Stephen (Charters 22–25) did, and one issued under Henry (Charter 16) probably did.

54. Bishop, *Scriptores Regis,* p. 28. It should also be noted that Salisbury supplied Gilbert Foliot with his chief clerk, Richard of Salisbury. He is probably not John of Salisbury's brother, Richard, however. See *Foliot Charters,* pp. 28–29. Salisbury may have also given Roger the Great of Sicily his chancellor, Robert; see Chapter 2, Note 110.

55. Charter 24.

land. This writ, witnessed by the constable, Robert de Ver, followed the exchequer pattern for such writs.[56]

In this period (1137–1138), also, Roger and Archbishop Thurstan of York called a council at Northampton, where they checked into reports of some miracles, but otherwise its achievements were not notable.[57] As always, Roger still kept abreast of his diocesan cares, such as regulating teaching at Reading and advising lay lords about gifts to monasteries.[58]

The king's Norman campaign was a complete failure. At first, he was welcomed because the Angevins had plundered the land, but he relied heavily upon Flemish mercenaries who were equally hard on the populace. Moreover, internal struggles between his vassals and his mercenaries nearly wrecked the army, and at one point his Flemish captain, William of Ypres, persuaded Stephen to ambush Robert of Gloucester. Worse yet, the trap failed. The two were outwardly reconciled, but Robert remained in Normandy when the king sailed for home.[59]

Stephen spent money lavishly. The mercenaries were a constant drain, but he retained them because they proved more loyal than baronial troops. He paid his older brother, Theobald of Blois, two thousand marks for not pursuing his own claim to the English throne, and he purchased a truce from Geoffrey of Anjou for two thousand marks a year.[60] The monarch returned to England claiming to have

56. Charter 25.
57. John of Worcester, pp. 44–48; Florence of Worcester (Continuator's part), 2:99, 105; Nicholl, *Thurstan Archbishop of York,* p. 217.
58. Charter 22. He helped obtain a meadow for St. Frideswide's, Oxford, *Regesta,* 3, no. 638, and Robert of Lincoln gave land at Holme to the Montacute monks "with the advice and consent of the bishop of Salisbury," *Two Cartularies of the Augustinian Priory of Bruton and the Cluniac Priory of Montacute,* p. 160, no. 118. An endowment was also established for Bradenstoke Priory in Wiltshire, see Chapter 4, Note 5.
59. William of Malmesbury, *H.N.,* p. 21; Robert of Torigni, *Chronicle,* p. 136; Davis, *King Stephen,* p. 27.
60. Robert of Torigni, *Chronicle,* p. 124.

accomplished a great deal, but actually he brought no peace to Normandy, and he never returned there.[61]

Roger met the king at the dock in late November 1137, but his news was not good.[62] There was increasing discontent throughout the country, and even Roger's nephew, Nigel of Ely, had uncovered a conspiracy in his diocese. A former Glastonbury monk, a clerk named Ranulf of Salisbury, was identified as the ringleader; according to Orderic Vitalis and the author of the *Liber Eliensis,* there was a widespread plot to kill all Normans in which the rebels were to find allies in the Scots and Welsh. This puzzling affair, which had apparently been brewing for two years, has been studied in detail by E. O. Blake, who proposes several alternative explanations.[63] It could have been a purely local dispute at Ely in which Ranulf, the bishop's deputy, had been promoting his own policy at his superior's expense or there might have been strong dissatisfaction with Nigel's policy of creating additional knight's fees from the cathedral abbey holdings. Perhaps Ranulf remained loyal to the empress after Nigel had declared for Stephen, and the clerk was fortifying the see to prepare for an Angevin invasion. Or maybe it was Nigel who remained loyal to Matilda. In effect, Blake favors the last explanation and suggests that such an affair was too big to have been fomented by Ranulf alone, and that Nigel therefore was actually responsible for these seditious acts. The rumors that Stephen, and even Bishop Roger, had died in 1136 may have brought the Ely crisis to a head prematurely. When Stephen returned safely from Normandy in late 1137, Nigel had to find a scapegoat to cover the treason, and Ranulf was the best candidate. The episode is very confused, and Blake's admittedly speculative interpretation

61. Richard of Hexham, *Historia,* p. 351; Orderic Vitalis, 5:81–91; Henry of Huntingdon, p. 260.

62. *Regesta,* 3, no. 827.

63. Orderic Vitalis, 5:92–93; *Liber Eliensis,* pp. 287–305; E. O. Blake, "The *Historia Eliensis* as a Source for Twelfth Century History."

is based in part upon Nigel's suspicious activity in June 1139 when his uncle was captured and upon his vengeful resistance to Stephen after Bishop Roger's death.

The troubles at Ely coincided with frequent Scottish raids against the north. Despite the fact that King David had come to the Oxford court, he still regarded himself as being pledged to support the empress.[64] His frequent invasions were partly in her behalf and largely to secure his own firmer control over the northern shires. Rarely have sentiment and policy better agreed.

Shortly after Whitsunday, May 22, 1138, in the best feudal fashion, Robert of Gloucester formally renounced his fealty and friendship with the king and went over to the Angevin forces of his half-sister. He certainly chose his moment. In late August one of the most ferocious battles of the century, the Battle of the Standard, was fought at Northallerton in Yorkshire.[65] The Scots came pouring over the border devastating the countryside, but old Archbishop Thurstan of York organized heroic resistance under the standards of the saints of his diocese. His armored knights and sharp-eyed bowmen fought desperately against the Danes, Germans, and terrible Galloway Picts under King David's command. But although the archbishop's men won this important battle, the border remained in danger and much of it subsequently fell to David. Robert of Gloucester's defection also took advantage of the continual warfare along the Welsh frontier, and it caused fresh rebellions throughout the southwestern shires, particularly near his own strongholds of Bristol and Gloucester.[66]

The intrigue and struggle for power at Stephen's court intensified after his Norman debacle. These contests could hardly have surprised Bishop Roger, whose own experience

64. *Gesta Stephani,* pp. 35–36.
65. Ailred of Rievaulx, *Relatio de Standardo,* is the best account. See also, Beeler, *Warfare in England,* pp. 84–96.
66. *Gesta Stephani,* pp. 9–14, 18–48.

confirmed that the palace guard changed with each new ruler, but he and his family had powerful claims on the king's attention, based on ability, experience, and gratitude. On the other hand, Stephen's ambitious brother, the wealthy Cluniac bishop Henry of Winchester, called for fraternal cooperation and reminded the monarch that he owed his crown to Henry's intervention, as well. Then too, Robert of Gloucester was one of the largest landowners in the kingdom and would have been an important ally had Stephen been able to retain him, but he was an early casualty in the curial competition, and when he lost out, he decided to seek favors elsewhere. William of Ypres and his mercenaries, while very expensive, were at least thoroughly loyal to Stephen; unfortunately for Roger, they made common cause with some young knights who had lived all their lives under Roger's careful administration and who now simply—and brutally—wanted to move the old man out.

Conflict between Stephen and Matilda compounded the intrigue. The "new" men Henry I had raised from the dust to be his administrators were not ignoble, but they were completely dependent upon him; he usually had rewarded them with lands taken from less faithful vassals, who thereby had become part of a group of "disinherited" knights. Under Stephen these knights and their sons saw their opportunity and urged the king to dispossess the interlopers. Henry had mastered the workings of his own government and hence feared none of his ministers, but Stephen was not so able or so confident. As he replaced Henry's officials, he thereby created a new group of displaced men, many of whom eventually turned to Matilda.

In brief, Roger and his local counterparts, men like Baldwin de Redvers and Miles of Gloucester, were to be replaced. Since Roger's and Henry's men were usually sheriffs, the resurgent, more aristocratic, barons took the title *earl,* and R. H. C. Davis has demonstrated how such earls systematically superseded sheriffs throughout the country in 1138, 1139, and 1140.[67]

Countless men demanded their supposed places at court, but Waleran, Count of Meulan and after 1138 Earl of Worcester, soon emerged as the champion of baronial interests.[68] He was an exceptionally able nobleman and Stephen's chief supporter in Normandy. Thirty-four-year-old Waleran and his twin brother, Robert Earl of Leicester, were two of the best educated laymen in the country, sons of Count Robert of Meulan, who had opposed Archbishop Anselm's reforms. In his youth Waleran had supported William Clito against King Henry and had been imprisoned until 1129. Now he was fully restored to power and was, moreover, engaged to Stephen's two-year-old daughter. Whether it was policy or personal antagonism which set Waleran against Roger is unknown, but the earl seemed determined to replace all the viceroy's men with his own Beaumont friends.[69] The bishop tenaciously clung to power, however, and Waleran and his allies were soon forced to desperate measures to dislodge him.

In the midst of the intrigue and rebellion of 1138 a papal legate, the Cluniac Gregorian Alberic of Ostia, arrived in England. He had come to urge continual church reform and to hasten the election of a successor to Archbishop William of Canterbury, who had died in 1136. Alberic, a good and effective legate who traveled extensively in England, assembled a synod at Westminster in mid-December 1138.[70] He opened the session by joyfully announcing the end of

67. Davis, *King Stephen,* pp. 32–33, 129–144; Davis, "What Happened in Stephen's Reign." Morris in *Medieval English Sheriff,* p. 103, noted that more than half of the sheriffs in 1130 were from the newer nobility.

68. Geoffrey H. White, "The Career of Waleran, Count of Meulan and Earl of Worcester (1104–1166)."

69. Davis, *King Stephen,* pp. 30–31. See Charter 21 for a gift Roger made to a Beaumont foundation in a possible attempt to win their regard.

70. Richard of Hexham, *Historia,* pp. 167–171; John of Hexham, *Historia,* pp. 297–299; Knowles, *Monastic Order in England,* pp. 253–254.

the eight-year papal schism and the complete triumph of Innocent II, the legitimate pope. Despite considerable adverse pressure from his bishops, Henry I had recognized Innocent in May 1130.[71] The Westminster council reaffirmed a number of reform decrees; lay investiture was condemned; luxuries for nuns were outlawed; clerics were forbidden to engage in war; and schoolmasters were enjoined not to employ substitutes.

A new archbishop was also chosen. Henry of Winchester yearned for the honor and may even have been elected in 1136, but he could not obtain papal consent to be translated from Winchester. Stephen did not help his brother, which the bishop did not forget. The choice of the Canterbury monks fell upon Theobald, the abbot of Bec, who was elected without protest and consecrated on January 8, 1139.[72] This election, although not well recorded, is significantly different from previous Canterbury elections. No dispute over the place of monks was reported, the elective power of the suffragan bishops was not prominent, and there is no indication that Bishop Roger was much concerned about the election. From the consecration the whole court moved to Oxford, and from there the king, the papal legate, the new archbishop, Roger, Alexander, and several other prelates went to the consecration of the nearby nunnery of Godstow.[73] Shortly thereafter Theobald left for the second Lateran Council, evidently not to return to England until August.[74]

71. Bethell, "Episcopal Elections," pp. 692–693.

72. Avrom Saltman, *Theobald, Archbishop of Canterbury*, pp. 7–13; Gervase of Canterbury, *Opera*, 1:109. Neither William of Malmesbury or the *Gesta Stephani* mentioned this election.

73. *Regesta*, 3, nos. 366, 473, 667. Earlier Roger had given this house a mill to help establish itself, *The English Register of Godstow Nunnery Near Oxford*, ed. Andrew Clark, pp. 27–28. Bishop Alexander was a major benefactor of the house; later Godstow became famous as the burial place of Henry II's fair Rosamund.

74. Walther Holtzman suggested that Roger and his nephews attended the Lateran Council, *Registrum Antiquissimum*, 1:193, but only the archbishop, Ernulf of Rochester, Simon of Worcester, Roger

Stephen undoubtedly thought he would gain support from his new archbishop, and he was pleased to have a primate to whom he owed no obligations. Despite the revolts against him, many of which he had crushed in 1138, he believed his position was secure because he retained the backing of the church. Through miscalculation he was about to lose that needed support.

---

of Coventry, and Robert of Exeter went. See Richard of Hexham, *Historia,* pp. 176–177; John Horace Round, "Nigel, Bishop of Ely," EHR, 8(1893):514–519; Reginald Lane Poole, "The English Bishops at the Lateran Council of 1139," EHR, 38(1923):60–63; and a reply by William Hunt to Poole's article, EHR, 38(1923):557–560; *Liber Eliensis,* pp. 316–317; Appelby, *Stephen's Reign,* p. 61.

6

The Turn of
Fortune's Wheel,
June 1139

DESPITE TEMPORARY VICTORIES in 1138, the next year saw
Stephen again struggling against enemies. His own apologist depicted him as Hercules battling the Hydra—when one
head of rebellion was cut off, two others sprang up in its
place.[1] To make matters worse, the king was quickly ex-
hausting the treasure it had taken King Henry thirty-five
years to accumulate. Great sums went to Rome for confirmation of his coronation, to Anjou for a Norman truce, and to
Blois for an offended brother's pride. His military campaigns scattered silver pounds like leaves in a winter wind.
In the three-month 1136 seige of Exeter alone, Stephen
spent ten thousand pounds, almost a tenth of his predecessor's treasure.[2] Moreover, Stephen was a spendthrift, and
his habit of lavishing presents upon his favorites, while
true to the chivalric code, was disastrous for an impoverished king. Unfortunately, his revenues cannot be estimated,
since his exchequer and chamber records are lost, but his
income must have declined as more and more shires felt the
fires of rebellion.[3]

Distraught lest they should lose their accustomed rewards,

1. *Gesta Stephani*, p. 48.
2. *Ibid.*, pp. 10–13, 22–25; William of Newburgh, 1:32, 38; Richard of Hexham, *Historia*, p. 145.
3. William of Malmesbury, H.N., pp. 17, 23, called him a spendthrift and later, p. 42, noted that he debased the coinage. See also
Prestwick, "War and Finance," pp. 38–42. Beeler, *Warfare in England*, pp. 301–303, believed Stephen usually had money to pay his
soldiers.

Stephen's fawning counselors told him not to worry about money as long as the monasteries were full of treasure. It was an unthinkable suggestion, and it came from desperate men. Evidently, some churches were plundered and their property distributed to laymen, but the king hesitated to order any outright spoliation of the church, probably because he realized it remained the one secure prop to his throne.[4] A more justifiable expropriation would have to be devised.

Spring breezes in 1139 carried rumors that Robert of Gloucester was about to sail and challenge England for his half-sister. The violated oath of 1127 would be his pretext for unseating the king.[5] At this news Stephen's greedy barons demanded even more money for themselves. The king was so worried that he broke the peace of his own court to arrest several knights there on the mere suspicion that they might side against him.[6]

It was a time of hasty preparation. Friend and foe stocked castles with arms and provisions and readied for war. Even Bishop Roger strengthened his great keeps at Salisbury, Sherborn, Malmesbury, and Devizes.[7] Other prelates also fortified their holdings. Bishop Alexander garrisoned Newark in Nottinghamshire and Sleaford in Lincolnshire, Bishop Nigel repaired Ely's defenses, and Henry of Winchester provisioned at least six towers.[8]

Although much of his money was spent on great building projects like his cathedral and castles, people generally believed that Roger was immensely wealthy.[9] Although he made no secret of his success, William of Malmesbury once

4. William of Newburgh, 1:29; *Gesta Stephani*, p. 18; William of Malmesbury, *H.N.*, p. 20.

5. *Ibid.*, p. 25.   6. *Ibid.*   7. *Gesta Stephani*, p. 48.

8. Winchester, Farnham, Waltham, Dunton, Taunton, and Merton, "Annals of Winchester," in *Annales Monastici*, 2:51.

9. William of Malmesbury, *G.R.*, 2:483; *H.N.*, p. 38; *Gesta Stephani*, p. 64; Orderic Vitalis, 5:120; John of Worcester, p. 58; Christina of Markyate, p. 167; Florence of Worcester (Continuator's part), 2:113.

complimented Roger for his modesty in not bragging about his family. But the author of the *Gesta Stephani,* certainly not an impartial observer, did criticize the bishop and his nephews for ostentatiously parading their good fortune.[10] Age, like charity, can sometimes cover many sins, but for Roger the passing years only increased the numbers of men who envied his magnificence. Orderic Vitalis took a slightly different view and wrote that the viceroy and his nephews harassed the lords of their neighborhoods with various outrages, thus turning the barons against them.[11] Since no specifics were given and since no English writer uttered a similar complaint, it is doubtful that this was a significant factor in the campaign against him. The bishop's baronial enemies were motivated more by jealousy than by outrage.

Count Waleran and his supporters plagued the king, urging him to ruin Roger and his family. Some complained that the bishops had become obsessed with building castles, an odd charge and certainly no more true in 1139 than it had been for some years past.[12] Roger put it out that his fortifications were for the adornment of the church, but that was a weak reply and no one believed him. Most damaging of all, these courtiers repeated that no one should doubt that Roger and his nephews were preparing to turn their strongholds over to Matilda at the first opportunity.[13] The pompous bishops, they said, wanted to steal the king's majesty and give it to the empress.[14] Stephen was therefore urged to seize the initiative, imprison these bishops, and add their strength to his own.

Although he was usually easily influenced by his intimates, Stephen resisted these demands. He hesitated out of respect for the sacred character of the bishops' office and, as the Malmesbury monk further wrote, because he knew that such

10. William of Malmesbury, *H.N.,* p. 38; *Gesta Stephani,* pp. 48–49.

11. Orderic Vitalis, 5:120.

12. William of Malmesbury, *H.N.,* p. 25.   13. *Ibid.,* p. 27.

14. *Gesta Stephani,* p. 49.

an attack on the clergy would be severely criticized.[15] Men
like Waleran countered by arguing that, when the bishops
devoted so much attention to military pursuits, they disre-
garded the holy and simple life a Christian priest should
lead.[16] Stephen should remember, they contended, that as
a monarch anxious to preserve the peace of his country he
could confiscate whatever might give rise to strife. To
succeed, he should imprison Roger and his nephews without further formalities. Afterwards, in pious and Catholic
fashion, he could eventually return to them whatever per-
tained to the church and to the sacred character of bishops.
The prelates were not to be captured as bishops, but rather
as sinners against the peaceful character of a bishop and as
men suspected of advocating rebellion.

These hypocritical arguments were persuasive, and the
king's trying circumstances and weak character made him
increasingly receptive to them. The barons did have an
interesting point in precisely distinguishing between a man's
role as bishop, on one hand, and as a crown minister, on the
other; but this almost insoluble question and—in view of the
times—utterly unreasonable demand could not be put to
Roger alone. The mixture of his responsibilities had always
been a special source of his power, but it had given him
problems throughout his life; and from his earliest days he
had recognized the tensions inherent in his dual role.[17]
Stephen acknowledged the oversimplification of his counselors' justification by refusing to decide on any action for
the moment. There is no doubt that he had to cope with his
barons in a way other kings had not, and that the diverging
interests of monarchy and landed baronage were factors
in these years, but Stephen's personality still seems crucial in

15. William of Malmesbury, *H.N.*, p. 26.
16. *Gesta Stephani,* p. 49.
17. His repeated efforts to resign his position under King Henry
must indicate such recognition; William of Malmesbury, *G.R.*,
2:483–484. Years later Richard Fitz Nigel (p. 1) wondered if priests
should act as government ministers, but he rationalized that all
power came from God and hence such men could serve their kings.

BISHOP ROGER'S EFFIGY IN SALISBURY CATHEDRAL

This beardless, black marble bishop wears vestments embroidered with
stars, holds a crosier which pierces a dragon, blesses his viewer, and is surrounded by a border of birds and foliage. The head and miter originally
belonged to another monument and were attached to Roger's sepulchre
at an unknown date centuries ago.

AN AERIAL VIEW OF OLD SARUM FROM THE EAST

Old Sarum was constructed on two different levels. The lower bailey housed the town and the great cathedral, whose groundplan, cloister, and crypt are clearly outlined. The inner motte, also surrounded by a dry moat, supported Roger's well appointed castle.

A RECONSTRUCTION OF ROGER'S CATHEDRAL AT OLD SARUM ABOUT 1130

Alan Sorrell's sketch shows Saint Mary's cathedral from the south. To Bishop Osmund's nave Roger added a greatly lengthened chancel, central tower, wide transepts, south porch, western facade with twin turrets, crypt and chapter house (not visible), and unusually placed cloister.

A RECONSTRUCTION OF ROGER'S CASTLE AT OLD SARUM IN 1135

Roger's tower keep and its attendant buildings form an open quadrangle and the effect is palatial rather than military. Two chapels, one above another, are housed in the building with arched windows directly across from the covered well. In Alan Sorrell's drawing the cathedral and town buildings of the lower bailey are shown below the rear wall.

A VIEW OF SHERBORNE CASTLE FROM THE SOUTH

This engraving made in 1733 by Samuel and Nathaniel Buck depicts the ruins of Roger's most luxurious fortification. The great gatehouse is at the left and part of the surrounding octagonal curtain wall is in the foreground; interior buildings create an open quadrangle with the main keep to the west.

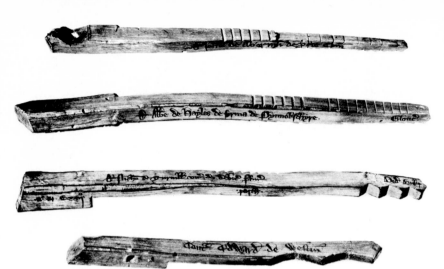

EXCHEQUER TALLIES AND SILVER PENNIES

Wooden tallies were carved and split lengthwise to record sheriffs' deposits at the exchequer; these examples were made in the thirteenth century. The coins were struck in the years 1125-1139. From top to bottom they are: Type XIII of Henry I minted by Alfwine at London; Type XIV of Henry I minted by Godwine at Thetford; Type I of Stephen minted by Gilpatric at Pembroke.

A PAGE FROM JOHN OF WORCESTER'S CHRONICLE

In Normandy in 1130 Henry I dreams of angry, abused bishops and abbots; later he returns to England in a perilous storm. This manuscript composed about 1140 is one of the very few known illustrated secular chronicles; the page is 9½ x 12½ inches in size. (Source: MS. CCC 157, fo. 383.)

BISHOP ROGER'S GRANT TO GEOFFREY THE CONSTABLE

Very few of Roger's original parchment charters have survived and only this one preserves a seal and it is badly damaged. This grant (approximately 4 x 6½ inches) seems to be a strictly private arrangement regarding Roger's London tenements. (Source: Ancient Deeds A/Box 24/1351.)

the early decisions of the reign. And in this case he took shelter in the refuge of all weak men, vacillation.[18]

It is impossible to determine the validity of the charges against Roger. Obviously, the king's dissatisfied lay advisers had no definite evidence that the bishop was plotting treason, for if they had, they would certainly have produced it. Nor were the contemporary chroniclers positive that Roger intended to help Matilda. William of Malmesbury, who probably knew Roger best but who personally supported Robert of Gloucester, gave no indication of whom he thought the bishop favored in 1139, even though he wrote a few years after Roger's death. Orderic Vitalis merely repeated court gossip about Roger's reputation for leaning to the Angevins.[19] It was only the king's own apologist, the author of the *Gesta Stephani,* who claimed that Roger always sympathized with Henry's children and promised to aid them. According to him, Roger received frequent messages from abroad and expected Robert of Gloucester at any moment; and this accounted for his traveling about with armed retainers, as he wanted to be able to switch his allegiance to Matilda immediately. Nevertheless, the same writer also believed that the baron's accusations against Roger were advanced with more envy than justice.[20] Even this information seems to be largely gossip which proves nothing and seems intended mostly to excuse the monarch's guilt in the sordid affair.

Why should Roger turn against Stephen? He had skillfully helped Stephen seize the throne, for which he had been well rewarded. A brooding conscience would hardly have driven him to revolt.[21] Was he so disappointed in his new ruler as to risk war to try another? He had no reason to expect Matilda to be a better monarch, nor could he hope

18. For a slightly different view which stresses Stephen's baronial policy more than his own personality see Donald J. Matthew's book review of Davis, *King Stephen,* EHR, 83(1968):559–563.

19. Orderic Vitalis, 5:120–121.   20. *Gesta Stephani,* p. 48.

21. This is the suggestion of Isabel Megaw, who thought Stephen was quite justified in capturing the bishops because they posed a

that she would consult him more than Stephen did. The king had not proved much of a champion of the church, but at least he recognized its power. There was no cause to believe the empress would do more, if that much, for it was her followers who were the first to abuse a prelate when they captured the bishop of Bath.[22] More money and possessions might have tempted Roger's nephews, but not the aging bishop. He knew that war would break out if Matilda landed in England, and it is highly unlikely he preferred that to the sporadic uprisings bothering Stephen. Although there is no decisive evidence one way or another, it appears that rumor spoke falsely and that Roger never did conspire against his king, for he could anticipate no personal, political, religious, or national advantage which would justify such a course.

Regardless of the lack of definite evidence, the barons continued to pressure the wavering king to capture the bishop of Salisbury, and their insistent demands finally had the desired effect. Stephen's apologist wrote that the king feared that it would be a slight to go against the advice of his magnates.[23] Stephen's weakness as a statesman was never more evident. Obviously he was led astray by his advisers, as the chroniclers explained it, but the final choice was his own.[24] It was a gamble, however; had he pulled it off successfully, there would have been fewer to fault his action.

Stephen's reasons for accepting such flimsy charges against Roger and his family can only be conjectured. Had he really considered them a threat to his power, he would undoubtedly have acted sooner. He might only have feared what

real threat to his rule as they were either in league with the empress or at least keeping a foot in each camp; "The Ecclesiastical Policy of Stephen, 1135–1139: A Reinterpretation," pp. 33–38. Appelby, *Stephen's Reign,* pp. 68–69, assumed Roger was guilty, but gave no reasons why he should favor Matilda. Davis, *King Stephen,* p. 31, felt the question could not be decided.

22. *Gesta Stephani,* p. 40.

23. *Ibid.,* pp. 50–51; William of Malmesbury, *H.N.,* pp. 17, 26.

24. *Gesta Stephani,* pp. 50–51; William of Malmesbury, *H.N.,* p. 20; William of Newburgh, 1:26; Christina of Markyate, p. 169.

they could do, rather than what they were likely to do; but, in view of the king's pressing need for money, it seems more reasonable to suggest that his principal motive in ordering the arrest of the bishops was to confiscate their treasures. His advisers had suggested that he pillage the monasteries, but that would have created lasting ill will at home and a furor throughout Christendom. How much easier it was to direct one swift blow against a wealthy and unpopular bishop! The rumors of Roger's impending desertion, which Stephen's cronies were busily circulating, would serve as a pretext to imprison the bishop and his nephews and would cover the king's financial motives. To prevent a family alliance against the king, the other members of Roger's clan, the bishops of Lincoln and of Ely, the royal chancellor, and the royal treasurer, were also to be taken into custody.

Stephen knew that the wrath of the church would descend upon him if he violated his own pledged word and mistreated her ministers, but he guessed that he could bully the hierarchy into accepting this one deed. Theobald, the new archbishop of Canterbury, was still in Rome, and Thurstan, the archbishop of York, was old and infirm. The only other powerful prelate was his own brother, Henry of Winchester, in whose case Stephen made a fatal miscalculation in thinking he would cooperate in an attack on the episcopate. It is ironic that, judged from one perspective, Roger was being sacrificed to save the very monasteries some people thought he so thoroughly hated.

After arranging peace with David of Scotland, Stephen returned to Oxford in June and summoned Bishop Roger to wait on him at a council called there for June 24, 1139.[25] What had Roger been doing since his last known appearance

25. Henry of Huntingdon, p. 67; William of Malmesbury, *H.N.*, pp. 25–26. Some other writers oddly confused the date of these important events. Florence of Worcester's continuator put them in 1138, the *Anglo-Saxon Chronicle* in 1137, and Gervase of Canterbury in 1138; Round, *Geoffrey de Mandeville*, pp. 384–385, discussed these errors.

at court in early January? Had anyone defended him and
his polices before the king? Neither question can be an-
swered, for we know nothing of his activity in this crucial
half-year.[26] It cannot even be proved that his son, Roger the
Pauper, the royal chancellor, ever spoke in his father's behalf, or indeed that he was even at the court in those trying
days. The chroniclers and magnates complained that Bishop
Roger was provisioning his castles, which indicates that he
may have been in his own diocese. Yet that was nothing exceptional; everyone was preparing for war. Perhaps Roger
had retired somewhat from the government and was con-
centrating more upon his religious obligations. He was well
on in years and may have sought a more restful life; and it
has already been suggested that he tried several times to
resign from his secular administrative duties.[27] The government he had organized could now run fairly well on its own,
given the right climate of order. It is the very lack of order
in those last months which makes one most suspect that
Roger was less active than before.

Roger was inspecting Malmesbury abbey and castle when
he received the royal command to come to Oxford. He had
a foreboding and was very reluctant to go. He said to the
monk William, "By my Blessed Lady Mary, somehow I am
disinclined to this journey. This I know, that I shall be as
useful at court as a colt in a battle." [28] This certainly does
not sound like the all-powerful viceroy of but a few months
previous. Although he expected to be out of place amidst
Stephen's new advisers, he surely did not think he was riding
to his own disgrace, which shows how out of touch he was
with recent developments and to what extent his old information service was being overcome in the shires.

26. He was with the king at Westminster sometime between August 1138 and June 1139; at Archbishop Theobald's election and
consecration and at Oxford and Godstow nunnery in January 1139;
and he helped erect Bradenstoke Priory in mid 1139, *Regesta,* 3, nos.
366, 473, 638, 667; *Cirencester Cartulary,* 1:144.
27. William of Malmesbury, *G.R.,* 2:483–484.
28. William of Malmesbury, *H.N.,* p. 26.

Unwillingly, he left the peace of Malmesbury and slowly followed the highway to Oxford. His nephews, Alexander and Nigel, who had been visiting with him, joined his column and headed for the council.[29] We would give much to know the purpose of their visit and their conversations along the road. By the time they reached the city gate, they had resolved to put up a good front and therefore made their usual ostentatious entrance into the town.[30] Bags, animals, servants, retainers, and armed attendants graced their progress and noised it about. Such display was one of the very practices which so irked the barons. Roger's rather arrogant nephews were much more flamboyant than he. After all, the diocese of Salisbury had enfeoffed only about thirty-eight knights, while tiny Ely had fifty-six and enormous Lincoln had more than one hundred men to fill its service quota of sixty.[31] Each bishop may have hired soldiers above these numbers, and it is not known how many guarded their procession to Oxford; furthermore, many knights would have remained behind to garrison the diocesan castles. All the same, it was an impressive array which marched into the quiet, scholarly town.

The prelates marched into a trap. Waleran of Meulan, aided by his twin, Robert of Leicester, and by Alan Dinan, Count of Brittany, had plotted to attack the supporters of the bishops.[32] One none-too-accurate writer said that Stephen was so alarmed by the number of Roger's retainers that he

29. Florence of Worcester (Continuator's part), 2:108; he also said Stephen sent for Roger because he heard Devizes was being fortified against him.

30. *Gesta Stephani*, p. 51.

31. The actual figures are 38⅝, 56¼, 101½; Round, *Feudal England*, p. 253; Helena Chew, *Ecclesiastical Tenants in Chief and Knights' Service*, pp. 2–10. Canterbury had enfeoffed 84¾, York 43⅔, and Winchester 70⅓. At this time Bishop Nigel was increasing the number of Ely knights, Edward Miller, *The Abbey and Bishopric of Ely*, pp. 167, 172–173. Roger could have added a few knights from the enfeoffments of Malmesbury, Abbotsbury, and Sherborne, but together these did not exceed ten knights.

32. *Gesta Stephani*, p. 51; Orderic Vitalis, 5:120. Megew, "Ecclesiastical Policy," p. 33, said the quarrel was accidental.

warned his own men to be ready for treason, but this must be apocryphal, as the king was personally very courageous and hardly feared trouble in his own court.[33]

As it turns out, Stephen was the devious one, for Roger and his nephews were honorably received and were conducted to pay their respects to the king. Meanwhile, their retainers were establishing lodgings, but they had hardly sat down to eat before a quarrel over accommodations had arisen between them and the men of the count of Brittany. Besides the obvious attempt to force Roger's men to violate the king's peace, something else was odd here. Roger and Alexander both owned properties and churches in Oxford and had attended councils there before, so the lodging issue seems artificial. Even in a pinch there would have been little difficulty in finding quarters for their men. In any event, a regular donnybrook ensued as the unarmed Salisbury men jumped up from their half-eaten meal and at first tried to shout down their tormentors. The melee turned ugly, and several men were wounded and a few killed before the fighting stopped. Although William of Malmesbury boasted that the Sarum men put their opponents to flight, just the reverse seems to have been true.[34] No one remained to defend the bishops, and their baggage was stolen by the royal knights, true brigands at heart. Later the same men regrouped and sought out the bishops themselves.

Roger seems to have been completely unaware of what was happening. He was in the chamber (*camera curie*), probably discussing its fiscal records, when the king's soldiers burst in and dragged him off to Stephen.[35] The others of Roger's party seem to have heard the news faster. Alexander was seized in his lodgings as he was trying to escape, and Roger's

33. Florence of Worcester (Continuator's part), 2:108.

34. William of Malmesbury, *H.N.*, p. 27; *Gesta Stephani*, p. 51; Florence of Worcester (Continuator's part), 2:108.

35. William of Malmesbury, *H.N.*, p. 29; at one point he seems to suggest that a day elapsed between the brawl itself and the bishops' capture.

son, Roger the chancellor, was also caught.[36] Bishop Nigel
was more fortunate. He had quarters outside the city, and,
when the first wind of what had happened reached him, he
raced from Oxford as fast as his horse could carry him and
rode all the way to Roger's great castle at Devizes. There he
laid waste the countryside surrounding the huge stone fortress and prepared to withstand a siege.[37] With him escaped
Adelelm, royal treasurer, archdeacon of Dorset, and kinsman
of Roger and Alexander.[38]

The two trapped bishops were taken before Stephen who
justified his actions by claiming that they had been arrested
for disturbing the peace. This was a patent falsehood. Their
capture at the royal court was an outrageous breach of hos-
pitality and a flagrant breach of the king's peace; Stephen in
effect had violated his own majesty.[39] It had happened before
when Eustace Fitz John had been arrested at the king's
court in 1138. Moreover, it would happen again when Geoffrey de Mandeville and Earl Ranulf of Chester were similarly
arrested years later. Even Henry of Huntingdon noted the
parallels with Bishop Roger's capture.[40] These schemes
reveal a treacherous side to Stephen's character which his
vacillation and reputed courtesy do little to excuse.

The king was furious when he learned that Nigel had
escaped. Glaring at the astonished bishops who knelt before
him, he demanded the keys of their castles as proof of their
trust. Roger and Alexander offered compensation for the
breach of the royal peace, but hesitated to surrender their
proud castles. It was a demand out of all proportion to their
supposed offense; Henry of Huntingdon, Alexander's archdeacon, said the bishops refused nothing which justice demanded.[41] The king spurned their offer and cried that now

36. *Gesta Stephani,* pp. 51–52.   37. Orderic Vitalis, 5:120.
38. "Annals of Oseney," in *Annales Monastici,* 4.23. This is a
thirteenth-century source, written about 1233.
39. Davis, *King Stephen,* p. 34.
40. Henry of Huntingdon, p. 276; Davis, "What Happened,"
p. 3.
41. Henry of Huntingdon, p. 265.

he was convinced that they were disloyal to him and that Nigel's bearing arms against him proved the charges of treason his courtiers had made against Roger and his family.[42] Stephen was almost hysterical, but his slip of the tongue revealed that he had not actually considered the bishops disloyal in the first place. Nevertheless, the king certainly wanted the castles and the gold they protected, and he immediately marshaled his troops and headed for Devizes. The *Gesta Stephani* said that he took both bishops with him, but Henry of Huntingdon, who was in a position to know better, noted that Alexander was left behind, rudely imprisoned at Oxford.[43] Roger the Pauper was bound in chains and taken along with his old father to the great castle on the Salisbury Plain.[44]

The siege of Devizes lasted three days. At first Nigel confidently paced the battlements of his uncle's fortress, realizing that this stone pile was well nigh impregnable and that he could easily disdain the royal troops who were attempting to invest its outer works. Stephen also knew that he could not carry the castle by assault and resorted to other tactics. He sent his Flemish captain, William of Ypres, forward under a flag of truce to warn Nigel that Bishop Roger would be kept without food until the tower surrendered, but arrogant Ely remained unmoved and boasted that he would continue the resistance.[45] Some authorities think that Roger went on a voluntary fast, but more state that he was deliberately starved by the king.[46]

42. *Gesta Stephani*, p. 52. Orderic Vitalis, 5:120, suggested Nigel had a guilty conscience when he fled to Devizes.
43. *Gesta Stephani*, p. 52; Henry of Huntingdon, pp. 256–266.
44. William of Malmesbury, *H.N.*, p. 27.
45. Orderic Vitalis, 5:120–121.
46. Voluntary fast, William of Malmesbury, *H.N.*, p. 27; Florence of Worcester (Continuator's part), 2:109. Forced starvation, *Gesta Stephani*, p. 52; Henry of Huntingdon, pp. 265–266; Robert of Torigni, *Chronicle*, p. 136; John of Hexham, *Historia*, p. 300. It is interesting that it is the *Gesta Stephani* which generally stresses Roger's hardships in these days, while William of Malmesbury underplays them.

Meanwhile, Roger lay in the filthy cowshed which the king had spitefully chosen as his prison; similar accommodations had been found for Alexander in Oxford.[47] The handful of friends—or so-called friends—whom the former viceroy had left at the court sought him out and urged him to save his life at all costs, for nothing could be exchanged for a man's life. They even used the phrase, "what belongs to Caesar, must be returned to Caesar," which Stephen's counselors had also employed in persuading him to capture the bishops.[48] When these men told Roger that he owed it to himself and to his church to end his dishonorable state, the bishop sadly agreed. Apparently no one thought that any great principles were at stake. Humiliated, but grasping for pride in his family and in his own ability, Roger thought that he could still influence his nephew, and he therefore obtained the king's permission to confer with Nigel personally.[49]

Weak from hunger the bishop slowly approached his own castle to confront his stubborn nephew, but when they met his anger blared forth, and he roundly upbraided the rash young bishop for not fleeing to his own diocese instead of running off to someone else's refuge. Especially concerned about his injured tenants, he thundered at Nigel, demanding to know what he meant by reducing thousands to want by burning over the whole area. It is not clear that Roger ever did come around to asking Nigel to surrender, but in any case Ely remained unmoved and, urged on by the castle guard, he determined to continue the fight. Roger, though perhaps psychologically relieved by his outburst, retired in even greater disgrace than before, a man beaten by king and family.

Stephen was enraged at such persistence and ordered Roger's son to be dragged forth in his chains and placed on a high platform with a noose around his neck. Unless the

47. Florence of Worcester (Continuator's part), 2:108. The *Gesta Stephani*, p. 52, simply noted the bishops were lodged dishonorably; William of Malmesbury made no observation about it.

48. *Gesta Stephani*, pp. 49–52.   49. Orderic Vitalis, 5:120–121.

castle were to surrender immediately, he cried, he would hang young Roger on the spot.[50] Although Nigel of Ely liked to act as if he were in charge of Devizes, he was not the commander of the castle. The prisoner's mother, Roger's mistress, Matilda of Ramsbury, had kept in the background so far, but she actually held the main fortifications of the ponderous keep. Whereas the threatened starvation of her old lover must have upset her, she would have realized that not even this headstrong king would dare kill a bishop. But her son had no such episcopal dignity to protect him, and Stephen was quite capable of carrying out his latest threat.

When Nigel thoughtlessly proposed to hold out still longer, Matilda jumped up and cried for the life of her child. "It was I that bore him," she groaned, "and I ought not to lend a hand to his destruction. Yea, rather, I ought to lay down my life to save his." [51] She then notified the king that she would surrender the keys to save her son and her friends. Shamed by her resolution Ely sullenly consented to surrender the whole castle.

Bishop Nigel's part in these events is somewhat mysterious. If it seems unlikely that Roger favored the empress, the same cannot be said so definitely of Nigel. He may have become friendly with her on his many trips to Normandy before 1135, and he certainly worked with her at times after 1140. The Ely conspiracy in 1137 was suspicious, too, as was his whole conduct at Devizes castle. Bishop Roger's own question is still the key—why did Nigel go to Devizes at all? It was, of course, closer than his own fenland stronghold, but he seems to have prepared for a siege even before he could have known Stephen's demands. It is stretching the evidence to suggest that he wanted to hold this important and strategic tower for the empress and Roger of Gloucester, but it is clear that Bishop Roger's policies were not necessarily his.

Stephen wasted no time in celebrating the fall of Devizes. Sherborne, Malmesbury, and Salisbury were also quickly

50. *Ibid.; Gesta Stephani*, p. 52.   51. Orderic Vitalis, 5:120–121.

besieged. After their surrender the king marched Alexander
off to accomplish the capture of Newark and Sleaford.[52]
The Lincoln canon, Henry of Huntingdon, reported that
Stephen also threatened to starve Alexander if his staunch
garrisons did not surrender.[53] William of Malmesbury was
critical of the various castle defenders, complaining that
Alexander did not show any more resolution than Roger
had.[54] Their knights could have put up a good fight, and
might well have, had their episcopal lords been in league
with the empress. As it was, there was not much point to
prolonged resistance. What Stephen did to Nigel immediately after his capture is not recorded, but he seems to have
banished Roger the Pauper from the realm.[55]

The king quickly seized the gold and silver Roger had
stored in his castles. One writer naively expressed surprise at
the king's good fortune, marveling that, after almost ex-
hausting his own treasure, Stephen was now able to enjoy
the fruits of another's toil.[56] The money, part of which a
Worcester writer extravagantly estimated at forty thousand
pounds, did not last long, however, for the king promptly
sent a large measure of Roger's hoard to France to obtain the
hand of Constance, sister of King Louis VII, for his son
Eustace.[57]

To indicate that he had completely separated his government from Bishop Roger's influence, Stephen even had a
new royal seal designed which would enable him to tell at a
glance which orders, gifts, and privileges had been granted
before the fall of the old viceroy and his officials.[58] Having
taken their castles, offices, and coin, the king had no further

52. William of Malmesbury, *H.N.*, p. 27.
53. Henry of Huntingdon, p. 266.
54. William of Malmesbury, *H.N.*, p. 27.
55. John of Hexham, *Historia,* p. 310. For Nigel, see Henry of
Huntingdon, p. 267; *Liber Eliensis,* pp. 433-436.
56. *Gesta Stephani,* p. 53.
57. Florence of Worcester (Continuator's part), 2:113; Henry of
Huntingdon, p. 266. For more on Roger's wealth, see Chapter 8.
58. *Regesta, 3:xii-xv.*

use for his once mighty bishops. He kept them in some sort of custody, but allowed them to return to their bishoprics. Roger went back to Sarum to try to recover from the hardest summer of his life.[59]

Despite their release, Stephen still regarded the bishops as beyond his favor and chose to ignore their existence. His attitude is evident in the way he treated the temporalities of the diocese of Lincoln. Sometime between late June and the first of September, Stephen granted the earl of Lincoln several parcels of land belonging to the bishopric, without consulting Alexander about this outright spoliation of his diocese. The grant stated that if Alexander ever made his peace with the king or, more significantly, if another bishop were appointed, Stephen would compensate the see for the loss incurred through his gift.[60] Clearly, he was contemplating appointing someone else if Alexander did not beg his complete forgiveness.

Few of the chroniclers who recorded the bishops' disgrace expressed shock at their treatment. Henry of Huntingdon did call it "a deed of infamy," but William of Malmesbury merely related others' outrage without giving his own opinion.[61] Only Stephen's champion, Bishop Robert of Bath, the probable author of the Gesta Stephani, really censured the king. He tried to excuse him by explaining that he had yielded to "foolish, or rather mad, advice," but he still considered the action a monstrous sin against God.[62] Of course, this bishop was also in effect protesting his own earlier mistreatment at the hands of Robert of Gloucester's allies.[63] Stephen even found an advocate in Hugh, the archbishop of Rouen and former abbot of Reading, who sanctimoniously declared that the bishops had been rightly deprived of their

59. Gesta Stephani, p. 53; Orderic Vitalis, 5:266.

60. John Horace Round, Ancient Charters, pp. 39-41, no. 3; Regesta, 3, no. 493.

61. Henry of Huntingdon, p. 266; William of Malmesbury, H.N., p. 28.

62. Gesta Stephani, pp. 50-51.   63. Ibid., pp. 39-41.

castles, which had been erected in defiance of canon law. He chanted the old song that churchmen should be evangelists of peace, not builders of houses where evil men could find refuge.[64]

Stephen's brother disagreed. Henry of Winchester was the lord of many castles, himself, and he was still annoyed at the king's refusing to support him in the Canterbury election. He reasoned that if the bishops had indeed transgressed justice they should have been judged by canon law, not by the king, for no bishop should be deprived of his property except by a general council of churchmen.[65] This was not what Stephen had hoped for from his brother, who was now someone important to reckon with, since Pope Innocent had recently appointed him a papal legate.

The bishop of Winchester charged that the king had not acted out of any concern for righteousness, but rather to serve his own advantage. Stephen had not returned the seized castles to those churches at whose expense they had been erected, but had handed them over to irreligious laymen. Henry appealed for the complete freedom of Roger and his nephews and the restoration of all their property, but Stephen turned him a deaf ear. Bishop Henry then summoned up both his courage and his legatine authority and commanded his brother, the king of England, to attend a church council he was calling for Winchester on August 29, 1139.

64. William of Malmesbury, *H.N.*, p. 28.   65. *Ibid.*

7

The Trial of a Bishop,
August 1139

THE ECCLESIASTICAL COUNCIL which opened at Winchester on
August 29, 1139, was not the magnificent clerical triumph
Henry of Winchester had planned. Although the attendance
was large, some bishops were conspicuously absent; Archbishop Thurstan, for example, was too ill to come south. A
few other prelates gave the uprisings then troubling the
country as their reason for not attending, but they probably
welcomed any excuse which allowed them to avoid a conference clearly intended to criticize the king. For some unexplained reason Alexander of Lincoln was not at the council, and, since Nigel of Ely was not mentioned, he also may
have been absent, thus leaving Bishop Roger to bear the
strain of the meeting alone.

Archbishop Theobald had recently returned from Rome
and was there, but Bishop Henry was the guiding voice in
all the deliberations. Abbot Geoffrey of Saint Albans, who
was also present, told the renowned anchorite, Christina of
Markyate, all about it, but most chroniclers recorded its proceedings in very cursory fashion.[1] The *Gesta Stephani* mentioned that a council was held at which the king excused his
conduct to the clergy, and Henry of Huntingdon merely
reported that the assembled prelates begged the king to
restore the bishops' possessions, and he refused.[2] Were it not
for the very detailed account by William of Malmesbury,

1. Christina of Markyate, p. 167.
2. *Gesta Stephani,* p. 53; Henry of Huntingdon, p. 266. Neither
Orderic Vitalis nor Robert of Torigni mentioned it.

who seems to have been an eyewitness, this intriguing confrontation of church and state would have been lost forever.[3]

At the opening session the bull of Innocent II creating Henry papal legate for all England was read. Since the commission actually dated from March 1, 1139, the assembly commented favorably on the bishop of Winchester's tact in not rushing to flaunt his new distinction. Still, it was a bitter pill for Archbishop Theobald, since recent papal practice had called for the archbishop of Canterbury to be permanent papal legate in England.

Bishop Henry wasted no time on preliminaries, but immediately launched into the subject of the bishops' arrest. He spoke in Latin, William of Malmesbury observed, since he was addressing educated men. Henry lamented that Stephen had been led by evil advisers to violate the peace of his own court by seizing bishops there, but stated also that the monarch had compounded his sin by then robbing their churches. With climactic eloquence Henry cried that he would rather have suffered injury to himself than that the dignity of the episcopate should have been hurt by such a humiliation. He noted that the king had not rejected his summons to the council, and therefore the assembly must decide what should be done. For his own part, he would carry out the synod's decision, whatever it was, even though the man in question was both his brother and his sovereign. Neither loss of property nor danger to his very life would deter him. The speech was a dramatic challenge to the church fathers, but in view of Henry's later ready acceptance of some of Roger's property one cannot help feeling that his oratory was greater than his sincerity.

Stephen, who the Malmesbury monk said had confidence in the justice of his own position, then sent several earls to ask the council why he had been summoned. Bishop Henry gave them a haughty answer to take back to their master, reminding them that a true and obedient Christian should

3. William of Malmesbury, *H.N.*, pp. 29–34.

not complain at being summoned by Christ's ministers, particularly if he were guilty of an unprecedented offense and were called to make satisfaction. Only in pagan days had bishops been imprisoned and stripped of their property. Let the messengers tell his brother that if he would calmly acquiesce in the legate's advice, Henry would give him counsel which neither the Church of Rome, the court of France, nor even their own wise and religious brother, Count Theobald of Blois, would consider objectionable. Stephen should either give an account of what he had done or submit to judgment according to canon law. Let him remember, Henry pointedly remarked, that it was through the favor of the church, not the prowess of knights, that he had become king. At this pause the earls rushed out of the council, furious, but nevertheless relieved to be away before the proud, sharp-tongued bishop thought of anything else to say.

A larger number of earls and lay magnates returned shortly and stationed themselves near their speaker, Aubrey de Vere, who was to give the king's reply to the legate's address. Aubrey was the royal master chamberlain and well experienced in many types of litigation.[4] Although he used no abusive language, he made no attempt to be gentle with Bishop Roger, who must have followed his presentation with a certain wry detachment since he probably had had a hand in the chamberlain's training. The barons, however, were in a restless mood, angered that the king had been brought to task for following the course they advised, and they often interrupted de Vere's speech to shout abuse at the pitiable former viceroy.

Aubrey was a direct man and made his point quickly: Roger had inflicted many wrongs on King Stephen. Rare was the occasion when his retainers had not raised a brawl

4. He obtained the master chamberlainship in 1130, and in that year was also one of the most powerful sheriffs in the country; *Regesta*, 2, no. 1777; *Pipe Roll, passim.*

at court, and the disgraceful episode at Oxford differed only in that men of more important lords, like Alan of Brittany and Hervey de Lyon, were injured. The absent bishop of Lincoln was to blame for this riot because he had deliberately stirred up a fight against his old enemy Alan of Dinan.[5] De Vere next directly accused Roger of treason, declaring that he had secretly favored the king's enemies and only pretended to be loyal to Stephen. Many proofs convinced the king of his treason, especially the bishop's refusal to shelter Roger de Mortimer and his royal troops at Malmesbury castle when they were in danger from the Bristol rebels. Moreover, everyone said that when the empress landed Roger and his nephews were going to join her cause and hand their castles over to her.

Satisfied that he had branded Roger a traitor, the chamberlain turned to answer the criticism raised by the papal legate, asserting that Roger had not been arrested as a bishop, but as a servant of the king, who had managed his affairs and received his pay. Aubrey calmly stated that Stephen had not taken the castles by force, but rather the bishops had gladly surrendered them to avoid facing charges for the commotion stirred up at the Oxford court. True, the king had found money in these castles, but it really belonged to him, anyway. After all, it was wealth Roger had amassed from the returns to the royal treasury in the reign of King Henry. Furthermore, Roger had willingly surrendered this money. Therefore, Aubrey concluded, Stephen wished the agreement between himself and the bishops to remain in force.

Roger could hardly contain himself during this tirade. Finally he cried out that he had never been King Stephen's servant or received his pay. Apparently, he chiefly objected to the insulting description of himself as a servant. Unlike the chamberlain, the justiciar was not a member of the royal household and did not receive a regular salary. Roger was a

5. I have been unable to discover what it was made these men enemies.

proud man, quick to note an affront, and this slight put him on his mettle, for, as the Malmesbury monk observed, he was a man of spirit and ashamed to be broken by misfortune.

Unfortunately, the rest of Roger's defense was not recorded. His earlier refusal to admit Roger de Mortimer to Malmesbury castle was a telling point against him, but, although the circumstances are lost, it is easy to understand why he may have been reluctant to expose his well-stocked castle to the rowdy, thieving troops who served the king. For the rest, Roger must have felt contempt for the poor case the king made against him. Much of the indictment for treason rested on unsubstantiated rumors and other parts of de Vere's speech were bold-faced lies. It was ridiculous to believe he ever freely surrendered his castles or his wealth. But what did it matter? When the king decided to break a man, he was not deterred by the subject's loyalty or prestige.

Roger did not give up without a fight, however. He still had one trump card. Rallying his spirits, he declared that if he could not find justice in this council for what had been taken from him, he would seek it in another place. Everyone recognized the threat to appeal to Rome, and it threw the meeting into an uproar.

At this point, determined that things should not fall completely out of hand, Henry of Winchester broke in, demanding that the bishops should be reinstated in their property, for they should not plead if they were already dispossessed. "All the charges against the bishops," he announced, "should have been made, and their truth investigated, in a Church council rather then sentence pronounced, contrary to canon law, against men who had not been proved guilty." [6] These were perfectly reasonable demands, in keep-

6. William of Malmesbury, *H.N.*, p. 32. Stephen's coronation charter had promised that jurisdiction over churchmen and their property was to remain in the hands of the bishops. For somewhat similar prosecutions see the trials of Bishop Odo of Bayeux under the Conqueror and Bishop William of Durham under William Ru-

ing with standard legal practice, but there was little likelihood that they would be fulfilled.

The council fathers thus discussed legal and ecclesiastical procedure, rather than the validity of the charges originally made against Roger. The principles were more important than the individuals involved, but Roger could not have been pleased with the direction the debate took. He wanted vindication and his property, but the legate was fighting for the independence of the church courts and the right of clerical immunity. After some further desultory discussion, the meeting recessed at the king's request until the next day.

The council actually remained in recess for three days. Stephen was not pleased with its proceedings, and he awaited the arrival of his own episcopal advocate, Archbishop Hugh of Rouen. His address on September 1 startled the clergy. Hugh was a good but tricky debater, and he proved it that day. He declared that he would allow Roger and his nephews to repossess their castles if they could prove by canon law that they should have them. The bishops had claimed that they could only be judged by canon law, and now Hugh turned the argument against them. Next he actually accused *them* of wickedly striving against the canons of the church.

Shifting his attack, Hugh focused on the charge of treason. Ignoring the direct indictment against Roger, he presented a hypothetical case, instead. If, for the sake of argument, he would grant that the bishops could hold castles, he began, it was clear that in time of danger all the chief men of the realm, according to custom, ought to hand their strongholds over to the king. Since it was the monarch's duty to fight for everyone's peace, surely he could demand the means to achieve it. Although English holdings did ultimately belong to the king, Hugh was greatly oversimplifying the relations

fus, where a similar demand for the restitution of stolen property was made; Poole, *From Domesday Book to Magna Carta*, pp. 102–104; Symeon of Durham, 1:179 ff.; David Douglas and G. W. Greenway, *English Historical Documents* 2:609–624.

between men, and much of what he said was not all that self-evident. Nevertheless, he pressed on and triumphantly reviewed his case against Bishop Roger and his family. "So the bishops' whole case will fall to the ground," he smiled, "for either it is unjust according to the canon law for them to have castles, or, if this be permitted by the king as an act of grace, they ought to yield to the emergencies of the time by delivering up the keys." [7]

Roger must have wondered how the Norman archbishop could so basely desert his episcopal colleagues in their defense of clerical privileges and legal principles. His relations with Hugh stretched back over many years, but whether important personal differences contributed to Hugh's position in 1139 will probably never be known. His speech was a severe blow to Roger's cause, and it serves as a reminder that the Anglo-Norman hierarchy never really did act as a unit in those years.

At this juncture, Aubrey de Vere again intervened, determined to reestablish royal supremacy over the troubled prelates. He acknowledged Roger's obvious threat to appeal to Rome and warned the assembly that the king forbade any such action. If anyone did leave the country against his will, that individual would find it very difficult to return. De Vere then announced Stephen's own move. He said the king felt injured by the prelates' accusations and he therefore was appealing his own case to the pope.

The recluse Christina of Markyate picked up a little information about this appeal from Abbot Geoffrey of Saint Albans. She credited the council fathers with more backbone than did William of Malmesbury. Christina was told that Stephen refused to submit to any judgment on his conduct unless it were favorable to him and his party. When the bishops asked for mercy, he refused it. They then threatened to excommunicate him. Realizing that he had been ill-advised and that the enemies of the church were attempting

7. William of Malmesbury, *H.N.,* p. 32.

to create a split between himself and his clergy, Stephen then appealed to Rome to avoid excommunication. Both sides chose delegates to go to the pope, but they never set out.[8]

William of Malmesbury specifically recorded that the bishops thought it would be rash to excommunicate the king without Rome's permission.[9] Thus there was more talk about excommunication than there was actual intent to use it. Yet Stephen realized that he had overreached himself, bitterly antagonizing the English church and its legate. An appeal to Rome might temper his own courtiers' extreme demands for ecclesiastical wealth and at the same time enable him to regain the support of some other clerics besides Hugh of Rouen.

Stephen's bombshell effectively terminated the council. The lay barons had again become very restless during the chamberlain's second speech, and they conspicuously fingered their swords and made threatening gestures at some of the already frightened bishops and abbots. The meeting hurriedly disbanded.

The few decrees of the council which have been preserved demonstrate Stephen's ascendancy in its closing hours: The wars raging throughout the country prompted men to entrust their valuables to bishops for safekeeping, but a decree at this Winchester council ordered that such goods must be handed over to the king as his own property.[10] All customs, towns, and forts should yield to the king, according to the decree, and the prelates of England should keep vigilant watch to see that their flocks were not harmed. If need arose, the prelates should speak out in their defense.[11] There was something plaintive about this last decree. Shorn of their castles and wealth, there was little left to some prelates except talk.

8. Christina of Markyate, pp. 167–169.
9. William of Malmesbury, *H.N.,* p. 34.
10. *Gesta Stephani,* p. 53; John of Hexham, *Historia,* p. 301.
11. John of Worcester, p. 55; Florence of Worcester (Continuator's part), 2:116.

After the council ended, the legate and the archbishop of Canterbury sought out the king and tried to salvage what they could from the situation. On bended knee they begged their lord to have pity on the church and end the divisions between the monarchy and the clergy. Stephen had carefully avoided attending any of the sessions in person, but the quarrel had gone far beyond what he had expected. His apologist wrote that he agreed to do penance for his fault, but the monk William gave a different account, saying of the king, "Though he rose respectfully and removed the stigma that their act had laid upon him, yet, taken up with the advice of wicked men, he showed no fulfillment of righteous promises." [12] Nevertheless, it would have been consistent with Stephen's character for him to go through some form of penance and make promises without ever intending to mend his ways or to return the bishops' property.

Bishop Henry seemed to believe that as papal legate he was strong enough to humble the king. Certainly he was far more concerned with criticizing him than with justifying Roger's conduct or securing the return of his castles. Stephen could also be stubborn, vain, and shifty, and he refused to submit to his brother's high-handed condemnation, calling upon Hugh of Rouen to hint broadly that all bishops should keep to their clerical business and not interfere in the affairs of the kingdom. Both brothers misjudged each other in this struggle. They ended the contest by breaking not only the peace of the realm but also the tolerable relations between church and state which Bishop Roger had done so much to create in the previous reign.

There was almost an anticlerical element running through the discussions at Oxford and Winchester. A better educated lay baronage was eager to establish its own privileges and hereditary rights and to gain control of the government apparatus, and it momentarily saw the episcopate as a real

12. *Gesta Stephani*, p. 53; William of Malmesbury, *H.N.*, p. 34.

enemy. Yet this synod also revealed post-Gregorian bishops fiercely aware of their own special status and highly resentful of lay interference. Such views are harder to imagine forty years earlier.

Bishop Roger was somewhat lost in the current of these fast-moving events. The struggle and debate were over his fate, but for the first time the issue had escaped his control. He must have felt justified in his previous opposition to monastic bishops, because he certainly was not well served by Winchester, Canterbury, or Rouen. He fought hard for his life, his possessions, his governmental creations, and his clerical dignity, but, even as he spoke, he must have sensed that he was using the terms of a bygone age. His carefully constructed world of good government and a prosperous church had fallen victim to the onslaughts of dynastic rivalry and family intrigue.

The Winchester council ended on the first of September. On the thirteenth of the same month, the long-expected forces of Robert of Gloucester and the Empress Matilda landed on the southern coast at Arundel.[13] Stephen was soon to learn that his triumph over the bishops was but a Pyrrhic victory. The money from Roger's castles had produced a bride for his son and money for his captains, but the church withdrew its unqualified backing and alternated its support between him and the empress for much of the remainder of the reign. More than that, the superb administration Roger had created in the days of Henry's rule suffered a general breakdown and reflected the disorder and anarchy of parts of the countryside. The famed nineteenth-century authority William Stubbs put the case as strongly as possible:

The arrest of Bishop Roger was perhaps the most important constitutional event that had taken place since the Conquest, the whole administration of the country ceased to work, and the whole power of the clergy was arrayed in

13. William of Malmesbury, *H.N.*, p. 34.

opposition to the king. It was also the signal for the civil war, which lasted with more or less activity for fourteen years.[14]

Modern scholarship has qualified some of the exaggerated claims of anarchy and bureaucratic disruption in the rest of Stephen's reign, but it is nonetheless clear that his government suffered a blow from which it never fully recovered.[15] Conversely, the fact that the exchequer and the courts continued to function more than it once was thought they did is in itself the strongest tribute to the genius of Bishop Roger; he had created a system which outlived his own supervision.

14. William Stubbs, *The Constitutional History of England*, 1:326. Richard Fitz Nigel certainly believed the government collapsed during Stephen's reign (p. 50).

15. *Regesta*, 3:ix–xxvi; Megaw, "Ecclesiastical Policy," pp. 38–39; Morris, *Medieval English Sheriff*, p. 105; West, *Justiciarship in England*, pp. 25–26. Davis, *King Stephen*, p. 48, suggested that after 1139 the king's intelligence service broke down almost completely. Stenton, *English Justice*, p. 26, felt "the collapse of the machinery of government in Stephen's reign had almost been complete."

Eventide

It was an old and broken Bishop Roger who returned to Sarum after the Winchester council. The meeting had accomplished nothing for him, neither exonerating his conduct nor restoring his possessions, and he would need to make private arrangements with the king. He never did regain control of his great castles; Malmesbury briefly passed to the bandit Robert Fitz Hubert, Devizes was garrisoned by the king's forces, and Sherborne remained in royal hands for many years despite petitions by later bishops and the pope.[1] On the other hand, Roger did at least arrive at a written understanding with Stephen regarding some of his lost churches, for the king ordered that the bishop was again to hold the church and lands of Saint Martin-le-Grand, London, and whatever he, his church, and his canons had been desseised of there "after the quarrel broke out between us."[2] Yet it was easier to direct this than to accomplish it, and a whole series of subsequent writs to much the same effect show that the men who had taken Roger's city lands were in no hurry to return them and that Stephen lacked the strength or the will to enforce his commands properly.[3]

Regardless of what action Roger might take, his nephews were determined to protest the confiscation of their castles. Bishop Alexander's tower at Newark had been given to Robert of Leicester, the twin of Count Waleran, and when he refused to return the castle Alexander excommunicated him and appealed to the pope for confirmation. A badly

1. Fowler, *Medieval Sherborne*, pp. 115–116.
2. *Regesta*, 3, no. 525.   3. *Ibid.*, nos. 526–534.

damaged copy of Innocent's mandate preserves the pope's order to the papal legate and the archbishop of Canterbury to uphold Alexander.[4] The papal letter can be dated in 1140, but it must have been requested in 1139. A similar letter confirmed an excommunication Bishop Nigel of Ely launched against some men who had despoiled his church.[5] These documents are not explicit enough to gauge Rome's reaction to the mistreatment of the bishops, but they do indicate that these two aggrieved prelates were prepared to take the strongest measures against Stephen's counselors.

Such recriminations meant less to Roger, and no record of his having excommunicated anyone has survived. When he returned to Salisbury, he realized that he had returned to his own cathedral to die, so he quietly set about putting his affairs in order and trying to make amends for past misdeeds. The habits of a lifetime linger on, however, and even his final letters breathe the passion for precision and efficiency which characterized his whole career.

He began by considering his position as bishop and cathedral canon. To Legate Henry, Archbishop Theobald, and all the bishops and nobles of England he wrote that, acting on the advice of his whole chapter at Sarum, he had returned to the Church of Saint Mary, his cathedral, "all the prebends which I held in my hands." [6] Then he directed that his life interests in parts of the endowment of Cirencester abbey be terminated and returned to the monastery.[7] Three other charters addressed to the papal legate declared Roger's intention of returning to the canons of Saint Frideswide's

---

4. *Registrum Antiquissimum*, 1:239–241, no. 283. Earl Robert later made restitution in the form of ten burgesses for the damage his men caused, *ibid.*, 2:16–17.

5. P. Jaffee, *Regesta Pontificum Romanorum*, 1:894, no. 8101, dated October 5, 1140. This referred principally to Nigel's expulsion from his see during his rebellion after Roger's death; see *Liber Eliensis*, p. 318. For Nigel's activities between late 1139 and 1144 see *ibid.*, pp. 433–436. He made his peace with Stephen in 1144; *Regesta*, 3, no. 267.

6. Charter 26.   7. Charter 27.

"whatever I had unjustly taken away" from them.[8] The bishop had always been an active patron of this Oxford house, and, on balance, his interest had been more beneficial than detrimental; but it was a mixed record, and this was his last opportunity to make reparations.

One of his most interesting depositions concerned the church of Saint Mary of Wolverhampton in the diocese of Worcester. To glimpse the bishop's somber mood in those last days, it should be read in its entirety:

Roger, Bishop of Salisbury, to all the faithful men in the Holy Church. Greetings. Know that through ambition and secular power I have unjustly and without judgment deprived the monks of the diocese of Worcester of their church of Wolverhampton which Bishop Samson gave them following the gift of King Henry. Moreover, I realize that, because of this grave sin and on account of my misdeeds, the hand of the Lord has touched me and rightly afflicted me. Therefore, fleeing to the mercy of Mary, the most pious Mother of God, I ask pardon for my great crime and I beg the brothers of Worcester out of respect for the divine mercy to forgive this injury which I have done against them and to pardon me in the presence of God at whose tribunal I now stand.[9]

The particulars of this episode are lost, but even in this confession Roger's love of order and procedure asserts itself, as he repents both for treating the church unjustly and for taking it without judgment, for that betrayed his own governmental system.

Although he tried to make amends for some of his past exactions, the toll of Roger's own misfortunes was not yet complete. William of Malmesbury summarized his sad decline:

In later years fortune that had followed him excessively for long at last stung the man cruelly with a scorpion's tail. What a grief it was that he saw before his own eyes a man who had deserved well of him being wounded, a knight

8. Charters 29, 30, 31.　9. Charter 28.

who was close to him cut down, on the next day his own arrest, as I have related above, and of two nephews, bishops of great power, one put to flight and one arrested, while a third young man whom he dearly loved was put in chains; after the surrender of his castles, the plunder of his treasure and himself in the council lashed with the vilest abuse; finally when he was almost breathing his last at Salisbury, the carrying off against his will of all the money and precious vessels he had left, which he had placed on the altar for the completion of the cathedral. I think it is the crown of his misfortunes, and I am very sorry for it myself, that while to many he seemed a man of sorrows, yet very few were sorry for him, so much envy and hatred had he acquired by his excessive power, undeservedly too among some whom he had even advanced to posts of distinction.[10]

Others also wrote of the cruel blow fate had dealt Roger. Henry of Huntingdon, for example, marveled at how the bishop's career had been an uninterrupted triumph until he was overwhelmed at the end, and he moralized in terms of a favorite medieval image—no one should "think that he could long maintain his position erect on fortune's revolving wheel."[11]

Roger suffered a final outrage before he died. The details are confusing, but, strange as it seems, the king had evidently not taken all of Roger's treasure when he pillaged his castles. The bishop left the remnants to his church at Salisbury, symbolically placing on the cathedral altar his remaining wealth, a great mound of gold and silver coins and splendidly worked ornaments.[12] A Worcester monk, a none-too-reliable reporter, estimated the silver pennies alone to be worth more than forty thousand pounds.[13] If he were correct—and it seems highly unlikely—this was equal to almost half the hoard King Henry had stored. Roger's original treasure must, then, have been stupendous!

10. William of Malmesbury, *H.N.*, p. 39.
11. Henry of Huntingdon, pp. 266–269.
12. *Gesta Stephani*, p. 64.
13. Florence of Worcester (Continuator's part), 2:113.

The chroniclers disagreed about what happened to Roger's bequest. William of Malmesbury claimed that the failing prelate was helpless to prevent its being taken away, but Stephen's champion said the Salisbury canons voluntarily offered the money to the king, who returned some of it to roof their cathedral and some for their own needs.[14] The untrustworthy monk of Worcester wrote that Roger had not left his treasure to the cathedral at all, but to the king.[15]

King Stephen spent Christmas 1139 at Salisbury, where the Worcester writer said the Sarum canons offered him two thousand pounds on his arrival. The king then exempted them from all taxes on their lands and gave them forty marks for roofing the cathedral and twenty more for their own use. He promised he would refund the rest when he was able.[16] What happened seems fairly obvious, for Roger was being continuously watched. The bequest money was not used as Roger had intended. Rather, as soon as he had donated it to his cathedral, a royal representative claimed it for the crown. Later, the canons tried to bribe the king by offering him a part of the treasure, but he took it all and returned a mere pittance for repairs and for their own use. The roofing fund probably refers to the new cloister Roger was building, rather than to the magnificent cathedral, itself. Stephen's two protagonists later tried to put the best face on the affair, so they suggested that the king was offered the money, rather than taking it outright.

Bishop Roger died two weeks before Christmas, on December 11, 1139.[17] His end was as sad as his life had been productive. Broken in fortune, bereft of friends, and perhaps even betrayed by his own cathedral clergy, he suffered

14. *Gesta Stephani*, p. 64. See also Michael Sheehan, *The Will in Medieval England*, pp. 243–244.

15. Florence of Worcester (Continuator's part), 2:113.

16. *Ibid.*, p. 122; John of Worcester, p. 59.

17. William of Malmesbury, *H.N.*, p. 37. Florence of Worcester (Continuator's part), 2:113, under the year 1138 said he died on December 4.

a hard death. William of Newburgh, who never thought well of Roger and who wrote sixty years after his death, claimed that the bishop was driven to madness at the end, saying and doing things unbecoming a prelate.[18] However, William of Malmesbury, who could have been at his bedside, stated that Roger died of a quartan fever contracted from the mental anguish he had endured when being assailed by the king.[19] Henry of Huntingdon merely recorded that the former viceroy died, worn out by the weight of his troubles and his years.[20] An anonymous writer thought he died in prison.[21] That was surely an exaggeration, but it confirmed the fact that Stephen kept him carefully guarded.[22]

In Roger's passing different commentators saw the mutability of human fortunes; this was certainly true of the bishop's memory in his own cathedral see. From his magnificent possessions the thirteenth century remembered only a few jeweled and brocaded vestments—eloquent testimony to Stephen's thorough confiscations. Even Roger's very name was sometimes omitted from the cathedral list of prayers for the dead.[23]

What manner of man was he? Contemporaries glimpsed some sides of Roger's activity and personality, and we can see more, but the complete individual eludes us. Chaplain, chancellor, bishop, justiciar, procurator, titular abbot, and viceroy—these and other titles marked his forty-year progress

18. William of Newburgh, 1:38.
19. William of Malmesbury, *H.N.,* p. 37.
20. Henry of Huntingdon, pp. 266–267.
21. "Tewkesbury Annals," in *Annales Monastici,* 1:46.
22. Henry of Huntingdon, pp. 266–267; *Gesta Stephani,* p. 64; William of Malmesbury, *H.N.,* pp. 37, 39.
23. *Register of St. Osmund,* 1:129–133; W. H. Jones, "The Bishops of Old Sarum, 1075–1225," p. 182. However, charters issued at Sarum and throughout the kingdom after his death did use the stock formula, "Roger of blessed memory," *Sarum Documents, e.g.,* pp. 16, 31, 89, 358. In the *Register of St. Osmund,* 2:lii, the editor said there was an annual commemoration of Roger on December 4. On the other hand, the Lincoln obit book, Gerald of Wales, *Opera,* 7:162, remembered him on December 11.

from obscurity to fame, from power to disgrace. The love of a strong woman, a modest pride in his own family, incessant church- and castle-building, unending demands for order and efficiency, an abiding interest in education, benign concern for Austin priories, and possibly even a reflective pleasure in fishing, were qualities to be balanced against his concrete achievements in monetary reform, diocesan organization, exchequer experimentation, and itinerant justice. Many medieval men are remembered because as saints, kings, and archbishops they staked out independent positions for their lives, or because as barons, monks, or peasants they were supposedly typical of the times. Roger's story is more complex because he struggled with the demands put upon him and apparently balanced what he wanted, what pleased his kings, and what benefited much of the country. Until almost the end he was hidden by his success. He was ambitious and yet surprisingly reluctant to take up government work; he was envied by monks and lay lords, but faced little opposition until the end of his career; he was sincerely interested in certain aspects of church reform, but not above trying to force his will upon monasteries and bishops; he was long-range in his thought, but derived his ideas from others and valued compromise. His personal contradictions, administrative talents, and diverse preoccupations seem to herald a later age. When his hand was withdrawn from the government, peace vanished and anarchy appeared. The good times of a strong king and an able viceroy disappeared until Henry II resurrected and expanded in his own reign policies Roger had introduced decades earlier.

Bishop Roger was quietly buried in his Sarum cathedral of Saint Mary. His tomb of black purbeck marble boasts the full-length, low-relief sculpture of a beardless bishop holding a crozier and blessing his viewer.[24] In 1226 Roger's bones

24. The present head on the tomb is not original, however. For the identification of this tomb and the problems surrounding it see Hugh Shortt, "Three Early Episcopal Tombs in Salisbury Cathedral."

were moved to the new cathedral in the present city of Salisbury. Unappreciated in death as he was misunderstood in life, his monument is passed by thousands of tourists and worshipers every year, unaware that they are looking at the remains of one of England's greatest statesmen.

Appendix 1

ROGER OF SALISBURY'S
ITINERARY

FEW EVENTS in Bishop Roger's long career can be dated precisely, but a detailed itinerary and chronology do suggest something about his movements and his changing interests. Like the kings he served, Roger appears to have traveled incessantly, rarely spending much time in any one spot. Frequently it is possible to locate him at a given place only because he witnessed a royal charter issued there (for this itinerary, I have assumed that he actually was at the location named in the charter he attested). Since Roger's life was so intimately connected with those of Henry I and Stephen, I have integrated some of their travels, particularly their journeys to Normandy, into his itinerary. A line in the right margin denotes the length of such royal excursions. The information available about Roger's activity varies with the king's whereabouts. When the monarch is abroad, charter and chronicle details about English affairs are sparse; when he returns to his kingdom, records are much more plentiful. Thus, the period we wish most to examine, the months and years when Roger ruled the country on his own, are the very times for which there is least evidence.

In the following scheme definite dates are simply calendered, but brackets enclose those portions of a date which must be estimated. For example, if the year were 1102

May 9 indicates that the event occurred, or Roger
definitely witnessed on May 9, 1102.

[*May 9*] indicates that the event occurred in 1102,
probably on May 9.

? indicates that the event occurred in 1102,

but the month is unknown and the event
is scheduled at a likely interval.

May 9 [*1102*]   indicates that the event occurred on May 9,
probably in the year 1102.

[*May 9, 1102*]   indicates that the event probably occurred
in that month and year.

[*1102*]   indicates that the event probably occurred
in 1102, but it cannot be approximated
more closely.

Documentation for all the events listed can be found either
in the notes or in the full text.

[1065]   birth in Normandy
[1091]   first meeting of Roger and Henry
1100
                                a priest in the diocese of Avranches
                                chaplain and adviser to Prince Henry in
                                Normandy
        August 2 King William II dies in the New Forest
        August 5 Henry is crowned at Westminster
    November 11 Henry marries Edith (Matilda)
    December 25 Christmas court at Westminster: Roger
                                witnesses as chaplain [1]
1101
  April 2, Easter Roger is made royal chancellor
    September 3 Roger witnesses as chancellor at the great
                                court at Windsor, Henry chooses him as
                                bishop of Salisbury
1102
        April 13 Roger is elected bishop
    September 29 Roger is invested as bishop at Westmin-
                                ster
 September 30–31 Roger attends church council at West-
                                minster
      [*Autumn*] Roger witnesses at Sutton [2]
      [*Autumn*] Roger witnesses at Newnham-on-Severn [3]
              ? Roger resigns his post as chancellor
              ? Roger avoids consecration by the arch-
                                bishop of York

1. *Regesta*, 2, no. 507.   2. *Ibid.*, nos. 595–596.
3. *Ibid.*, nos. 592–593.

December 25 [1102] Roger witnesses at Westminster [4]

1103

January 13 Roger witnesses at Salisbury; this is his first recorded visit [5]

March 29, Easter Archbishop Anselm begins his second exile

[May 17, 1103] Roger witnesses at Windsor [6]

September 25 [1103] Roger witnesses at Westminster [7]

1104

August 4 King Henry goes to Normandy

December Henry returns to England

1105

February 13 Henry sails for Normandy and Roger sees him off at Romsey [8]

July Henry and Anselm are reconciled at Laigle

August Henry returns to England

[October 18, 1105] Roger witnesses at Cornbury [9]

1106

[May 13, 1106] Roger witnesses at Sarum "as justiciar" he receives writ to protect Abbotsbury abbey [10]

August 1 Henry sails for Normandy

August 15 Henry and Anselm meet at Bec

September 28 Henry victorious at Tinchebrai

? Roger given great prisoner, Duke Robert Curthose, to guard

? Roger receives marcher lordship of Kidwelly in Wales

1107

March/April Henry returns to England

[after May 1, 1107] Roger witnesses at Westminster [11]

4. *Ibid.*, nos. 613, 615.   5. *Ibid.*, no. 626.
6. *Ibid.*, no. 649. May 17 was Pentecost Sunday in 1103.
7. *Ibid.*, no. 653.   8. *Ibid.*, no. 682.   9. *Ibid.*, no. 703.
10. *Ibid.*, nos. 754–755.   11. *Ibid.*, no. 812.

Pentecost [*1107*]   Roger witnesses at Westminster [12]

August 1–3   end of investiture controversy; Roger attends great council at London [13]

December 25 [*1107*]   Roger witnesses at Westminster [14]

1108

mid-February   near London; Henry sends Roger and others to Anselm to settle quarrel over consecration of Abbot Hugh

[*March 1108*]   Roger witnesses at Windsor [15]

Easter [*1108*]   Roger witnesses at Winchester [16]

[*May 9, 1108*]   Roger witnesses at Norwich [17]

Pentecost [*1108*]   Roger witnesses at Westminster [18]

May–July   Roger witnesses at Reading [19]

[*May–July 1108*]   Roger witnesses at Dunstable [20]

May–July   Roger witnesses at Windsor [21]

July   Henry goes abroad

July 26   at Paggaham, Roger coconsecrates Richard, Bishop of London [22]

Roger probably begins to act as viceroy about this time

1109

Roger's earliest writ issued

April 21   Archbishop Anselm dies

May 31–June 2   Henry returns to England

June 13   Roger witnesses at Westminster; [23] joyous Whitsuntide court; Roger and fellow bishops support Anselm's mandate

October 17   Roger witnesses at Nottingham; [24] diocese of Ely created

1110

May 29, Pentecost   Roger witnesses at Windsor [25]

c. May   Roger witnesses at Reading [26]

12. *Ibid.*, no. 813. In 1107 Pentecost was June 2.
13. *Ibid.*, no. 825.   14. *Ibid.*, no. 839.
15. *Ibid.*, no. 871.
16. *Ibid.*, nos. 873, 874. In 1108 Easter was April 5.
17. *Ibid.*, nos. 875–876.
18. *Ibid.*, nos. 878, 881, 883, 884. In 1108 Pentecost was May 24.
19. *Ibid.*, no. 892.
20. *Ibid.*, no. 897. This is Queen Matilda's foundation charter for the convent of Holy Trinity, London.
21. *Ibid.*, no. 899.   22. Eadmer, *H.N.*, p. 198.
23. *Regesta*, 2, no. 915.   24. *Ibid.*, no. 919.
25. *Ibid.*, nos. 945–948.   26. *Ibid.*, no. 949.

feudal aid for Princess Matilda collected
this year; first mention of exchequer [27]

? Roger witnesses at Romsey [28]

? Roger witnesses at Woodstock [29]

1111

August 8 Roger witnesses at Bishop's Waltham [30]

August 13 Roger sees the king off at Portsmouth
Henry sails for Normandy [31]

September 30 Roger is a judge at the Winchester treasury when the queen's court hears pleas of
Abingdon abbey [32]

? Roger exchanges land with Faritius of
Abingdon and erects a convent of regular
canons at Saint Frideswide's, Oxford

? Dean Robert of Salisbury dies [33]

1112

[*1111–1113*] Correspondence with Bishop Herbert
Losinga about Thorpe manor

King Henry abroad all year

1113

? Roger entertains Laon canons visiting
Sarum

July Henry returns to England

[*1113*] Roger witnesses at Ditton [34]

? Devizes castle burned this year

1114

January 7 Princess Matilda marries Henry of Germany

[*February or
March 1114*] Roger witnesses at Woodstock [35]

April 26 at Windsor Roger successfully opposes the
election of Abbot Faritius as archbishop

Spring Henry leads an expedition to Wales

[*May*] Roger witnesses at Tewkesbury [36]

27. *Ibid.*, no. 963.   28. *Ibid.*, no. 956.   29. *Ibid.*, no. 958.
30. *Ibid.*, nos. 988–990.   31. *Ibid.*, nos. 991–992.
32. *Ibid.*, no. 1000.
33. "Annals of Margan," in *Annales Monastici*, 1:6.
34. *Regesta*, 2, nos. 1027, 1028.   35. *Ibid.*, no. 1034.
36. *Ibid.*, no. 1041.

July 19 at Kidwelly Roger gives Sherborne priory land; his brother, Humphrey, attends him [37]

July 21 at Kidwelly Roger consecrates a cemetery

? Roger witnesses at Thetford [38]

[1114] Roger witnesses at Eye castle [39]

September 13 Roger witnesses at Westbourne [40]

[September 21, 1114] at Portsmouth Roger witnesses with Henry, who sails for Normandy [41]

? earliest mention of the pipe rolls

1115

June 27 at Canterbury Roger coconsecrates Theobald of Worcester [42]

July Henry returns to England

September 13 [1115] Roger witnesses at Westminster [43]

September 16 Roger witnesses at Westminster in council [44]

September 19 at Westminster Roger coconsecrates Bernard, Bishop of Saint David's; many Salisbury canons are present [45]

[1115] at Westminster Roger arranges for Saint Botolph's Aldersgate to be given to Saint Martin-le-Grand [46]

[1115] Roger witnesses at Winchester [47]

December 28 Roger helps dedicate Saint Alban's abbey [48]

1116

February 2 Roger witnesses at Windsor [49]

? Roger at Brampton with Ralph Basset [50]

37. Charter 4.   38. *Regesta*, 2, no. 1057.   39. *Ibid.*, no. 1059.
40. *Ibid.*, nos. 1061–1063, 1070.   41. *Ibid.*, no. 1056.
42. Eadmer, *H.N.*, p. 230.   43. *Regesta*, 2, no. 1090.
44. *Ibid.*, no. 1091.   45. *Eadmer, H.N.*, p. 235.
46. *Regesta*, 2, nos. 1105–1107.   47. *Ibid.*, no. 1098a.
48. *Ibid.*, no. 1102.   49. *Ibid.*, no. 1124.
50. Stenton, *English Justice*, p. 62.

March 20 Roger must have been at Salisbury for the oath to Prince William; Archbishop Thurstan of York refuses to profess obedience to Canterbury

April Henry goes abroad

1117

February 23 Abbot Faritius dies at Abingdon; he orders word of his passing to be sent to Bishop Roger

Henry abroad all year

1118

? Roger deposes Abbot Edulf of Malmesbury

May 1 Queen Matilda dies

May at Westminster Roger celebrates Matilda's funeral[51]

Henry abroad all year

1119

[September 29] Abingdon monks appear before Roger's court; case sent back to shire court[52]

Henry abroad all year

1120

April 4 at Westminster Roger coconsecrates David, Bishop of Bangor[53]

November 25 the White Ship wrecked

November 25–26 Henry returns to England

---

51. *Liber Monasterii de Hyda,* ed. Edward Edwards, pp. 311–312.
52. *Regesta,* 2, no. 1211.   53. Eadmer, *H.N.,* p. 260.

[*late November, 1120*] Roger witnesses at Portsmouth with the grieving king [54]

[*December 25, 1120*] Roger witnesses at Brampton [55]

1121

[*January 7, 1121*] Roger witnesses at Westminster [56]

[*January, 1121*] Roger witnesses at London [57]

January 29 at Windsor Roger tries to marry Henry and his new queen, Adeliza

[*January 30, 1121*] Roger witnesses at Windsor [58]

? Roger ceremoniously escorts Abbot Vincent to his new high seat at Abingdon

[*March, 1121*] Roger witnesses at Woodstock [59]

April 10, Easter Roger witnesses at Berkeley, Gloucester [60]

[*April*] Roger witnesses at Cheddar, Gloucester [61]

[*April*] Roger witnesses at Alveston, Gloucester [62]

April 10–May 29 Roger witnesses at Winchester [63]

June Henry in Wales

[*Summer, 1121*] Roger witnesses at Hereford [64]

July Reading abbey founded

September 21 Roger ordains Gregory at Devizes castle [65]

October 2 at Lambeth Roger coconsecrates Gregory, Bishop of Dublin [66]

? Roger helps Merton priory

1122

[*March 1122*] Roger witnesses at Northampton [67]

? Sherborne absorbs Horton and becomes an abbey; Thurstan elected abbot

? Roger confirms prebend gifts of Serlo of Devon [68]

1123

January 10 at Woodstock Bishop Robert Bloet dies in the arms of Henry and Roger

54. *Regesta*, 2, no. 1238.
55. *Ibid.*, no. 1240.
56. *Ibid.*, nos. 1242–1243, 1245.
57. *Ibid.*, no. 1246.
58. *Ibid.*, nos. 1247–1249.
59. *Ibid.*, nos. 1259–1264.
60. *Ibid.*, no. 1265.
61. *Ibid.*, no. 1268.
62. *Ibid.*, no. 1267.
63. *Ibid.*, no. 1280.
64. *Ibid.*, no. 1294.
65. Eadmer, *H.N.*, p. 298; John of Worcester, p. 16; Florence of Worcester (Continuator's part), 2:76.
66. John of Worcester, p. 16; Florence of Worcester (Continuator's part), 2:76.
67. *Regesta*, 2, nos. 1313–1314.   68. Charter no. 7.

February 2 at Gloucester Roger opposes a monk's election as archbishop of Canterbury

February 25 at Canterbury Roger coconsecrates Archbishop William Corbeil[69]

April 15, Easter Roger witnesses at Winchester;[70] he also arranges Alexander's election to bishopric of Lincoln

[June 1123] Roger witnesses at Winchester[71]

[June 3–10, 1123] Roger witnesses at Portsmouth and sees Henry off to Normandy[72]

July 22 at Canterbury, Alexander consecrated bishop; Roger was probably there[73]
Roger clearly supreme as viceroy

1124

Henry abroad all year

1123–1125 Roger corresponds about enlarging endowments of Reading abbey

? Roger gives wardship of Battle abbey temporalities to Aelward, a Battle monk[74]
very hard winter; famine

December Ralph Basset hangs forty men in Leicester

Christmastide at Winchester, following royal order, Roger has many minters blinded and castrated

1125

January 6, Roger completes mutilation of coiners at
Twelfth Night Winchester

September 8–11 at London, Legate John of Crema holds church council; clerical marriage condemned

69. Symeon of Durham, 2:269. 70. *Regesta*, 2, no. 1391.
71. *Ibid.*, no. 1394. 72. *Ibid.*, no. 1397.
73. John of Worcester, p. 17; Florence of Worcester (Continuator's part), 2:78.
74. *Chronicon Monasterii de Bello*, ed. J. S. Brewer, p. 60.

Henry abroad all year

1126

January 1, 1125/1126 Pope Honorius II confirms Roger's monastic holdings

September 11 Henry returns from Normandy with daughter, widowed Empress Matilda

after September 29 Roger loses custody of Duke Robert Curthose

[*Autumn 1126*] Roger witnesses at Rockingham [75]

? Roger witnesses at Woodstock [76]

1127

January 1 great council at London; Roger speaks in favor of oath to Matilda; he and other barons pledge to support her

[*January*] Roger witnesses at Winchester [77]

May 13-16 Roger attends church council at Westminster; he witnesses there and at London [78]

May betrothal of Empress Matilda and Geoffrey of Anjou in Normandy

[*May*] Roger helps Vincent of Abingdon in court

[*May 22*] Roger witnesses at Winchester [79]

? Roger orders Plympton canons to be freed from gelds of Ralph Basset [80]

[*August 26, 1127*] Roger witnesses at Eling when Henry sails for Normandy; Roger possibly visits Normandy [81]

December 8 [*1127*] Osbert of Clare celebrates Immaculate Conception near London; Roger intervenes

75. *Regesta*, 2, no. 1459.   76. *Ibid.*, no. 1466.
77. *Ibid.*, no. 1475.   78. *Ibid.*, nos. 1476–1477, 1483.
79. *Ibid.*, nos. 1485–1489.   80. Charter 11.
81. *Regesta*, 2, nos. 1499–1509; Chapter 5, Note 11.

1128

King Henry abroad all year

April 29   Roger urges council at London to renew
             oath to Matilda
June 17   Matilda marries Geoffrey at Le Mans
July 27   William Clito, son of William Curthose,
             dies

1129

early July   Roger possibly visits Normandy [82]
[July 15, 1129]   Roger witnesses at Portsmouth with re-
                    turning king [83]
September 29–   Roger participates in London legatine
October 4   council which approves celebration of Im-
                    maculate Conception and condemns cler-
                    ical marriage
Autumn 1129 through   general reorganization in government
Autumn 1130

1130

[March 29–August]   Roger witnesses at Winchester; king gives
                      Abingdon abbey to Ingulf [84]
?   Roger consecrates Ingulf at Woodstock [85]
May 4   Roger helps dedicate choir of Christ
                      Church, Canterbury [86]
May 8   Roger helps dedicate Saint Andrew's ca-
                      thedral, Rochester [87]
[1130]   Roger witnesses at Waltham, Westmin-
                      ster, and Windsor [88]
August   Henry sails for Normandy
September 29   first surviving pipe roll composed

1131

[August 1131]   Roger witnesses at Westbourne as Henry
                  returns from abroad [89]

82. *Ibid.*, nos. 1575–1576; Chapter 5, Note 11.
83. *Ibid.*, no. 1603. Offler, *Durham Charters*, p. 107, dated this
writ late August 1127.
84. *Ibid.*, no. 1641.
85. John of Worcester, p. 30; Florence of Worcester (Continuator's part), 2:92.
86. *Saxon Chronicle*, 2:196.   87. *Ibid.*
88. *Regesta*, 2, no. 1668, 1649, 1650, 1656.   89. *Ibid.*, no. 1710.

[*August*] Roger witnesses at Waltham [90]

September 8 Roger witnesses at Northampton; great council renews oath to Matilda; Henry restores Malmesbury to Roger

[*1131*] Roger witnesses at Woodstock [91]

1132

[*April 29*] Roger witnesses at Westminster [92]

? Roger helps preserve Peterborough abbey's independence

? Roger witnesses at Marden, Sussex [93]

? Roger witnesses at Gillingham [94]

[*December 25*] Roger witnesses at Windsor; Henry is ill [95]

1133

[*1133*] Roger witnesses at Blackmore, Essex [96]

May 28 at Bury, Roger's nephew Nigel is chosen bishop of Ely; Roger was probably there [97]

[*June*] Roger witnesses at Woodstock [98]

[*June*] Roger witnesses at Westminster [99]

[*June*] Roger witnesses at Winchester [100]

July Roger witnesses at Fareham, Sussex [101]

July Roger witnesses at Westbourne [102]

August 2 Roger sees Henry off to Normandy; eclipse of the moon

October 1 at Lambeth Nigel is consecrated bishop; Roger was probably there [103]

1134

Henry abroad all year

1135

Henry abroad all year

December 1 Henry dies at Lyons-la-Forêt

90. *Ibid.*, no. 1711.
91. *Ibid.*, no. 1724.
92. *Ibid.*, no. 1736–1737.
93. *Ibid.*, no. 1742.
94. *Ibid.*, no. 1746.
95. *Ibid.*, nos. 1740–1741.
96. *Ibid.*, no. 1791, 1792.
97. *Liber Eliensis*, pp. 283–284.
98. *Regesta*, 2, no. 1757.
99. *Ibid.*, nos. 1759, 1761.
100. *Ibid.*, no. 1764.
101. *Ibid.*, 1770–1777.
102. *Ibid.*, nos. 1784, 1787.
103. *Liber Eliensis*, pp. 283–284.

Roger at Winchester with royal treasure, which Stephen of Blois claims

December 22–26   Stephen's coronation and council at Westminster; Roger one of three prelates assisting

1136

January 4   at Reading, Roger assists at the burial of Henry [104]

March 22, Easter   large gathering at Westminster court; church council at London immediately after

early April   at Oxford; coronation oath reissued

Spring   rumors of Stephen's death

May 10   Roger is ill at Sarum; King Stephen hastens there from Portsmouth on hearing rumor of his death

June–August   Roger witnesses with king at seige of Exeter castle [105]

Easter–December   at Gillingham, Dorset [106]

December 1   at Reading, with Queen Adeliza Roger attends memorial service for Henry [107]

1137

mid-March   at Portsmouth, Roger bids farewell to Stephen, who sails for Normandy [108]

November 5   trouble at Ely

[November 28]   Roger witnesses at Portsmouth and greets returning king [109]

?   Roger witnesses at Westminster [110]

1138

?   at Malmesbury, Roger issues writ "on behalf of the king and myself" [111]

late May   Robert of Gloucester renounces fealty to Stephen

August 22   Battle of the Standard

104. *Regesta*, 3, no. 386.   105. *Ibid.*, nos. 572, 592.
106. *Ibid.*, no. 818.
107. British Museum Manuscript, Egerton 3031, fo. 16.
108. Orderic Vitalis, 5:63, 83; also see Note 50 in Chapter 5.
109. *Regesta*, 3, no. 827.   110. *Ibid.*, no. 681.
111. Charter 25.

December 11–25 at Westminster; Legate Alberic of Ostia holds church council; Theobald elected archbishop of Canterbury, December 24

1139

January 8 Roger helps consecrate Archbishop Theobald at Canterbury

January 8–13 Roger witnesses at Oxford and attends dedication of nearby Godstow nunnery [112]

rumors and court intrigue

April 26 Pope Innocent II confirms Roger's holdings

mid-June at Malmesbury, Roger receives summons to court in Oxford; Alexander and Nigel are with him

June 24–25 at Oxford, Bishops Roger and Alexander captured

c. June 27–30 Devizes castle beseiged; Nigel resists, and Matilda of Ramsbury surrenders

early July Stephen captures Roger's other castles: Salisbury, Sherborne, Malmesbury

mid- or late July Alexander's castles fall

August 29 to September 1 legatine council at Winchester to defend Roger

September 30 Robert of Gloucester lands in England

October 7 to 22 Robert Fitz Hubert seizes Malmesbury

autumn at Sarum Roger writes bequests; [113] money is stolen from his cathedral

December 11 Bishop Roger dies at Sarum

December 25 at Sarum Stephen confiscates Roger's other treasures

1226

Roger's body is moved from Old Sarum to the spot in the new cathedral, where it now lies

112. *Regesta,* 3, nos. 366, 473.   113. Charters 26–31.

Appendix 2

ROGER OF SALISBURY'S
CHARTERS AND WRITS

THE FOLLOWING Latin texts of thirty-one charters and writs of Bishop Roger of Salisbury have never before been gathered together in one place. The small parchment originals, the varied cartulary copies, later transcripts, facsimilies, printed editions, abstracts, and translations are all indicated in the listings. References to further discussions of these texts are also given, including the pertinent chapters in this biographical study of the great justiciar.

Although most of Bishop Roger's charters have been mentioned elsewhere in one way or another, five (1, 6, 8, 14, 21) have not been published previously, one (19) has only been printed incompletely, and several others have been in part incorrectly edited. Many of those which have been published are in volumes no longer readily accessible. One writ, long associated with Bishop Roger, can now be demonstrated to belong to a later bishop.

Although these documents include both longer, more formal charters and brief, direct writs, I have used the two terms interchangeably. Roger's instructions, gifts, and confirmations contain little personal information which would warrant their being called letters, but several of them can be related to royal writs issued about the same time. It is unfortunate that so few of the bishop's written charters and writs have survived; those collected here surely represent only a small fraction of the viceregal and episcopal directives he must have issued during forty active years in England.

I have arranged Roger's thirty-one instructions in their

most probable chronological order, but they can also be classified in several other ways. Fifteen (1–5, 7, 19–21, 26–31) are episcopal charters, six of them (26–31) deathbed bequests. One (6) is largely a personal charter. Eleven (11–18, 23–25) are writs issued as justiciar and viceroy. Four (8–10, 22) entail mixed episcopal and viceregal responsibilites. They were issued throughout Roger's career, but not one of them contains a precise date. Seventeen, however, can be accurately placed, while fourteen have wider limits. In several instances I have offered more definitive dates than previous editors have. Six of the charters come from the first twenty years of the twelfth century; seven are from the decade of the 1120s; and ten originated in the years between 1135 and 1139; eight others are very hard to place.

Strictly speaking, only three of the documents are the original writs Roger could have handled himself (1, 6, 25; 9 is a disputed possibility). The others were all copied at different times by scribes onto rolls or into great bound charter collections called cartularies, and the originals lost. Twenty-five different cartularies and three rolls preserved one or more of Roger's dictated orders. Ten of these writs were recorded in more than one place, and two charters were even copied twice in the same cartularies. The Salisbury cathedral register, the Register of Saint Osmund, contained four of Roger's varied instructions, one of which was later copied into three other Sarum cartularies. The Reading abbey cartularies preserved four charters in multiple copies (the Egerton manuscript 3031 recorded three, Harley 1708 inscribed four, and Cotton Vespasian E XXV preserved three). The Saint Frideswide priory cartulary contained three writs, and there were two each in the Sherborne and Oseney abbey cartularies. In all, I therefore know of forty-eight extant copies of Roger's texts, although there are only thirty-one individual documents.

Most of Roger's extant charters and writs concerned religious foundations. This reflects the cause which preserved

them more than anything else. Normally, the great ecclesiastical establishments, the monasteries and cathedrals,
kept the best proofs of their goods and privileges, but even
these cartulary records, many of which have descended to
our own day, offer no way of estimating how many writs
a scribe or archivist decided not to record. About half of the
bishop's remaining directives related to houses intimately
connected with him: five concerned Saint Frideswide's
priory, Oxford, where he was patron; four concerned
Reading abbey, Berkshire, founded by Henry I in the Salisbury diocese; three concerned Salisbury cathedral chapter
affairs; and two concerned Sherborne abbey, Dorset, where
Roger had been titular abbot. On the other hand, many of
the viceroy's lost commands probably concerned laymen or
clerks who never bothered to enroll their parchment writs
in cartularies, but who may have tried to preserve the
originals themselves. It is interesting, for example, that two
of his three extant original charters (6, 25) concerned individuals rather than religious corporations.

Roger's viceregal writs closely followed the chancery
style for royal writs, and he probably dictated all his commands to clerks who regularly served him. His words were
thus rather straightforward and impersonal in form and
had an intelligent, no-nonsense air about them. In some
ways the resulting charters and writs are therefore more
valuable for their witness lists and for glimpses of Roger's
activity than for their content. The cumulative effect, however, confirms the view that Roger was a conscientious and
effective diocesan and a forceful and imaginative viceroy.
His deathbed bequests, moreover, breathe an air of resigna-
tion and tragedy which is in marked contrast to the com-
pelling vigor of his earlier formulations.

Stylistic patterns are evident in the total collection. Roger
usually referred to himself simply as the bishop of Salisbury,
but in four instances (4, 5, 8, 19) he added *dei gratia* to this
designation. Once he wrote, *"dei permissione Saresberiensis*

ecclesie minister humilis," (12) a formula that would become more common among bishops later in the century. Most important, he twice added an additional title, *"regni Angliae procurator sub domino nostro rege Henrico,"* and *"sub domino nostro rege Henrico regni Anglie procurator,"* (9, 10).

His name was usually abbreviated and appeared twelve times as simply *R.*, but *Rogerus* appeared eleven times and *Rogerius,* five. His name was omitted once (24), was illegible another time (31), and was written mistakenly as *Robert* (16) and in one of two copies of a writ as *Ralph* (14). I have extended the abbreviations to read *R[ogerus]*, but twelfth-century scribes wrote all three forms.

The name *Salisbury* showed even greater variation. The standard abbreviation *Sar'* appeared in twenty-one of the texts, but one also finds *Seriberiensis, Salesbir', Saresberie, Salesb'* (twice), *Sarr', Saresburiensis, Saresb', Sarum,* and *Salobriensis.* Although some prefer *Sar[isberiensis]*, I have arbitrarily extended *Sar'* to read *Sar[esberiensis]*. The many divergent spellings can be accounted for rather easily, especially when one recalls that many writs were copied years, or even centuries, after they were first issued. The abbreviation for Salisbury, *Sar',* has an interesting history. It originally stood for the long form of the word, but the peculiar medieval writing of the final letter *r* also served as a contraction for *rum.* Thus, some clerks and readers began to spell the word *Sarum,* and Roger's deserted town is called Old Sarum to this day.

Roger's greeting was very direct. *Salutem* appeared twenty-three times. Variations of *salutem in domino, salutem et honoris dignitatem, salutem et dei benedictionem,* and a destroyed particle, *salutem et* ———, also appeared. Four documents lacked any greeting.

Not surprisingly, the notifications showed greatest variety. Roger wrote: *sciatis nos, sciatis me, sciatis quod, sciatis quia, universitati vestrae innotescimus, attendentes, notum sit vobis.* Commands were also direct: *precipio quod* appeared four times, and the variations *precipio vobis quod, precipio tibi quod,* and *precipio tibi ex parte regis et mea quod,* appeared thrice, twice, and once. The last form was an especially striking illustration of Roger's viceregal authority. Other forms used included: *do, prohibeo quod, concedo quod, dimittite habere,* and *fac habere.* The deathbed bequests all began in a similar way: *notum vobis facio quoniam* was used three times, *notum facio dignitati vestre quoniam* appeared twice and *notum vobis facio quia,* once.

Writ and charter endings were equally direct, but less varied. Two ended with *valete;* one, with a postscript warning. Six were issued *per breve regis.* Nineteen texts identified the place of issue: seven were issued at Westminster, five at Salisbury, two at Winchester, and one each at Wilton, Sherborne, Malmesbury, Brackley, and Kidwelly. The witness lists are most important, for it is from them that the documents can be approximately or precisely dated. Thirteen documents had witness lists. None of the viceregal writs issued under King Henry had them, but each of the four viceregal writs definitely issued under Stephen had the witness of a single man (Charter 16 may have had witnesses).

In presenting these documents, I have tried to follow the styles of the individual scribes. Thus, spelling and punctuation are not always consistent; in some cases copyists even spelled a word differently within the same writ. I have, however, modernized some lettering. Thus, although some writers favored a *c* rather than a *t* (*tocius* for *totius*) or a *u* for a *v* (*donauimus* for *donavimus*), I have followed present usage. I have also capitalized all names of persons and places, even when contemporary writers did not. Furthermore, all abbreviations have been extended to full words, but in proper names the inserts have been bracketed, thus, Rog[er]i[us]. There are no significant differences among the several copies of single writs, but variant readings are listed along with odd readings from printed sources. When more than one copy of a writ survives, an asterisk indicates the manuscript version used. My remarks on each text are usually quite restricted and mainly are intended to date the document, to identify the persons and places mentioned, and to indicate related royal actions. Other observations may be found in the designated chapters of the text, for which these documents constitute partial evidence. However, some few details from that biography have been repeated here for convenience and clarity.

1

Bishop Roger promises obedience to Archbishop Anselm of Canterbury, the "Primate of All Britain."

Ego Rogerus Seriberiensis ecclesiae electus et ad te reverende pater Anselme Sanctae Cantuariensis ecclesiae archiepiscope et totius Britanniae primas antistes consecrandus, tibi et omnibus successoribus tuis canonice succedentibus canonicam obedientiam me per omnia servaturum promitto.

SOURCE: original charter, *Canterbury Cathedral Manuscript, C 115, no. 12; copy on roll, Canterbury Cathedral Manuscript, C 117, no. 11; cartulary copy, British Museum Manuscript, Cotton Cleopatra E I, fo. 29v.

DISCUSSED: Chapter 1.

DATE: 1107. Roger was appointed Bishop of Salisbury in 1101, but the investiture controversy delayed his consecration until August 1107.

REMARKS: This is the standard short form of profession to Canterbury. Other bishops, like William of Exeter and Reinhelm of Hereford, used exactly the same formula. Their professions are also preserved in the Canterbury manuscripts. For the later misuse of such professions in the Cleopatra manuscript cartulary, see R. W. Southern, "The Canterbury Forgeries." The official notification to Archbishop Anselm of Roger's election as bishop has been preserved in British Museum Manuscript, Harley Roll A 3, no. 4.[1] This is also a ritual formula, but it reveals that at the time of his election Roger was a priest of the diocese of Avranches. Roger was elected by the clergy and the people; later bishops would be elected by the cathedral chapter.

2

Bishop Roger confirms to Tewkesbury abbey the gifts of Robert Fitz Hamon, including the church of Saint Mary of Cranborne.

Carta Rogeri Salesbir[iensis] [a] episcopi confirmantis ecclesie de Theok[esberia] dona R. filii H. et militum suorum anno incarnationis domini M.C.IX. In primis ecclesiam sancte Marie de Craneburna, cum omnibus pertinentis suiis, ecclesias quae fuerunt R. capellani, videlicet ecclesiam de Pentrich, ecclesiam de Essemer, ecclesiam de Froma, cum omnibus quae ad eam pertinent, decimam de Tarente Roberti de Haia, decimas de Chaldewelle et de Fifhida, decimam de Develisc, decimam de Thornecumba, decimam de Muleberna, Odonis de Hemdeswicha, decimam de Blachesberga, decimam de Eschetilestuna, decimam de Wichometon, quandam decimam apud Suttonam, decimam dominii de Chenuca, decimam Willielmi de Hectredesbiria, in Purbica duas decimas de elemosina Aelfredi de Nichola, videlicet decimam de Tachetona et de la Harpine, decimam dominii de Occheberna, Gaufridi de Mersi,[b] decimam dominii de Werftona.

SOURCE: charter roll abstract, *British Museum Manuscript, Cotton Cleopatra A VII, fo. 74v; printed, Dugdale *Monasticon Anglicanum,* 2:69–70 (citing above manuscript as fo. 75b).
VARIATIONS: a. Dugdale reads *Salesburiensis;* b. Dugdale reads *Meili.*
DISCUSSED: VCH, Dorset 2:70. Chapter 2.

1. A partial facsimile of this charter was included in N. R. Ker, *English Manuscripts in the Century After the Norman Conquest,* plate 9a; also see pp. 17–18, 27–28.

DATE: 1109

REMARKS: This thirteenth-century charter roll contained only abstracts; witnesses were omitted. Robert Fitz Hamon lost his reason in 1105 and died in 1107.[2] It is interesting that Bishop Roger's charter therefore seems to have been issued a few years after the gifts were made. In 1102 Cranborne abbey was reduced to priory status, as Tewkesbury became the mother abbey.[3] Robert de la Hay became a monk of Montacute by at latest 1121, and possibly much earlier.[4] The places mentioned are all in the diocese of Salisbury, and, unless otherwise indicated, in the county of Dorset. In order they are: Cranborne, Pentridge, Ashmore, Frome, Tarrant Monachorum (Monkton), Chettle, Fifehead Magdalen, Dewlish (Devil's Brook), Thorncombe, Milborne Saint Andrew, Hemsworth, Bradbury, Shillingstone, Witchampton, Sutton, Knook (Wiltshire), William of Heytesbury (Wiltshire), Purbeck, Alfred of Lincoln, Tatton, Hurpston, Ogbourne and Wroughton (Wiltshire).

3

Bishop Roger orders Adelelmus of Kingston and Robert of Bagpuize to do right by Abingdon abbey regarding the church of Kingston, or he will interdict services at Kingston.

Rogerus episcopus Saresberie Adelelmo de Kingestuna et Roberto de Bachepuz, salutem. Precipio vobis quod reddatis ecclesie de Abbendona rectitudines quas illi debetis de ecclesia vestra de Kingestuna. Et nisi feceritis, Ilbertus decanus interdicat divinum officium apud Kingestuna. Apud West [monasterium].

SOURCE: cartulary copy, *British Museum Manuscript, Claudius B VI, fo. 148v; printed, *Abingdon Chronicle* 2:121; Melville Madison Bigelow, *Placita Anglo-Normannica*, p. 105.

2. *Regesta*, 2, no. 721; Orderic Vitalis, 4:203; William of Malmesbury, *G.R.*, 2:475.
3. For royal confirmations of Tewkesbury's endowments see *Regesta*, 2, nos. 847 (spurious), 1069, 1535, 1978.
4. *Ibid.*, no. 1307.

DISCUSSED: earlier in the *Abingdon Chronicle* 2:30. VCH, Berkshire 4:352. Chapter 3.

DATE: in or shortly before 1113, at Westminster

REMARKS: This writ concerns a matter which would have come to Roger's attention as diocesan bishop, and he does threaten the ecclesiastical penalty of interdict, but the tone is that of a viceregal writ. Kingston Bagpuize, Berkshire, was originally part of Longworth, Berkshire. Adelelmus of Kingston and Ralph of Bagpuize built a chapel there and agreed to pay the parent church, Abingdon abbey, thirty-two pence a year. Ralph's son and heir, Henry, neglected to continue payment, and it was probably at about that time that Roger issued this threatening charter.[5] In any event, Henry suddenly died, and his heir and brother, Robert, quickly paid the debt in 1113. Ilbert the dean is not otherwise known; rather than being a dean of the Salisbury cathedral chapter, he was probably a rural dean in Berkshire.

4

Bishop Roger grants lands at Kidwelly, Wales, to Sherborne convent and its prior, Thurstan. A record of Roger's consecration of a Kidwelly cemetery is attached.

In nomine Sanctae et individuae Trinitatis ego Rogerius gratia dei Salesb[iriensis] [a] episcopus pro salute et incolumitate domini mei Henrici regis et Mathildis reginae et filiorum suorum cum consensu eorundem pro salute animae meae et parentum meorum et antecessorum meorum, do sanctae Scireburnensi [b] ecclesiae et Turstino priori et successoribus suis sibi regulariter succedentibus unam carrucatam terrae apud Catweli [c] sicut perambulavi eam, scilicet a novo fossato novi molendini per rivulum qui illic hieme defluit usque ad domum quondam babbae [d] et inde ad rivulum currentum per medium alnetum usque ad viam et a via sicut rivulus idem decurrit in mare, et totum montem qui dicitur mons Salomonis usque ad mare porrectum et ex alia parte sicut quaedam pulla vadit usque ad predictam viam, solutam

5. The editor of the *Abingdon Chronicle*, 2:340, suggested the year 1111.

et quietam et liberam ab omni famulorum impedimento et saeculari exactione et servitio et omnis decimas meas in annona, in vitulis, in porcis, in agnis, in caseis, in piscibus, et in pasnagio [e] porcorum, et concedo ut suos proprios porcos quietos a pasnagio [f] habeat [g] in bosco meo et pasturam animalium suorum cum meis dominicis habeant. Videntibus et audientibus plurimis clericis et laicis quorum nomina hic subnotantur. Radulfus capellanus, Rog[erius] subdiaconus, Unfridus frater episcopi, Osmundus dapifer, Alricus de Halsuei,[h] Ricardus Latemerus, Hildebrandus, Earnaldus [i] pincerna, Will[el]m[us] de Lund[oniam], Rog[erius] de Reinni,[j] Ricardus Foliot, Rob[er]t[us] vetus dapifer, et Rodb[er]t[us] filius ejus, Will[el]m[us] conestabularius, Will[el]m[us] Esturmit, Rad[ulfus] filius Warini, Rodb[er]t[us] de Sagio, Rodb[er]t[us] de Maisi, et Walteri[us] frater ejus, Picot[us], Gaufridus Rufus, Rodb[er]t[us] Niger, Philippus de Bealfou, Osmundus filius Everardi, Rog[erius] Fol[iot], Henricus filius Walt[er]i[us] de Poterna, Albri de Felgeria,[k] Eadmundus qui tunc castellum de Caduelli custodiebat, Alwinus presbiter villae. Haec donatio facta est xiiii kalendas Augusti in domo castelli de Caduelli,[l] testimonio istorum et aliorum multorum quorum nomina ignoro.

Post haec tertia die domus Rogeri[us] episcopus licentia et consensu Wlfridi [m] episcopi de Sancto David dedicavit cimiterium in eodem loco, et in eadem dedicatione predicatione et concessu [n] ejusdem episcopi dederunt omnes burgenses, et Franci et Angli et Flandrenses decimas suas de Penbrai et de Pennald, testimonio omnium illorum supradictorum.

SOURCE: cartulary copy, *British Museum Manuscript, Additional Manuscript 46487, fos. 14–15v; printed, Thomas Hearne, *Remarks and Collections,* 3:449 (incomplete text), see also p. 417. Dugdale, *Monasticon Anglicanum,* 3:64, also printed this charter but used an untraced 1301 inspeximus copy of Bishop David of Saint David's, which was in an ancient roll in the Augmentation Office. Between 1642 and 1649 this had been transcribed by Roger Dodsworth from the same roll; see Bodleian Manuscript, Dodsworth 63, fos. 90–91; abstract, *Regesta,* 2, no. 1042.

VARIATIONS: a. Dugdale reads *Sarisbiriensis;* b. Dugdale reads

Shyrbornensi; c. Dugdale reads *Cadweli;* d. Dugdale reads *Balbe;* e. Dugdale reads *pannagio.* f. Dugdale reads *pannagio;* g. Dugdale reads *habeant, et boscum in bosco meo;* h. Dugdale reads *Halver;* i. Dugdale reads *Cornaldus;* j. Dugdale reads *Reigni;* k. Dugdale reads *Albericus;* l. Dugdale reads *Kadweli;* m. Dugdale reads *Wilfridi;* n. Dugdale reads *consensu.*

DISCUSSED: Lloyd, *The History of Carmarthenshire* 1:350. Chapter 3.

DATE: July 19, 1114, at Kidwelly; July 21, 1114, at Kidwelly (cemetery consecration). Bishop Winfrid died in 1115, and the charter could have been prepared any time before then, but most likely it was issued in 1114, when Roger was in Wales in connection with Henry's summer military campaign.

REMARKS: The magnificent Sherborne cartulary which records these gifts was made in the middle of the twelfth century. It contains some splendid illuminations and even retains its original wooden binding.[6] This text sounds as if it might have been slightly altered by the Sherborne scribe as he copied it into the cartulary. Phrases like "Edmund who was then castellan," "I pass over the names of many others," and "Robert and his brother," suggest minor changes. Furthermore, the note about the cemetery consecration is clearly a scribal entry rather than an actual charter. Pembury and Saint Ishmael's, Penalt, are both in Carmarthenshire. This charter lists several members of Bishop Roger's household, including his brother, Humphrey. Osmund was a frequent witness to Roger's episcopal charters and was still his steward in 1139.[7] Walter de Maisi was also a regular companion. William of London was the father of Maurice of London, who later assumed lordship of Kidwelly after Roger. William of Sturminster was involved in legal disputes in 1127 and after Roger's death.[8] Geoffrey Rufus may have been the future royal chancellor who after 1133 was bishop of Durham.

6. See F. Wormald, "The Sherborne Cartulary," in *Fritz Saxl Memorial Essays,* ed. D. J. Gordon (London, 1957), pp. 101–119; M. A. F. Borrie, "The Binding of the Sherborne Chartulary," *The British Museum Quarterly,* XXXII, nos. 3–4, pp. 96–98.

7. See Charters 26, 27, 31.

8. For William of London see Lloyd, *A History of Wales,* 1:430. For William of Sturminster, see *Regesta,* 2, nos. 825, 1509; John of Salisbury; *Letters,* 1:131–132.

5

Bishop Roger concedes that Arnulf the Falconer and his
heirs have rights of presentment, saving the king's interest,
for the prebends Arnulf gave to Sarum.

Rogerus dei gratia Sar[esberiensis] episcopus universis
sancte ecclesie filiis, salutem in domino. Sciatis nos concessisse
et presenti carta confirmasse Arnulfo Falcario et heredibus
suis ut ipsi eligant et presentent clericos idoneos qui in-
stituantur prebendas quae ipse Arnulfus adquisivit ecclesie
nostre consensu et voluntate Henrici regis Anglie.

SOURCE: cartulary copy, *Salisbury Cathedral Manuscript, Register of Saint Osmund, fo. 114; printed, *Register of St. Osmund* 1:383.
DISCUSSED: Chapter 3.
DATE: c. 1115–1116. In William Rufus's time Arnulf had given
a prebend to Salisbury for his son, G. Later he wished to endow one for another son, Humphrey. King Henry wrote to
Bishop Roger and Dean S[erlo] and the Salisbury chapter,
reviewing Arnulf's plan and his complaint that they were
not observing the conditions of his first grant.[9] The king reminded them that they had recognized the agreement in a
royal court and in a court of the archbishop, and he commanded it be kept. Henry then notified his justiciars of the
new prebend.[10] Accordingly, Roger issued the above writ conceding Arnulf's right of presentment to the prebends. The
exact order of these three documents may vary, but they were
all related. Roger's charter can thus be dated in terms of the
two royal commands. The editor of the *Register of St. Osmund* suggested dates of 1118 for Roger's concession, 1120
for Henry's command that the covenant be observed, and
1130 for his confirmation of the prebend. The witness list in-
validates the last suggestion, and the others are also probably
incorrect. Serlo can only have been dean from some time after

9. *Register of St. Osmund*, 1:383; this writ was omitted from
Regesta, 2.
10. *Register of St. Osmund*, 1:196; *Regesta*, 2, no. 1163.

IIII until before 1125, when he was mentioned at Merton priory as a former dean of Salisbury.[11] Henry's confirmation of the prebend, witnessed by Queen Matilda, cannot be later than April 1116. Thus, the wide limits for these texts seem to be between 1111 and 1116. The court discussion was probably held before the archbishop of Canterbury, but that office was vacant until April 1114. Henry and Roger appear to have gone to Wales immediately thereafter. Following this, in September, the king left for Normandy, where he remained until July 1115. Thus, between July 1115 and his next departure in April 1116 seems most likely to be the time of his two charters and Roger's command.

REMARKS: It is unusual for Roger to have used the first person plural, *nos,* in this text, but the writ may have been issued originally by the bishop and the chapter, as was the writ preceding it in the cartulary and as seems called for by the circumstances here. Roger's reluctant grant of the rights of presentment to a layman was, of course, contrary to the spirit of the reforms of the twelfth-century church. The churches Arnulf the Falconer gave are Swinbrook and Shipton in Oxfordshire and Bricklesworth (Brixworth) in Northamptonshire, which for many years constituted one prebend, and Uffcot in Wiltshire.[12]

6

Bishop Roger grants Geoffrey the Constable the land at Ludgate which Hugh of Buckland had bought from Peter Futnud.

R[ogerus] episcopus Sar[esberiensis] hominibus et vice-comitibus London[ie] et ministris suis et omnibus hominibus suis, omnibus fidelibus et amicis suis de Lond[onia] Francis et Anglicis, salutem. Sciatis me concessisse Gaufrido Conestabulario terram quam Hugo de Bochelanda emit de Petro Futnud et quam ipse tenuit de me ad portam de Lutgata ad tenendam de me et de herede meo in feodo et hereditate sibi

11. College of Arms Manuscript, Arundel 28, fo. 12. Serlo was still dean in 1122, see Charter 7.

12. *Register of St. Osmund,* 1:201.

et heredi suo per idem servitium quod Hugo fecit inde mihi.
Scilicet per iii solidos reddendo mihi ad Pascha. Et iii solidos
ad festum Sancti Michaelis. Ea pro concessione ista dedit
mihi de Gersoma i unciam auri. Quapropter volo et precipio
quod bene et in pace et honorifice et libere et quiete teneat
terram illam et omnes homines in ea manentes. Valete.

SOURCE: *original charter with badly damaged white wax seal;
charter size, app. 4 × 6½ inches; Saint Paul's Cathedral Manuscript, Ancient Deeds, A/Box 24/1351.

DISCUSSED: Chapter 2.[13]

DATE: 1116–1139. Hugh of Buckland, the great sheriff of eight
counties, seems to have died in 1116 or 1117. Presumably, this
charter was issued shortly after his death. Apparently Hugh
was a cleric and held the prebend of Harleston in Saint Paul's
Cathedral, London.[14]

REMARKS: This may be called a personal charter. It is not an
episcopal or viceregal mandate and seems to be a strictly private arrangement regarding Roger's London tenements. The
charter address, however, is surely in a viceregal, or even royal,
style. On the other hand, Professor Pierre Chaplais has kindly
called my attention to the use of the valediction (*Valete*),
which was a peculiar feature of episcopal charters and rare in
royal charters, and which often replaced a list of witnesses.
I have not been able to identify the scribe of Roger's charter,
but Professor Chaplais suggested that he was contemporary
with Professor Bishop's Scriptor 8.[15] Bishop Roger's principal
London holding was the deanship of Saint Martin-le-Grand,
and this charter may have been issued in that connection,
which its place in the Saint Paul's archives further suggests.
The charter mentions Roger's heir, however, not his successor.
The use of the term *gersoma* for the payment Hugh made to

13. Although this charter has not been printed before, it was
mentioned in the *Historical Manuscripts Commission's Ninth Report* (London, 1883), p. 256, as a charter of "R. Bishop of Sar."
Norman Moore, *The History of St. Bartholomew's Hospital*, 1:33,
cited Roger's charter as did C. N. L. Brooke, "The Composition of
the Chapter of St. Paul's, 1086–1163," CHJ, 10(1950–1952):124,
n. 70.

14. *Regesta*, 2, nos. 1102, 1180. For his prebend see Greenway,
Fasti, 1:51.

15. For examples of Scriptor 8's work see Bishop, *Scriptores Regis*,
plate *XIIIa*.

Bishop Roger is interesting, for that term usually referred to the initial payment a sheriff made to the crown for the profitable privilege of farming a county. Geoffrey the Constable was probably the Geoffrey, constable of the bishop, who helped Maurice of London rout the Welsh near Roger's old castle of Kidwelly in an 1136 encounter.[16] A Geoffrey the Constable witnessed the 1137 charter of Rahere, prior of Saint Bartholomew's Smithfield.[17] Geoffrey the Constable held the prebend of Chamberlin Wood in Saint Paul's, and Rahere was his predecessor in the same prebend.[18] Geoffrey died between 1139 and 1154, when his London property passed to his nephew, Hugh Fitz Pinceon.[19] This Geoffrey also seems identifiable with Geoffrey the canon, who held the church of Saint Mary Magdalene in Milk Street and other lands in London.[20] Peter Futnud held three market stalls of Bishop Roger.[21] These were apparently rights Roger ultimately held as dean of Saint Martin's. In 1141 the houses and lands Peter held in London from the collegiate church of Saint Martin-le-Grand were given to Bishop Henry of Winchester, who succeeded Roger as dean.[22] Evidently, Peter died or was dispossessed shortly after Bishop Roger's disgrace. Futnud's tenement was north of Cripplegate and was still known by his name as late as 1171.[23] Years before, in 1131, King Henry had told Bishop Roger that he had granted to a Peter, the clerk of Saint Martin, Mara in Wilton.[24] This may have been the London Peter Futnud.

16. Gerald of Wales, *Opera*, 6:79.
17. Moore, *St. Bartholomew's Hospital*, 1:26–27.
18. Greenway, *Fasti*, 1:38.   19. *Regesta*, 3, no. 317.
20. Greenway, *Fasti*, 1:38; *Regesta*, 3, no. 1944. See also H. W. C. Davis, "London Lands and Liberties of St. Paul's, 1066–1135," in *Essays in Medieval History Presented to T. F. Tout*, ed. A. G. Little and F. M. Powicke (Manchester, 1925), p. 59.
21. *Regesta*, 3, no. 526.   22. *Ibid.*, no. 529.
23. Westminster Abbey Manuscript, no. 13251. Peter's tenement was later held by Ralph Lothair, a canon of St. Martin-le-Grand from at least 1158; *Ibid.*, no. 13247.
24. *Regesta*, 2, no. 1709. Peter, a clerk of Wilton, accounted in Wiltshire in 1130 (*Pipe Roll*, p. 20). It is tempting to connect this Peter (and Peter Futnud) with Peter the Scribe, Scribe 14 as identified by Professor Bishop in *Scriptores Regis*, pp. 24–25. This latter Peter may have been a clerk of St. Martin's, *Regesta*, 3:xiv, for which either he, or his scribe, wrote several writs. Peter the Scribe, however, lived into the 1160's.

7

Bishop Roger and his chapter certify the gifts with which
Serlo, the collector of Devon, endowed a prebend at Salisbury for his son and heirs.

Universis sancte matris ecclesie filiis, Archiepiscopis, Episcopis, Archidiaconis, Clericis, et omnibus ad quos ista carta
pervenerit, R[ogerius] episcopus, totusque conventus sancte
Marie Sarr[esberiensis], salutem. Universitati vestre innotescimus quod Serlo collector Devon[iae], concessu domini
regis H[enrici] et nostra petitione concessit et dedit Deo et
sancte Marie et ecclesie nostre Sarr[esberiensis], ecclesias
quas tenuerat in Devon[ia], videlicet, ecclesiam de Tein-
ton[ia], et illam de Herburnatam, et illam de Alienton[ia],
et illam de Alvinton[ia] cum capellis, decimis, et terris, et
singulis quibus beneficiis ad eas pertinentibus in prebendam,
et similiter domos et terram que fuit Rogeri Patin, et domos
et terram quae fuit Herfridi in civitate Winton[iensi], quas
ab eis emit concessu domini regis H[enrici]. Nos autem sub
gratia mutue dilectionis et recompensationis simul cum
caritatis intuitu, ipsam prebendam Ricardo ipsius Serlonis
nutrito dedimus, et post Ricardum, semper propinquiori in
progenie, qui aptus et idoneus ad servitium in ecclesia
nostra faciendum fuerit, in perpetuam elemosinam conces-
simus. Et ut haec elemosina nostra et donatio propinquis de
posteritate illorum rata et inconcussa conservetur, attesta-
tione litterarum nostrarum et impressione sigillorum nos-
trorum communivimus. His testibus, Serlone decano, God-
wino cantore, Hard[ingi] thesaurario, Nigello de Kaln, Joel
archidiacono, Willielmo subdecano, magistro Ailwino, Tur-
gis[o], Ainulfo, Waltero Gurmund[o], Ailwardo, Henrico,
Kenewardo, Galfrido Martel, et multis aliis.

Source: cartulary copy, *Salisbury Cathedral Manuscript, Regis-
    ter of Saint Osmund, fo. 113; printed, Register of St. Osmund
    1:381.
Discussed: Chapter 3.
Date: 1122. A royal writ definitely datable June–September 1122

to January 10, 1123, confirmed Roger's charter.[25] The *Register of St. Osmund* editor mistakenly dated Roger's charter in 1108 and Henry's in 1109.

REMARKS: The editor of the *Register of St. Osmund* misread *Godwin cantor* as *Godwin chancellor*. Godwin's tomb and that of a canon named Alward of Ramsbury (possibly Ailwardo of this charter) were found in the canons' cemetery at Old Sarum.[26] Nigel of Calne was a royal chaplain and a prebendary of Calne in the Sarum chapter.[27] The Devon churches mentioned are Taynton, Harberton, East Allington, and West Alvington.

8

Bishop Roger confirms Reading abbey's holdings in the diocese of Salisbury, including the churches of Cholsey and Wargrave obtained by the king from the abbey of Mont St. Michel, in exchange for twelve librates of land.

Ego dei gratia Saresburiensis [a] episcopus Rog[er]i[us] concedo et confirmo ecclesie Rading[ensi] et eius abbati primo Domno Hugoni et monachis in eadem ecclesia deo et Beate dei genitrici virgini Marie servientibus omnia illa que dominus noster rex Henricus eidem dedit ecclesie [b] in episcopatu meo. Hec sunt ecclesia sancte Marie que in eadem villa est, scilicet Radingia cum omni ad eam pertinente parrochia; et Tacheham et Chelseia [c] et terra centum solidorum in Chelseia [e] quam Will[el]mus filius Georldi de supradicto abbate et monachis tenet reddens illis inde centum solidos singulis annis.[d] Hec ita libere ita quiete, scilicet Radingiam, et Chelseiam,[c] et Tacheham, ut dominus noster rex Henricus eis dedit, ego concedo. Ecclesias quoque de Chelesia [c] et de Waregrava [e] ab abbate et monachis de periculo maris, ego suppliciter rogatus per eorum litteras supradicte ecclesie Rading[ensi] concedo. Eas enim per xii libratas terre ab

---

25. *Regesta*, 2, no. 1372.
26. Shortt, *Old Sarum*, p. 34. Since Godwin was ordained by Archbishop Anselm, Shortt's suggestion that he was still alive in 1160 seems unlikely. For more on Godwin see Chapter 3.
27. *Regesta*, 2, nos. 1018, 1164, 1204, 1209, 1230, 1231, p. *x*.

abbate predicto escambiavit dominus noster rex Henricus, et ecclesie Radingensi concessit.

SOURCE: cartulary copies, British Museum Manuscripts; *Egerton 3031, fos. 51–51v.; Harley 1708, fos. 189–189v.; Cotton Vespasian E XXV, fo. 109v.

VARIATIONS: a. Harley 1708 reads Sar'; b. Harley 1708 reads *eidem ecclesie dedit;* c. Harley 1708 reads *Chals[eia];* d. Harley 1708 reads *per singulos annos;* e. Harley 1708 reads *Wereg[re]ve.*

DISCUSSED: Chapter 2.

DATE: latter half of 1123. Reading abbey was founded in 1121, and its first abbot, Hugh of Amiens, the former prior of Lewes, was elected two years later. He served until he was consecrated archbishop of Rouen in 1130. Before resigning his position in 1123, another abbot, Roger of Mont Saint Michel, wrote to Bishop Roger, "vigorous administrator of the realm of England," noting that his abbey had given Reading the churches of Cholsey and Wargrave in Berkshire in exchange for twelve librates of land in Budleigh, Devon; Abbot Roger asked the viceroy to transfer these lands to his abbey as soon as possible.[28] King Henry had already announced this exchange in Normandy in 1123.[29]

REMARKS: In this charter Roger acts both as viceroy and as diocesan bishop. Normally, such a transaction would be a simple episcopal matter, but the king's personal interest in his own foundation at Reading, his repeated instructions from abroad, and Bishop Roger's other writs about this monastery, indicate the viceregal implications of his actions. Brian Kemp of the University of Reading is preparing a critical edition of the various Reading cartularies.[30]

28. British Museum Manuscripts, Egerton 3031, fo. 47; Harley 1708, fo. 195. The Egerton version of the abbot's charter is addressed: *Reverendo domino et patri R[ogero] Saresb[eriensis] episcopo gratia dei strenuo regni Anglie provisori.* The Harley version reads: *Reverendo patri et domino R[ogero] Sar[esberiensis] episcopo gratia dei strenuo regni Anglie provisori.*

29. *Regesta,* 2, no. 1418.

30. Some of his work has already appeared in a University of Reading Ph.D. thesis (1966), "The Foundation of Reading Abbey and the Growth of its Possessions and Privileges in England in the Twelfth Century." This charter is no. 5 in his Apepndix XI. Kemp has also written a short history of the abbey, *Reading Abbey: An Introduction to the History of the Abbey,* and of one of its dependent churches, "The Mother Church of Thatcham."

9

Bishop Roger, Procurator of England, issues a general confirmation of Reading abbey's churches and privileges.

Rogerius episcopus Saresb[eriensis] [a] sub domino nostro rege Henrico regni Anglie procurator, Archiepiscopis, Episcopis, Abbatibus, Comitibus, Vicecomitibus, et omnibus fidelibus et ministris regis, salutem. Sciatis quia rex et dominus noster H[enricus] hanc libertatem abbatie [b] Redingensi [c] dedit et decreto firmavit ut nulla persona parva vel magna per debitum seu per consuetudinem, aut per violentiam, aliquid ab hominibus et terris, et possessione Redingensis monasterii exigat, non equitationem, sive expeditionem non pontium vel castrorum edificationem, non vehicula, non summagia, non vectigalia, non navigia, non opera, non tributa, non xenia, sed habeant abbas et monachi Redingenses in tota possessione sua, in Redingia scilicet et Cealseia,[d] et Leoministria, et Thacheham,[e] et in his que habent [f] precedentium maneriorum appendiciis, omnem iusticiam, et quicquid rex in eisdem habuit, de geldis, et redditibus, et servitiis, et consuetudinibus, de assaltu, de sanguinis effusione, et pacis infractione quantum ad regiam pertinet potestatem, de furtis et murdris, et hamsochna et de omnibus forisfactis. Sintque abbatis et monachorum eius, sicut rex dedit et teneri mandavit, de prefata possessione Reding[ensis], tam de hominibus suis quam et de alienis in ea forisfacientibus, vel ibi cum forisfacto interceptis, hundreda et placita omnia cum socca et sacca, et toll, et theam, et infangentheof, et hutfangentheof,[g] in omnibus locis, cum omnibus causis que sunt, et esse possunt. Quod si abbas et monachi, eorumve ministri, de predictis forisfactis iusticiam facere neglexerint; rex fieri compellat, ita ut in nullo prefatam libertatem seu redditus Redingensis ecclesie minuat. Veniantque ad hundreda de Redingia et de Leoministria homines circumiacentium maneriorum secundum consuetudinem precedentium temporum. Et sint monachi Reding[enses], et familia eorum, et res ipsorum absoluti per totam Angliam ab omni theloneo et alia qualibet consuetudine in terris et aquis et silvis, in viis, et semitis, in transitibus pontium et portuum maris. Deditque rex monetam et unum monetarium abbati et monachis apud Redingiam.[h] Volo itaque et precipio ut libere et quiete et honorifice sicut rex precipit per cartam suam, abbas et monachi Redingenses omnia sua[i] teneant. Apud Westm[onasterium]. Per breve Regis.

SOURCE: supposed original charter, *British Museum Manuscript, Additional Charter 19575; cartulary copies, British Museum Manuscripts, Egerton 3031, fo. 51v.; Harley 1708, fo. 189v; Cotton Vespasian E XXV, fos. 109v–110. printed, Doris M. Stenton, "Roger of Salisbury, *Regni Anglie Procurator*", EHR 39 (1924): 79–80; Charles Johnson, "Some Early Charters of Henry I," pp. 139–143, with a facsimile. Johnson italicized the words which were identical with those of the royal charter of 1125; abstract, Hurry, *Reading Abbey*, p. 157; *Regesta, 2*, no. 1471.

VARIATIONS: a. The cartularies read *Sar'*. Stenton read the original as *Saresburiensis;* b. Egerton 3031 used the word *ecclesie;* c. The cartularies spell *Reading* with an *a* throughout, *Radingensi;* d. Egerton 3031 spells this *Chelseia;* Harley and Vespasian manuscripts read *Chalseia;* e. The cartularies spell this *Tacheham;* f. Johnson reads *habeat;* g. Egerton 3031 reads *et infangenetheot et utfangeneth';* Vespasian E XXV reads *infangenetheoff et utfangenetheff;* h. Egerton 3031 reads *unum monetarium apud Radingiam abbati et monachis;* i. This word is badly damaged in the original charter; to me it looks like *sua*. Stenton and Johnson read the original as *iu* and guess *ra,* thus, *iura*. The cartularies clearly read *sua*.

DISCUSSED: Naomi D. Hurnard, "The Anglo-Norman Franchises," pp. 442–443. Kemp, "The Foundations of Reading," pp. 400–405. Chapter 2.

DATE: c. 1124, at Westminster

REMARKS: It appears that this original charter and its cartulary copies are adaptations (forgeries) of a yet earlier charter. Johnson, Hurnard, and Kemp have analyzed this charter and found it wanting in form and style.[31] Its wording is clumsy and obscure, and it does mix grants of gelds, rents, and criminal jurisdictions. The fact that *utfangenetheof* is included is

31. These scholars also analyzed the related royal foundation charters of Henry I, abstracts of which are in *Regesta, 2*, nos. 1427, 1474.

unusual for this period, but not impossible. Miss Hurnard felt Roger's charter was "probably concocted simply to support the abbot's claim to sit with the itinerant justices and to take the profits of justice from his liberty;" this seems too severe a judgment. Better is the position of Johnson and Kemp that, while the document as it now stands may have been a later forgery, it was in all likelihood based on an actual writ and is basically correct in substance, if defective in form. Kemp further argues that "the unusual and primitive description of the justiciar as *'sub domino nostro rege Henrico regni Anglie procurator'* is itself an indication that this spurious text was probably based on a genuine original. Moreover, he points out that a papal bull of Honorius II dated April 13, 1125, contained many of these provisions, which an earlier bull of Calixtus II dated June 1123 lacked. There are several minor differences between the charter and the cartulary copies, of which the Egerton manuscript from the late twelfth century is the earliest. Either the scribes were rather careless or they, or the Egerton copyist alone, had seen the true original. Roger's confirmation refers to a moneyer at Reading and therefore is presumably earlier than the following charter (10), which mentions a coiner of the abbey at London. Three of Roger's charters concerning Reading lack witnesses, but they were issued after the king's own instructions. These charters demonstrate Roger's responsibilities both as viceroy representing the absent king and as local diocesan bishop governing his episcopal affairs.

10

Bishop Roger, Procurator of England, grants Reading abbey a London minter named Edgar.

R[ogerus] Sar[esberiensis] episcopus et regni Angliae procurator sub domino nostro rege H[e]nr[ico] A[lberico] vicecomiti et omnibus ministris regis tam presentibus quam futuris de London[ia], et de tota Angl[ia], salutem. Sciatis quod ex precepto domini nostri regis H[e]nr[ici] donavimus Hugoni abbati et monachis Rading[ensis] unum monetarium in London[ia], ubi et monetam faciat et cambium teneat, et omnia sicut ceteri monetarii regis, Edgaru[m] scilicet, qui concedente rege ita libere et quietus et absolutus cum domo et familia sua ab omni placito et omnibus causis et consuetudinibus manebit in manu abbatis et monachorum Rading[enses] ac si maneret Radingis. Quicunque etiam post Edgaru[m] vel loco ejus in moneta positus apud London[iam] per manum abbatis et monarchorum Rading[enses] fuerit, eodem modo liber et quietus et absolutus cum domo et familia sua apud Lond[oniam] manebit in manu abbatis et monachorum Rading[enses] ac si maneret Radi[n]g[ia]. Ipse vero Edgar[us] et quicunque post eum monetraius fuerit, solvet pro moneta abbati et monachis Radi[n]g[enses] omnes illas causas et consuetudines quas ceteri monetarii Lond[oniae] solvunt domino regi et cambiet in terra abbatis Rading[enses] ᵃ sicut ei abbas concesserit tam Edgar[us] quam ille qui post eum vel pro eo abbas seu monachi Rading[enses] fecerint monetarium. Quod eis concessum est facere in perpetuum.

SOURCE: cartulary copies, British Museum Manuscripts, *Harley 1708, fo. 113; Cotton Vespasian E XXV, fos. 60–60v; printed, Dugdale *Monasticon Anglicanum,* 4:41. Dugdale's text was reprinted by W. J. Andrew, *A Numismatic History of the Reign of Henry I (1100–1135),* pp. 371–376; abstract, *Regesta,* 2, no. 1472.

VARIATIONS: a. The Vespasian manuscript reads *abbatis et monachorum Rading [enses].*

DISCUSSED: Kemp, "The Foundations of Reading Abbey," Appendix, IX. Chapter 2.

DATE: c. 1125–1128. The *Regesta* editors suggested a date from about 1123 to 1126, but I think it must be slightly later. In the previous charter (9) the king gave the abbey a coiner at Reading sometime near 1124. For some reason, the minter's residence was later changed to London. It also seems likely that Bishop Roger's charter was issued after the great mutilation of moneyers at Winchester in the winter of 1124–1125.

REMARKS: Coins bearing Edgar's name are known to have been struck in London late in Henry's reign.[32] This charter addressed to the great sheriff, Aubrey de Vere, again illustrates the mingling of Bishop Roger's viceregal and episcopal duties.

32. Brooke, *English Coins,* p. *clxxix.*

11

Bishop Roger, acting as justiciar, orders Richard Fitz Baldwin to acquit the Plympton canons of the gelds of Ralph
Basset.

Rogerus episcopus Sarum Ricardo filio Bald[wino], salutem.
Precipio tibi quod in pace esse dimittas terram canonicorum
de Plimton, de quicquid inde requiris de geldis et assisis
Rad[ulfi] Basset, et omnibus aliis rebus, quia ipsa est quieta [a]
ex toto. Ita quod neque est in compoto hidarum cartae
R[egis] G[uillelmi] neque inde quicquam requiro. Apud
Winton[iam].

Source: cartulary transcript, *Bodleian Manuscript 3860 (James
23), fo. 152; printed, *Regesta*, 2, no. *CXCII;* abstract, *Regesta*,
2, no. 1488
Variations: a. The Regesta editors printed it as *quieta est.*
Discussed: Chapter 2.
Date: c. 1127, at Winchester. King Henry's writ, which confirmed and referred to Roger's writ, seems to have been issued
in 1127, before August when he went abroad.[33] Plympton
priory was founded in 1121; Ralph Basset died in 1127 or 1129;
and Richard Fitz Baldwin seems to have been replaced as
sheriff of Devon and Cornwall in 1128. The wide dates are,
thus, 1121–August 1127, but Roger's writ was probably issued
shortly before Henry's. In 1127 Roger seems to have been at
Winchester in January[34] and at Whitsuntide May 22.[35] He
may also have been there for the regular Easter exchequer
audit, a natural time for a writ like this to have been dictated.
Remarks: This writ is especially notable as evidence for the
continuous use of Domesday Book.

12

Bishop Roger, as justiciar, commands Restoldus the sheriff
and Turchil the reeve of Oxford to allow the canons of

33. *Regesta*, 2, no. 1515. 34. *Ibid.*, no. 1475.
35. *Ibid.*, nos. 1485–1489.

Saint Frideswide's priory to have their possessions in Headington, Oxfordshire.

Rogerus episcopus Sar[esberiensis] Restoldo vicecomiti et
Turchillo preposito Oxon[iae], salutem. Precipio vobis quod
permittatis habere canonicos Sancte Frid[eswidae] decimam
regis de manerio suo de Hedindona et de appendiciis eius
in omnibus rebus et hundredum suum et curiam bene et
iuste et honorifice sicut episcopus Sar[esberiensis] melius
habuit dum res canonicorum erant in dominio suo.

SOURCE: cartulary copy, *Christ Church Manuscript, A, fo. 75;
    printed, *St. Frideswide Cartulary*, 2:22, no. 709 (dated c. 1122).
DISCUSSED: Chapter 4.
DATE: c. 1122–1129. Restoldus, who was mentioned in the pipe
    roll of 1130, was apparently replaced as sheriff in 1129.[36]
REMARKS: Although Roger was acting as justiciar in this in-
    stance, he was also the principal patron of the Saint Frides-
    wide's canons.

13

Bishop Roger, acting as justiciar, orders Robert Fitz Walter
to see that the monks of Bury Saint Edmund's receive their
wardpenny.

R[ogerus] episcopus Sar[esberiensis] R[oberto] filio Walteri, salutem. Precipio quod abbas et monachi de Sancto
Aedmundo ita bene et honorifice habeant warpeni de viii
hundredis et dimidio sicut melius habuerunt tempore patris
et fratris mei et meo tempore. Et si quid inde retentum est
postquam novissime mare transivi reddatur cito et iuste et
nominatim de Glemesford et Herdest et de Nedding. Per
breve regis. Apud Wiltun.

SOURCE: cartulary copy, *Cambridge University Manuscript, Mn
    IV, 19, fo. 106; printed, Douglas, *Bury Documents*, p. 75, no.
    47. abstract, *Regesta*, 2, no. 1614.
DISCUSSED: West, *Justiciarship in England*, p. 19. Chapter 2.

    36. *Ibid.*, no. 1470.

DATE: c. 1129, at Wilton. Robert Fitz Walter was sheriff of Norfolk and Suffolk from perhaps as early as 1111 [37] until Michaelmas 1129.[38] The possible dates are thus between 1111 and 1129. Since two royal writs from about 1123 to 1129, addressed from Rouen to Robert and to Robert and Bishop Everard of Norwich,[39] and another one sent to Robert and Bishop Everard from Winchester in 1129 [40] all mention the wardpenny in terms which suggest that it was being violated, one may assume that Bury's rights were being contested in that period. Bishop Roger's charter probably falls into the same period. Abbot Anselm of Bury Saint Edmund's was in Normandy in 1125 [41] and may have brought the matter to King Henry's attention. If the phrase, "since I last crossed the sea," does refer to Bishop Roger, it is unlikely that his charter was issued at Wilton before September 1129. A royal charter to much the same effect was sent from Winchester before September 29, 1129, to Sheriff Robert.[42] Within the following year a similar writ was sent to Robert's successors, Richard Basset and Aubrey de Vere.[43] It must be noted, however, that exact dating of Roger's charter is not possible, especially because monks of Saint Edmund's frequently obtained charters guaranteeing their privileges in these lands.[44]

REMARKS: Admittedly, the text is odd, and it reads like a royal rather than a viceregal writ. It is entirely conceivable that the copyist may have slipped and written Roger's name when he meant to write King Henry's. In fact, in another, later fourteenth-century cartulary there is an identical text issued by the king and sent to Bishop Roger and Sheriff Robert Fitz Walter.[45] The phrase *tempore patris et fratris mei et meo tempore* certainly has little meaning in Roger's writ. The formula *post-*

37. *Ibid.,* no. 987.   38. *Ibid.,* no. 1608; *Pipe Roll,* p. 90.

39. *Regesta,* 2, nos. 1597–1598; Douglas, *Bury Documents,* pp. 77, 71.

40. *Regesta,* 2, no. 1605; Douglas, *Bury Documents,* p. 76.

41. *Regesta,* 2, nos. 1426–1427.

42. *Ibid.,* no. 1605 (already cited above in Note 40).

43. *Ibid.,* no. 1642.

44. *Ibid.,* nos. 656, 664, 777, 1079, 1227, 1812–1813; only no. 1227 mentioned the wardpenny, however.

45. British Museum Manuscript, Harley 743, fo. 148; printed by Douglas, *Bury Documents,* p. 75. The Cambridge manuscript containing Roger's writ was written in the late twelfth century with additions to the fourteenth century.

quam novissime mare transivi is also a royal usage. The *Regesta* editors translated it as "since the king's last crossing"; nevertheless, it could refer to Roger, himself, since he is thought to have been in Normandy sometime in the first six months of 1129.[46] It is also unusual for royal and viceregal writs to be issued from the same place. On the other hand, the phrase *per breve regis* is also rather unusual in a royal writ (but see Charter 14). Professor Douglas, who printed both versions, suggested that the royal writ from the Harley manuscript was a composite of an original *breve de ultra mare* writ (not yet found) and Bishop Roger's above justiciary writ, *per breve regis*. This may well be so, but, for my part, Roger's writ itself seems either to have been incorrectly copied or to have been inflated from an earlier true original. Glemsford, Hartest, and Nedging are all in Suffolk.

14

Bishop Roger, acting as justiciar, grants the abbot of Saint Augustine's Canterbury, warren in his lands in Stodmarsh and Littlebourne, Kent.

R[ogerus] [a] episcopus Sar[esberiensis] [b] archiepiscopo et vicecomiti et hominibus baronibus de Chent,[c] Francis et Anglicis,[d] salutem. Concedo quod abbas de Sancto Augustino habeat warennam in terra sua de Stotmersa et de Litelburna et in omnibus terris eis pertinentibus in bosco et plano [e] et nullus in ea fuget sine licentia sua super x libros forisfactem.[f] Apud Westm[onasterium]. Per breve regis.

SOURCE: cartulary copies, *British Museum Manuscript, Cotton Julius D II, fo. 89v.; Public Record Office Manuscript, E 164, 27, fo. 152 [47] translation, Richardson and Sayles, *Governance of Medieval England*, p. 163.

VARIATIONS: a. The P.R.O. manuscript reads *Radulfus,* but there was no Bishop Ralph of Salisbury in this period; b. The P.R.O. manuscript reads *Saresbir';* c. The P.R.O. manuscript reads

46. *Regesta,* 2, nos. 1575–1576.

47. A more complete reference would be Public Record Office Manuscript Exch. K. R. Misc. (E, 164), i, 27, fo. 152. *Regesta,* 2, no. 1814, incorrectly listed this as E, 163.

Kent; d. The P.R.O. manuscript reads *Anglis;* e. The P.R.O. manuscript makes two sentences: *plano. Et nullus.* . . . ; f. The P.R.O. manuscript reads *forisfacture.*

Discussed: Chapter 2.

Date: 1101–1133, at Westminster.

Remarks: Another version of this text contains the same wording, except that it was issued by King Henry.[48] In the royal version the warranty subscription *per breve regis* is again noteworthy (see Charter 13); the *Regesta* editors suggest that this royal writ was actually "issued by the justiciar in the king's name and under his own testimony." They also suggest it therefore was probably after the death of Queen Matilda in 1118.

15

Bishop Roger, acting as justiciar, orders William Fitz Robert to see that the monks of Saint Pancras of Lewes hold their land on the same conditions as the Count of Eu gave it to them.

Rogerus [a] episcopus Sar[esberiensis] Willelmo filio Roberti, salutem. Precipio tibi quod ita bene et in pace et libere facias habere et tenere monachis de sancto Pancratio terram suam et heredes suos in Bure'sarehea sicut comes de Augo eam eis dedit et concessit in elemosina et sicut carta eorum testatur quam inde habent et sicut etiam tenuerunt die qua rex mare novissime transivit. Et habeant iuste pacem regis firmam et omnes consuetudines suas quas iuste habere debent donec rex in Anglia veniat ne interim requiratur ab eis aliquid iniuste vel iniuria aliquid fiat super statutum Regis ne super hoc inde clamorem audiam. Apud Westm[onasterium]. Et quod inde captum est reddat.

Source: cartulary copy, *British Museum Manuscript, Cotton Vespasian F XV, fos. 85v–86; printed, Douglas, *Bury Doc-

48. *Regesta,* 2, no. 1814, from British Museum Manuscript, Cotton Claudius D X, fo. 59v. All three cartularies of Saint Augustine's, Canterbury, Cotton Julius D II, Cotton Claudius D X, and Public Record Office E, 164, are thirteenth-fourteenth century, but the folios in Julius D II seem slightly earlier, mid-thirteenth century.

uments, p. *xxxv.* translated, Salzman, *Lewes Cartulary* 1:154.

VARIATIONS: a. Douglas printed *Rogerius.*

DISCUSSED: Chapter 2.

DATE: 1105-1135, at Westminster. The king's second trip was made to Normandy in 1105.

REMARKS: Roger's writ is a particularly interesting example of the procedure followed by the justiciar. Complaint was made to him in the absence of the king, overseas; he checked the relevant charters, ordered the monks' goods returned, and postponed final judgment until the king returned to the country. Buscot, Berkshire, is apparently the place referred to in this writ.[49]

16

Bishop Roger, acting as justiciar, orders William de Albini Brito to see that the monks of Spalding hold their land in Ludford, Lincolnshire, with all its customary privileges.

R[ogerus] [a] episcopus Sal[esberiensis] [b] W[illelmo] de Alb[ini],[c] Brit[o],[d] salutem. Precipio quod facias priorem et monachos beate Marie et beati Nicholai de Spald[inge] tenere terram suam de Ludeford et omnes homines et res suas ita bene et in pace et juste et honorifice sicut unquam melius tenuerunt tempore W[illelmo] fratris regis et suo postea. Et super hoc prohibeo ne aliquis requirat aliquam consuetudinem ab eis quam tempore fratris regis non fecissent, et quam juste facere non debeant. Testibus. . . .

SOURCE: cartulary copy, *British Museum Manuscript, Harley 742, fo. 260; printed, *Regesta,* 2 no. *CCCXXII;* abstract, *Regesta,* 2, no. 1977.

VARIATIONS: The scribe seems to have been rather careless in his transcription of this text. I have reconstructed it to show how I think it must have appeared in the original writ. The cartulary, however, actually reads: a. *Robertus.* b. *Salobriensis.* c. *Alba.* d. *Britanno.*

49. A William Fitz Robert witnessed a royal writ in Normandy in 1131; *Regesta,* 2, no. 1693.

DISCUSSED: Chapter 2.

DATE: 1101–1135.

REMARKS: There is a related royal writ ordering William to see that the Spalding monks hold their land peacefully.[50]

17

Bishop Roger, acting as justiciar, orders Robert Revel to ensure the canons of Holy Trinity, Oxford, the enjoyment of the gifts of Earl Robert of Leicester.

Rogerus episcopus Sar[esberiensis] Roberto Revel et ministris suis, salutem. Precipio quod ecclesia Sancte Trinitatis Oxon[ia] et priori et canonicis teneant et habeant terras et domos et homines quas Robertus comes Legr[ecestria] eis in elemosinis [a] dedit, ita bene et in pace et honorifice cum omnibus illis consuetudinibus et quietantionibus [b] et libertatibus, cum quibus comes melius et liberius tenuit, dum res ille fuerunt in manu sua, et sicut melius erant tempore patris suis, et sicut rex percipit per brevia sua. Apud Brechelea.

SOURCE: cartulary copy, *Christ Church Manuscript, A, fo. 270; printed, *St. Frideswide Cartulary,* 2:323, no. 1120.

VARIATIONS: a. The printed cartulary reads *elemosinam;* b. The printed cartulary reads *quietacionibus.*

DISCUSSED: Chapter 4.

DATE: 1118–1133, at Brackley, Northamptonshire. Robert was earl of Leicester, 1118–1168; Robert Revel seems unknown. King Henry was in England last in 1133. Spencer Wigram, editor of the printed cartulary, suggested a date around 1130.

REMARKS: This writ was copied in a cartulary of Saint Frideswide's priory, Oxford, because Holy Trinity was a dependent chapel of that house. The royal writ Roger referred to may well have been the one immediately preceding his in the cartulary.[51] It is almost identical to his own except that the king sent it to Robert de Oilli from Woodstock, where it was witnessed by Geoffrey Fitz Payn.

50. *Ibid.,* no. 1976; also see no. 1975.
51. This writ was omitted from *Regesta,* 2.

18

Bishop Roger, acting as justiciar, orders the royal foresters to allow the archbishop of York and his men easements in the forests of the archbishopric.

R[ogerus] episcopus Sar[esberiensis] forestariis regis de Eboraciscira, salutem. Dimittite habere Thuristino archiepiscopo Eboracensi et hominibus suis omnia aisiamenta sua et [a] necessaria sua in nemoribus archiepiscopatus que rex posuit in forestam suam. Apud Westmonasterium. Per breve regis.

SOURCE: cartulary copies, *British Museum Manuscript, Cotton Claudius B III, fo. 95; York Cathedral Manuscript, Magnum Registrum Album, III, fo. 14; printed, William Farrar and Charles T. Clay, eds. *Early Yorkshire Charters,* 1:33–34, no. 19; abstract, *Regesta,* 2, no. 1989.

VARIATIONS: a. The York manuscript omitted *et.*

DISCUSSED: Chapter 2.

DATE: 1114–1135, at Westminister. Thurstan became archbishop in 1114. This reads like a writ issued under Henry, rather than Stephen.

REMARKS: The *Regesta* editors suggested that this was a writ of Roger in the absence of king *ultra mare.* The subscription *per breve regis* certainly suggests this. If Henry sent a related command from Normandy, it has not survived.[52]

19

Bishop Roger informs Thurstan, the abbot of Sherborne, that he has given many gifts to Sherborne abbey and to Nicholas, its sacrist, including Saint Swithun's fair (July 13–17) and the church of Saint Mary Magdalene.

Rogerius dei gratia Salesb[eriensis] episcopus Turstino abbati et omnibus tenentibus suis de Dorseta, salutem. Notum

52. *Regesta,* 2, no. 1328 also deals with Yorkshire easements, but Roger is not mentioned.

sit vobis presentibus et qui post vos sunt futuri me dedisse
et concessisse Nicolao sacriste de Scireb[urna] et eius successoribus ad suum ministerium et ad servitium ipsius ecclesiae feriam Sancti Swithuni de ipsa Scireb[urna] et
omnes eius exitus ita liberae et quietae tenendam et haben-
dam sicut eam melius et honorabilius dum in manu mea
esset ⁿ illam tenueram. Quae feria, sicut eam michi rex Henricus concesserat, duos dies ante festivitatem incipiat et duos
alios dies post festivitatem permaneat, ita scilicet ut per
totam villam per hos quinque dies quicquid rectitudinis ex
mercatu provenerit ecclesiae ipsius usibus conferatur. Concessi etiam ei ecclesiam Sanctae Mariae Magdelenae quae in
insula est ubi castellum situm esse conspicitur et omnes
eius reditus decimas scilicet, omnium quae ibi nascuntur
videlicet, de blado et vino et de omnibus quae decimari
solent, decimas etiam piscationis de vivariis tam de anguillis
quam de aliis piscibus. Preterea quidem contra singulas festi-
vitates beatae Mariae, quae quater per annum a fidelibus
celebrantur, per omnes vivarios ubicumque voluerunt unum
diem integrum et dimidium eiusdem ecclesiae monachis
piscandi licentiam contuli, ita scilicet ut post nonam die
quae vigiliam festivitatis praecidit, retia et alia ad piscandum
ingenia praeparent et aquis iniciant, et in crastino idest in
die vigiliae tota die et toto conamine ipsam piscationem
exerceant. Hoc etiam eis me recolo concessisse cum aliquam
personam episcopi scilicet aut abbatis hospitandi gratia ad
eos venire contigerit, in uno quolibet vivario cum uno videlicet reti eis ad piscandum duo tractus solummodo conce-
datur. De bestiis etiam quae capiuntur in parco ad usus
eorum hospitum armum eius dextrum concessi et ad operi-
endos eorum libros decimum corium. Et ad usus infir-
morum iiiiᵒʳ vaccarum et iiiiᵒʳ vitulorum pastum in parco.
Sed et molendinum quod iuxta ecclesiam Sancti Andreae et
iuxta vivarium occidentale situm esse dinoscitur, pro duobus
molendinis quae causa vivariorum aquis prefocata monachi
perdidisse noscuntur, eis me concessisse sciatis. Et ut haec
omnia eis et eorum successoribus libere et quietae perma-
neant pontificali auctoritate et anathematis sententia haec
studui roborare. Spatium quoque terrae et omnem eius am-
bitum ubi domus et mansio episcoporum antiquitus fuisse
noscuntur, cum parvo pomerio et quodam molendino quod
iuxta cimiterium residet, pro platea quam ad communes

transeuntium usus, et ad iter publicum iter agentibus in
australi parte, excidi ex eorum cimiterio feceram, eis me
dedisse et concessisse noveritis. Quod ideo me fecisse sciatis,
ut cimiterium quod in australi parte per me aliquantulum
minoratur in parte occidentis per me duppliciter augeatur.
Hanc autem meam donationem in die dedicationis pre-
dictae ecclesiae beatae Mariae Magdalenae coram omnibus
qui affuerant demonstravi et coram idoneis testibus postea
privilegii munimine confirmavi quorum nomina hic subtus
notantur. De clericis quidem hi testes extiterant: Azo decanus Salesb[eriensis]; Rog[erius], Arnaldus, Athelelmus,
archidiaconi; Radulf[us], Teodbaldus, Rog[erius], capellani
episcopi. De baronibus: Rodb[er]t[us] de Arundel; Rod-
b[er]t[us] de Nincol; Will[el]m[us] filius Walt[er]i; Ricardus de Monte Acuto; Radulfus Luvel. De militibus:
Osmundus dapifer; Nicolaus filius Hardingi; Arnaldus pincerna; Ricardus de Divisis; Jordanus Delestre; Ricard Foliot; Rog[erius] Foliot; et plures alii. Quisquis igitur hanc
meam donationem pro animae remedio in aliquo augere
voluerit, hic et in futuro donis ei bona omnia augeat. Qui
autem infringendo fraudulenter de aliquid auferre tempta-
verit in presenti saeculo pessimam celeriter pestem incurrat
et in futuro nisi ad satisfactionem venerit electorum con-
sortium et vitam eternam deus ei omnipotens auferat. Fiat.
Fiat. Amen.[b]

SOURCE: cartulary copy, *British Museum Manuscript, Additional
    Manuscript 46487, fos. 15–16; printed, Hearne, *Collections*
    3:449; Fowler, *Medieval Sherborne,* p. 135. Both of these ver-
    sions are incomplete; abstract, *Regesta*, 2, no. 1324.
VARIATIONS: a. Hearne and Fowler read *esset* as *et etiam;* b.
    Fowler's text is complete except that the postscript, *Quisquis
    igitur. . . . Amen,* is omitted.
DISCUSSED: Chapter 3.
DATE: c. 1130–1138. Sherborne became an abbey in 1122. The
    Regesta editors suggested that this charter was issued about
    then, but I cannot agree, for the dating really depends upon
    the witnesses, particularly Dean Azo. As late as September
    1129 he was still an archdeacon.[53] A terminal date may be

53. A dispute concerning Archdeacon Azo's brother, canon Roger
of Ramsbury, and his prebend of Heytesbury was transferred to
Archdeacon Adelelm (Athelelm) for settlement. Bishop Ranulf

found in 1138, the year Ralph Luvel rebelled against King
Stephen.[54] It would be unlikely for him to be publicly associated with Bishop Roger after that.

REMARKS: A keen interest in building and fishing animates this
generous gift. Osmund the dapifer, Arnald the pincerna, and
Richard Foliot were all with Bishop Roger in Kidwelly in
1114.[55] Harding may be Harding of Wilton; [56] he may also
be the Harding mentioned in Charter 5.

20

Bishop Roger writes to his archdeacons, confirming which
churches the abbey of Saint Wandrille controls in his
diocese.

R[ogerus] episcopus Sar[esberiensis] A[delelmo] archidiacono de Dorsete, et Rogero et Ern[aldo] archidiaconis de
Wiltesir[a], salutem. Precipio quod abbas de Sancto Wan-
drigesilo[a] teneat ita bene et honorifice et libere omnes ecclesias quae[b] in archidiaconatu vestro sunt cum decimis et
omnibus consuetudinibus suis[c] sicut unquam eas melius
habere et liberius tenere solebat. Et[d] nominatim ecclesiam
de Rusteshale cum decima sua, et ecclesiam de Bridetun[e]
cum decima sua, et ecclesiam de Brideport[f] cum decima
sua, et ecclesiam de Witchirche[g] cum capellis et decimis sibi
pertinentibus, et ecclesiam de Sorestane[h] cum tota decima
ville,[i] et ecclesiam de Wivelesford[j] cum decima et omnibus
consuetudinibus suis. Et si quis eis inde injuriam fecerit, etc.

SOURCE: original charter, *British Museum Manuscript, Additional Charter 8071, item 7. This is actually an inspeximus
charter of about 1200 from the abbot of Saint Wandrille, containing Roger's command and several other confirmations;
cartulary copy, Salisbury Cathedral Manuscript, Register of

Flambard, the former holder of Heytesbury, died in September 1128
and Salisbury cathedral regulations required that vacant prebends
revert to the common fund of all the canons for one year after the
last occupant's death. See *Register of St. Osmund*, 1:351, and 349;
and *Regesta*, 2, no. 753.

54. *Gesta Stephani*, p. 44; Orderic Vitalis, 4:110–111.
55. See Charter 4.   56. *Regesta*, 2, no. 622.

Saint Osmund, fo. 57; printed, *Register of St. Osmund* 1:232; Joseph Hunter, *Ecclesiastical Documents,* pp. 58–59.

VARIATIONS: a. The cartulary and the printed edition read *Wandragesilo;* b. The cartulary copy reads *que.* c. *Suis* was omitted in the cartulary and the printed edition; d. The cartulary reads one sentence: *solebat, et nominatim;* e. The cartulary and the printed edition read *Brideton;* Hunter's version reads *Bridetuna.* f. The cartulary reads *Bridiport;* g. The printed cartulary copy reads *Witcherche;* h. The printed cartulary copy reads *Sorestan;* i. The printed cartulary copy reads *villae;* j. The printed cartulary copy reads *Wivelford.*

DISCUSSED: Chapter 3.

DATE: c. 1130–1139. The dating of Roger's charter depends upon the dating of the archdeacons Roger and Ernald of Wiltshire and A. (probably Adelelm) of Dorset. Roger seems to have become an archdeacon only after 1129/1130; see Note 53.

REMARKS: The other charters in the abbot's letter included confirmations from King William I, Bishop Jocelin, Pope Innocent II, and Pope Eugenius III. Burton Bradstock, Bridport, and Whitchurch Canonicorum are in Dorset; Rushall, Sherston, and Wilsford are in Wiltshire.

21

Bishop Roger grants the tithes of Stuminister, Dorset, to the congregation of Saint Giles of Pont Audemer, Normandy.

R[ogerus] dei permissione Sar[esberiensis] ecclesie minister humilis Congregationi Sancti Egidii de Ponteaud[omare] que est in Christo, salutem et dei benedictionem. Attendentes domus Sancti Egidii de Ponteaud[omare] [a] tenues et modicis [b] esse facultates et nichilominus effusam in omnes transseuntes etiam super vires eiusdem domus caritatem. Solo caritatis intuitu et ut specialius de cetero vestris commendemur orationibus, dedimus vobis fratribus et sororibus apud Sanctum Egidium de Ponteaudom[are] [c] deo serventibus omnes maiores decimas ecclesie de Esturministre,[d] et in usus vestros auctoritate episcopali confirmavimus. Minori-

bus dumtaxat decimis de Esturministre^e ad sustentationem
vicarii qui pro tempore in ecclesia de Est[ur]ministre per-
sonaliter deserviet, in ordine sacerdotali reservatis. Rogamus
ergo vos attentius, quantinus tanto devotius pro nobis et pro
Sar[esberiensis] ecclesia deum sedulo interpellatis, quanto
liberalius et sincerius ad nullius instantiam sed solum deum
habendo per occulis vobis istud contulimus beneficium.
Valete.

SOURCE: cartulary copies, *Public Library of Rouen Manuscript,
Y 200, fos. 34, 48v. The same scribe copied this charter twice
in the same cartulary. I have used fo. 34 and listed variations
from fo. 48v; printed abstract, John Horace Round, *Calendar
of Documents Preserved in France* p. 83, no. 240.

VARIATIONS: a. Fo. 48 reads *Ponteaudom[are]*; b. Fo. 48 reads
modicas; c. Fo. 48 reads *Ponteaud[omare]*; d. Fo. 48 reads
Est[ur]menist[re]; e. Fo. 48 reads *Est[ur]menistre*

DISCUSSED: Chapter 3.

DATE: c. 1129–1139.

REMARKS: Saint Giles leprosarium was founded by Count Waleran of Meulan between 1129 and 1135; and this text suggests
that Bishop Roger was a visitor there. The date for a monastic
foundation is never exact, however, as the establishment proceedings usually took several years. Bishop Roger may have
been in Normandy about 1129,[57] and there is a very remote
possibility that he may also have been there about 1135.[58] The
form used here, "Roger, by divine permission humble minister
of the church of Salisbury," is not found in Roger's other
charters,[59] but this charter must be his, since other documents
in the Saint Giles cartulary indicate that this church was given
to Pont Audemer by the bishop.[60]

57. *Ibid.,* nos. 1575–1576, but see Chapter 5, Note 11.
58. *Ibid.,* no. 1915, prints a royal charter issued at Falaise regarding some properties of Ramsey Abbey. One version, *Ramsey Chronicle,* p. 284, lists the bishop of Salisbury as the second witness, but
the *Ramsey Cartulary,* 1:250, lists the bishop of Carlisle in this spot
and this seems more likely as Roger normally remained in England
while Henry was abroad.
59. Later bishops of Salisbury like Richard Poore regularly used
this formula, *e.g., Register of St. Osmund,* 1:382.
60. Round, *Feudal Documents,* nos. 243–246.

22

Bishop Roger forbids anyone to conduct a school in the town of Reading without the permission of the abbot and monks of Reading.

Rogerius [a] episcopus Sar[esberiensis] [b] archidiacono [c] de Berkesire [d] et omnibus decanis, et toti clero de Berkesire,[d] salutem. Prohibeo quod nullus regat scolas apud Radingiam,[e] nisi consensu et bona voluntate abbatis et conventus. Teste A[delelmo] th[esaurario] [f] apud Wintoniam.

SOURCE: cartulary copies, British Museum Manuscripts, *Egerton 3031, fo. 51v.; Harley 1708, fo. 190v; printed, Leach, *Educational Charters and Documents*, p. 94, using Harley 1708; translations, Leach, p. 95; VCH, Berkshire 2:245.

VARIATIONS: a. Harley 1708 reads *R;* b. Leach reads *Sarisberiensis;* c. Leach reads *archidiaconis;* d. Harley 1708 reads *Berk';* Leach reads *Berks;* e. Harley 1708 reads *Rading';* f. Harley 1708 reads *A. Th'.*

DISCUSSED: Richardson and Sayles, *Governance of Medieval England,* p. 221, Van Caenegam, *Royal Writs,* p. 184, Chapters 2, 3, 5.

DATE: December 1135–June 1139. The dating of this charter depends upon the identification of the cryptic witness *A. th'.* The most plausible suggestion, originally made by Richardson and Sayles, is to read this as *Adelelm* (or *Athelelm*), the treasurer of King Stephen from 1135 to 1139.[61]

REMARKS: This writ seems to have been added to the Harley cartulary by a smaller hand after the main body of the text was completed. Prof. Van Caenegam has pointed out that the diplomatic of this document is that of a chancery writ. The matter at first appears a purely diocesan concern, but the interest of Kings Henry and Stephen in Reading made it more than that. Moreover, it is not surprising that Bishop Roger would regularly use convenient chancery clerks to draft his own episcopal writs. Furthermore, the treasurer Adelelm was

---

61. Other, less satisfactory, possibilities include: *Teste* Archbishop Thurstan (of York), or Archbishop Theobald (of Canterbury).

probably his own son. It is unfortunate that the archdeacon of Berkshire was not named, but the writ does constitute early evidence for the existence of rural deans. Archdeacons were the normal officials to receive instructions like this, but Roger's prohibition also enlarges our knowledge of the early days of a Reading school. It seems as if a preexisting secular school was about to be suppressed by the recently founded black monk abbey. A somewhat similar writ issued by Bishop Henry of Winchester forbade unauthorized teaching in London.[62]

23

Bishop Roger, acting as justiciar, orders Sheriff Hugh Fitz Eudo and Reginald, the constable of Lincoln, to allow the bishop of Lincoln lands worth twenty shillings, as provided in the king's charter.

R[ogerus] episcopus Sar[esberiensis] Hugoni filio Eudonis vicecomiti et Reginaldo constabulario de Linc[olnia] et omnibus burgensibus de Linc[olnia], salutem. Precipio vobis quod faciatis habere episcopo Linc[olniensis] xx^{ti} solidatas terre sicut rex precipit per cartam quam habet et ubi rex precipit. Et eas ei fideliter et plenarie faciatis habere per sacramentum xii legalium hominum de civitate de Lincol[nia] et xii legalium hominum de visneto Linc[olniensis] qui non sint de eadem terra. Teste Roberto de Ver apud Westmonasterium.

SOURCE: cartulary copy, Lincoln Cathedral Manuscript, Registrum Antiquissimum, A, 757, 759; printed, *Registrum Antiquissimum,* 7:85, no. 2050; translated, W. O. Massingberd, "Lincoln Cathedral Charters," no. 757.

DISCUSSED: Chapter 5.

DATE: c. 1135–1139. Kathleen Major suggested the date 1135–1139 and indicated that this writ added another name to the list of sheriffs of Lincolnshire.[63]

REMARKS: The witness by Robert de Ver, the royal constable,

---

62. Arthur Leach, *Educational Charters and Documents,* p. 91.

63. Hugh Fitz Eudo, who founded Kirkstead Abbey, was mentioned in two writs of Stephen; *Regesta,* 3, nos. 427, 822.

260   APPENDIX 2

and the financial considerations involved suggest that this was an exchequer writ.[64] There seems to be no surviving related royal writ.

24

Bishop Roger, acting as justiciar, orders the sheriff of Hereford to see that the monks of Gloucester receive the alms of the late Payn Fitz John.

[Rogerus][a] episcopus Sar[esberiensis] vicecomiti de Hereford[ia], salutem. Fac habere monachos Glouc[estrie] lx solidos de elemosina regis quos habere solebant tempore[b] regis H[enrici] et quos Pag[anus] filius Joh[annis] eis dare solebat. Et nisi feceris, Milo Glouc[estrie] faciat fieri. Teste Milon[e] Glouc[estrie] apud Westm[onasterium].

SOURCE: cartulary copy, *Balliol College Manuscript, Manuscript 271, fo. 101; printed, *Regesta*, 3, no. 397.
VARIATIONS: a. The space was left blank in the cartulary; b. The *Regesta* printed *quos solebant habere tempore.*
DISCUSSED: West, *Justiciarship in England,* p. 24. Chapter 5.
DATE: July 10, 1137–June 25, 1139, at Westminister. The death of Payn Fitz John and Bishop Roger's disgrace are terminal indicators.
REMARKS: This is one of the strongest and best examples of Roger's viceregal style of command. He is known to have been at Westminster in 1137[65] and at the legatine council held there in December 1138.

25

Bishop Roger, acting as justiciar, orders Sibyl, the widow of Payn Fitz John, to return the property she has taken from her daughter, Cecilia.

R[ogerus] episcopus Sar[esberiensis] Sibille que fuit uxor Pag[ani] filii Joh[ann]is, salutem. Precipio tibi ex parte re-

64. Richard Fitz Nigel, pp. 16–19.   65. *Regesta,* 3, no. 681.

gis et mea quod sine dilatione resaisas omnes illas terras
que fuerunt de accatis domini tui de blado et feno, et nominatim de vino de Maurdina et de omnibus aliis rebus sicut
fuerunt die qua rex illas concessit Rogero filio Milon[is]
Gloec[estrie] cum Cecilia filia tua primogenita. Et bene et
in pace sint sicut rex precipit per breve suum.[a] Teste
R[ogero] Canc[ellario] apud Malmesb[ur]ias.

SOURCE: original writ (seal missing), *Public Record Office
Manuscript, Duchy of Lancaster Charter 25 no. 2 (D.L. 25/2);
facsimile, *Regesta,* 4, plate 50; printed, Round, *Ancient Charters,* pp. 38–39, no. 22; *Regesta,* 3, no. 313; abstract, Duchy of
Lancaster Calendar, p. 73.

VARIATIONS: a. This last line was read by the *Regesta* as *tua
primogenita, et bene et in pace sicut rex precepit per breve
suum.*

DISCUSSED: Poole, *From Domesday Book to Magna Carta,* p.
136. Richardson, *Memoranda Roll I John,* p. *lxxxiii.* West,
Justiciarship in England, p. 24. Bishop, *Scriptores Regis,* p. 28.
Chapter 5.

DATE: 1138, at Malmesbury. Payn Fitz John died July 10, 1137.
Professor Richardson said that Roger's writ must have been
issued in 1137 while the king was in Normandy, because it
was highly improbable that the justiciar would issue writs in
his own name while the king was in the country. But it
does not strike me as at all improbable. Moreover, Roger the
chancellor was in Normandy with Stephen, who did not return to England until November 28, 1137. Shortly thereafter
at Marlborough (Round and the *Regesta* editors suggest December), Stephen confirmed all Cecilia's lands to her and
Roger Fitz Milo.[66] Roger's charter follows this and refers to
it. The *Regesta* plausibly suggests a time in June 1138, when
Stephen and his chancellor may have passed through Malmesbury on the way to the siege of Exeter.

REMARKS: This document has attracted great attention because
it is one of Roger's very few surviving original writs and because of the extremely authoritative tone in which he issued
his command, "On behalf of the king and myself I order

66. Round, *Ancient Charters,* p. 38, no. 21; *Regesta,* 3, no. 312.
For further information on Miles of Gloucester and his son, Roger,
see David Walker's articles, "Miles of Gloucester, Earl of Hereford,"
and "The Honors of the Earls of Hereford in the Twelfth Century."

you. . . ." Dr. West conjectured from this that Stephen became annoyed at Roger's prideful stance, but I know of no
firm evidence for such a claim. And the tone may not have
been so novel; between 1093 and 1095 Archbishop Anselm had
used a similar expression in a purely episcopal instruction sent to
Bishop Osmund, *"ex parte regis ipso iubente et nostra. . . ."* [67]
The scribe who wrote Bishop Roger's order also composed two
of Stephen's charters at Salisbury in December 1139.[68] It is
probably a moot point whether he was a Salisbury clerk working for the government or a chancery scribe knowledgeable
about Salisbury affairs. Bishop Roger's viceregal writ was witnessed by his son, Roger the chancellor, at the bishop's great
castle-monastery-town complex, Malmesbury. Maurdina is
Mardon, Hereford.

26

Bishop Roger restores to the cathedral chapter of Salisbury
all the prebends he has held in his hands.

Henrico, Dei gratia apostolice sedis legato,[a] et Theobaldo
Cantuar[iensis] archiepiscopo, et omnibus episcopis, totique
clero, et omnibus baronibus totius Angliae, Francis et Anglis, Rogerus episcopus Sar[esberiensis], salutem. Notum
facio dignitati vestre quoniam in libera potestate mea [b] reddidi ecclesie sancte Marie Sar[esberiensi],[c] omnes prebendas
quas in manu mea tenueram. Et illas pro certo dedi provida
consideratione et communi consilio honestissimarum [d] personarum, et totius capituli Sar[esberiensis],[e] clerics eidem
ecclesie honeste servientibus. Et prebendam de Caninges
dedi eternaliter ecclesie et canonicis sancte Marie ad communam ecclesie manutenendam et sustentandam, et ita
quod quaedam honesta persona serviens ecclesie pro eadem
prebenda, habeat inde [f] singulis annis xl [g] solidos. Quare
precor vos omnes communiter, quod pro Dei amore et vestro honore, et pro salute animarum vestrarum et meae illud
concedatis, et stabile et firmum esse percipiatis. Et preterea
dedi et concessi ecclesie de Lavintona,[h] totam decimam de

67. Anselm, *Opera Omnia,* letter 195. See also *Regesta,* 3, no. 530.
68. Bishop, *Scriptores Regis,* p. 28; *Regesta,* 3, nos. 787–788.

dominio meo de Liteltona,[i] et decimam omnium hominum ejusdem ville. Testibus, Capitulo Sar[esberiensis], et Osmundo dapifero, et Ricardo filio Willielmi, et Waltero de Maisy, apud Sarum.[j]

SOURCE: cartulary copies, Salisbury Cathedral Manuscripts, *Register of Saint Osmund, fos. 48–49; Liber Evidentiarium B, fo. 13; Liber Evidentiarium C, fo. 71; Registrum Rubrum, fo. 9, repeated on fo. 176 on paper in a much later hand, probably sixteenth century; printed, *Register of St. Osmund*, 1:216–217, where it was mistakenly dated 1140–1142.

VARIATIONS: a. All the other manuscripts read *sedis apostolice legato;* b. *Mea* is omitted in the printed edition; c. Registrum Rubrum reads *Sarr[esberiensi]*; d.This is *honestarum* in Liber B and Registrum Rubrum; e. *Sar[esberiensis]* is omitted in Registrum Rubrum; f. This is printed as *in;* g. This is printed as *quadraginta;* h. This is printed as *Laventona;* i. This is printed as *Littleton;* j. *Sarum* appears with this spelling in the original Register of Saint Osmund, but the place is omitted altogether in the three other manuscripts.

DISCUSSED: VCH, Wiltshire 4:189. Sheehan, *The Will in Medieval England*, pp. 243–244. Chapter 8.

DATE: September–December 1139, at Salisbury.

REMARKS: This is a deathbed bequest. Henry of Blois announced his legateship in September, and Roger died on December 11, 1139. He had only recently received land at Lavington from King Stephen.[69] Bishop Cannings and Lavintgon are in Wiltshire; Littleton is in Hampshire.

27

Bishop Roger restores to the abbey of Cirencester those churches in which he had a life interest.

Stephano regi Anglorum ac sedis apostolice legato totique clero et omnibus baronibus Francis et Anglis totius Anglie, Rogerus episcopus Sar[esberiensis], salutem. Notum vobis facio quoniam reddidi abbati et conventui Cirecestr[ie] omnes ecclesias et terras et tenuras quas de tenura ecclesie

69. *Ibid.*, no. 786.

Cirecestr[ie] in manu mea tenebam, et postea omnes alias
ecclesias et terras tenuras post mortem illorum qui modo
inde saisiti sunt, de tenura dico predicte ecclesie. Quare precor vos omnes quod illud firmum et stabile esse faciatis.
Testibus Atio[ne] decano Sar[esberiensis], et Will[elm]o
subdecano, et Osm[undo] dap[ifero] et Walt[er]o de Maisy.
Apud Sar[esberiensem]

SOURCE: transcript, Longleat Manuscript 38b, p. 11, no. 2; printed,
  Baddeley, *A History of Cirencester,* pp. 111–112; *Regesta,* 3,
  no. 189 note (a much better text).
DISCUSSED: Ross, *Cirencester Cartulary,* 1:21–25, 141. Chapter 8.
DATE: September–December 1139.
REMARKS: This is another deathbed bequest. About Christmas
  1139, Stephen confirmed this charter and listed parts of Roger's
  bequest, namely, the churches of Frome in Somerset, Avebury
  in Wiltshire, and Shrivenham, Cookham, and Bray, and ten
  hides in Aston Upthorpe, all in Berkshire.[70] Roger's substantial
  life interest in the tenures of Regenbald the priest had been
  noted in the foundation charter of 1133.[71]

28

Bishop Roger admits despoiling the monks of Worcester
of the church of Wolverhampton, Staffordshire.

R[ogerus] episcopus Sar[esberiensis] omnibus sancte ecclesie
fidelibus, salutem. Notum vobis facio quia per ambitionem
et secularem potentiam iniuste et sine iudicio spolavi monachos Wigorn[iensis] ecclesie de ecclesia sua Wlfruneh[am-
tona] quam S[anson] episcopus eis dedit favente illius do-
nationi rege H[enrico]. Recognosco autem quia propter
hoc grave peccatum et propter delicta mea, manus domini
tetigit me, et digne afflixit. Ego igitur ad misericordiam
piisime dei genitricis Marie confugiens, tanit sceleris veniam
peto, et fratres Wigorn[iensis] exoro quatinus respectu mi-

70. *Ibid.,* no. 189. Henry of Winchester, acting as papal legate
forbade Abbot Serlo to account for the possessions the abbey received after Roger's death unless Henry himself were present; Baddeley, *Cirencester,* p. 112, no. 13.
71. *Regesta,* 2, no. 1782; Ross, *Cirencester Cartulary,* p. 21. Innocent II had confirmed Roger's life interests in 1136, *Ibid.,* p. 141.

sericordie dei hoc grave dampnum quod illis intuli mihi remittant, et coram deo, in cuius iam iudicio consisto, absolvant.

SOURCE: cartulary copy, *Worcester Cathedral Manuscript, Register I of Worcester Cathedral Priory, fo. 35; printed, Stebbing Shaw, *The History and Antiquities of Staffordshire*, 2:152; Darlington, *Worcester Cartulary*, p. 140, no. 266.

DISCUSSED: Dorothy Styles, "The Early History of the King's Chapels in Staffordshire." Chapter 8.

DATE: September–December 1139.

REMARKS: This is one of Rogers most interesting charters. It is his most intimate, moving, and religious text. Nevertheless, the habits of a lifetime linger on, and even here some legal and administrative formulae persist. Professor Darlington, for example, noted how the phrase "unjustly and without judgment" presaged the language of the later writs of novel disseisin.[72] Bishop Sampson of Worcester died in 1112. It is not known when Roger seized the church of Wolverhampton, but other writs in the Worcester cartulary suggest either 1114, or a period between October 1123 and January to March 1125. Either of these times seems more likely than Dorothy Styles's suggestion of some time in Stephen's reign. The exact nature of Roger's spoliation is not specified, and it may well have been nothing more than his assuming control of the church. Yet many of the church's thirty hides were apparently already held by the canons before this writ. Roger's penitent note directs no specific action, not even the return of the church to the cathedral monks. Moreover, it is clear from other documents that the monks did not receive it back for some time.[73] When the Wolverhampton canons appealed to Pope Eugenius III in about 1148, they used much the same language as parts of Roger's letter, but they also somewhat gratuitously added that Roger through his power had oppressed many other churches unjustly. Under Henry II Wolverhampton became a free chapel of the crown as it had been under the Conqueror.

29

Bishop Roger restores to the monastery of Saint Frideswide "whatever I had taken unjustly."

72. *Worcester Cartulary*, pp. *xlvii–xlix.*   73. *Ibid.*, nos. 263, 267.

Stephano Regi Anglie, et Henrico sedis apostolice legato, et Theob[aldo] Cantuar[iensis] Archiepiscopo, totique clero totius Anglie, Rogerus Episcopus Sar[esberiensis], salutem et honoris dignitatem. Notum facio dignitati vestre quoniam [a] reddidi pro salute anime mee ecclesie et priori totique conventui Sancte Frid [eswidis] Oxenford quicquid eisdem iniuste abstuleram, pratum quod dicitur Presteit,[b] et molendinum, et Bisshopesmore, et terram que est ante orreum, et terram in qua est orreum, et terras que de ara Sancte Frid[eswidis] dicuntur. Preterea reddo eis feriam unam in Oxenford et in toto suburbio eiusdem pertinentem eidem ecclesie cum omnibus libertatibus et liberis consuetudinibus suis. Et totum locum qui dicitur Beneseye, et totam terram pertinentem ad hidam ipsorum in Walton[e]. Omnes etiam terras suas et redditus suos infra civitatem Oxon[iae] et extra cum alibus [c] rebus et dignitatibus et libertatibus et consuetudinibus suis reddo eis fideliter. Quare dignitatem vestram humiliter requiro quod, pro Dei amore, et vestro honore, et pro salute animarum vestrarum et mee, illud firmum et stabile faciatis. Testibus A[tione] Decano et conventu apud Sar[esberiensem].

SOURCE: cartulary copy, *Christ Church Manuscript A, fo. 16; printed, St. Frideswide Cartulary, 1:17, no. 13.

VARIATIONS: a. The printed cartulary reads quod; b. The printed cartulary reads Prestent; c. The printed cartulary reads aliis.

DISCUSSED: Chapters 4, 8.

DATE: September–December 1139, at Salisbury.

REMARKS: Roger's relations with the Austin Canons of Saint Frideswide's priory were rather ambivalent. He was most instrumental in establishing them at Oxford and in increasing their endowments, but, as this charter shows, he also exploited them. This document is quite precise about what it returned, including a fair that had changed hands several times. Its overall impression, however, depends upon how strongly one translates iniuste abstuleram. A sworn recognition of Saint Frideswide's rents within and without Oxford in 1139 and 1140 totaled more than thirteen pounds.[74] Bishopesmore, Binsey, and Walton are all in Oxfordshire.[75]

74. Regesta, 3, no. 640.
75. These were all parts of the original grant of Henry I about 1122; Regesta, 2, nos. 1342-1343. Also see the empress' 1141 confirmation; Regesta, 3, no. 646.

30

Bishop Roger returns to Saint Frideswide's monastery a fair and the churches of Saint Mary Magdalene, Saint Michael, and All Saints.

H[enrico] dei gratia sedis apostolice legato et Theobaldo Cantuariensi archiepiscopo totique clero totius Anglie Rogerus episcopus Sar[esberiensis], salutem. Notum vobis facio quoniam pro salute anime mee reddidi ecclesie et priori et canonicis de Sancta Frideswida feriam et ecclesiam Sancte Marie Magdalene quam Wimundus prior disrationavit subiacere predicte ecclesie [et] preterea ecclesiam Sancti Michaelis supra portam aquilonis et ecclesiam Omnium Sanctorum quas Robertus presbiter eidem ecclesie donavit cum [molen]dino quod eis diu reddidi sicut ius eorum, sed eccelsias [suas predic]tas tunc retinui, et omnes alias res et dignitates [suas quas] eidem ecclesie iniuste absturam.[a] Quare precor [et fir]miter et fiducialiter requiro quod pro dei amore [   ][b] illud firmum et stabile esse facia[tis. Testibus Atione deca]no et Will[elmo sub]decano Sar[esberiensis] et Ricardo [filio Willelmi] et Gotso cam[erari]o apud [Saresberiensem.]

SOURCE: cartulary copy, *British Museum Manuscript, Cotton Vitellius E XV, fo. 17. Parts of this manuscript are very badly damaged. Conjectural readings, most of which follow those in Salter's edition, are italicized in brackets; printed, *The Cartulary of Oseney Abbey*, ed. H. E. Salter, 2:233, no. 793.

VARIATIONS: a. This must be a misspelling for *abstuleram*. b. In other charters Roger used the phrase *"et vestre honore, et pro salute animarum vestrarum et mee,"* at this spot, but the void in the manuscript seems a bit too small for all of that.

DISCUSSED: Chapter 8.

DATE: September–December 1139, at Salisbury (?)

REMARKS: This charter and the next one (31) are very similar, but it is a puzzle why they were preserved in only this cartulary of Oseney abbey and not among the Saint Frideswide records or other Oseney cartularies. Copies of Roger's charters seem to have been made by Saint Frideswide's priory about

1200 and then sent to Oseney along with confirmations by Archbishop Theobald and Legate Henry of Winchester. These were then enrolled in the cartulary itself.[76] Both Oseney and Saint Frideswide's claimed the church of Saint Mary Magdelene, but Oseney seems to have had the upper hand. Saint Frideswide's claimed it against Oseney in 1151, 1174, and 1220, but each time failed to win its case. King Henry I had given the church of Saint Mary to Saint George's chapel in Oxford castle, but apparently Bishop Roger later held it himself and in his last days gave it to Saint Frideswide's. This monastery's own cartulary contained a confirmation by Innocent II, dated January 8, 1141, which listed the Magdelene church among Saint Frideswide's possessions, but somehow the priory failed to retain it.[77] Between 1142 and 1148 the Empress Matilda confirmed the use of the church to Saint George's chapel.[78] Control of the other churches was not disputed.[79] Guimund was the first prior of Saint Frideswide's, but, according to the following charter, he had died by 1139.

31

In a second charter Bishop Roger returns to Saint Frideswide's monastery a fair and the churches of Saint Mary Magdalene, Saint Michael, and All Saints.

[*Henrico sedis*] apostolice legato et T[*heobaldo Cantuariensi archiepiscopo et*] omnibus episcopis [*totius Anglie, Rogerus*] episcopus Sar[esberiensis], salutem et [*benedictionem. Notum vobis facio*] quoniam reddidi pro salute anime mee ecclesie et priori totique conventui Sancte Frideswidis feriam pertinentem eidem ecclesie et ecclesiam Sancte Magdalene quam rex H[enricus] concessit eidem ecclesie disrationatione Wimundi qui fuit prior predicte ecclesie. Preterea reddo eis ecclesiam Sancti Michaelis supra portam aquilonis, et ecclesiam Omnium Sanctorum quas Robertus presbiter

76. *Oseney Cartulary*, 2, nos. 790–791.
77. *St. Frideswide Cartulary*, 1:20.
78. *Regesta*, 3, no. 632. She also confirmed the fair to Saint Frideswide's, and King Stephen confirmed all the gifts of Robert the priest; *ibid.*, nos. 645, 641.
79. *Ibid.*, no. 646.

eidem ecclesie donavit cum molendino quod eis diu est ᵃ
reddidi, sicut ius suum, sed ecclesias predictas suas predictas ᵃ
tunc retinui, et omnes alias res suas et consuetudines et dignitates suas quas eidem ecclesie iniuste abstuleram eis reddidi similiter. Quare dignitatem vestram humiliter requiro
quod pro dei amore et vestro honore et pro salute animarum
vestrarum et mee, illud firmum et stabile esse faciatis. Testibus, A[tione] decano, et Willelmo subdecano, et Ricardo
filio Willelmi, et Osmundo dapifero, et Waltero de Maisi,
et Serlone filio Eudonis apud Sar[esberiensem].

SOURCE: cartulary copy, *British Museum Manuscript, Cotton
  Vitellius E XV, fo. 17. The beginning of this charter is also
  badly damaged; printed, *Oseney Cartulary*, 2:234, no. 794.
VARIATIONS: a. Both of these unnecessary words are probably
  scribal errors.
DISCUSSED: Chapter 8.
DATE: September–December 1139, at Salisbury.
REMARKS: One wonders why Roger dictated two such similar
  letters as Charters 30 and 31. The differences between them
  are slight, but doubtless they were important to the canons.
  There are minor variations in phrasing and a few new witnesses, but the main distinction of this text is the novel attention to the king's role. Perhaps the first text seemed a bit
  weak, so the second noted that King Henry had given the
  church of Saint Mary Magdelene to the canons of Saint Frideswide's priory. Although a fair and a mill are mentioned, the
  two charters largely deal with spiritualities. Charter 29 also
  involves Saint Frideswide's, but it mainly treats temporalities.
  All three contain variations of the phrase, "what I have unjustly taken away."

* * *

The cartulary of Ramsey abbey, Public Record Office
Manuscript, E, 164, 28, contains on Folio 21 a list in which
three possible writs of Bishop Roger are noted. Unfortunately, I was unable to find the complete texts of the writs
either in the full cartulary or in other Ramsey abbey
cartularies. Thus, I cannot prove that the writs did belong

to the first Bishop Roger of Salisbury. William Henry Hart and P. A. Lyons edited the Public Record Office Manuscript as *Cartularium Monasterii de Rameseia,* RS 79(1857), 3 vols. Their edition also lacks full texts of these writs, but lists them in volume 1 (pp. 105–106):

#503. Breve R. episcopi Sarum, vicecomiti Fulquio, pro abbate de hundred de Hirstingstone.

Remarks: This may be one of Bishop Roger's writs. About 1114/1129 he witnessed a royal writ granting the abbot of Ramsey the farm of the hundred of Hurstingstone, Huntingdonshire.[80] There was also a sheriff Fulk in Huntingdon between about 1125 and 1129.

#509. Breve R. Sarum episcopi de protectione terrarum de Terfelde.

Remarks: There seems little way to identify this.

#511. Rogerus episcopus Sarum, custos regni, Reginaldo abbate pro terris quas ipse acquisivit.

Remarks: Hart and Lyons correctly note that the manuscript actually reads *H. episcopus; Rogerus* is thus their own guess, working from the viceregal title *custos regni.* The word *regis* should also be added to the end of the entry. Identification of this writ with Bishop Roger is thus very tenuous. A Reginald was abbot of Ramsey from 1114 to 1130, however.[81]

One writ long identified as Bishop Roger's work clearly belongs to a later bishop of Salisbury. The Salisbury Cathedral Manuscript, *Registrum Rubrum,* fo. 2, contains a grant in French of the assize of bread and ale at Stratford-sub-Castle, dated Wodeford, March 10, the thirteenth year of the bishop's episcopate. The manuscript copyist headed the entry with a note that this was Bishop Roger's charter; the nineteenth-century editors printed it with the date 1120, assuming that it was a charter of the first Bishop Roger of

80. *Regesta,* 2, no. 1632. See also nos. 1788, 1860 for other royal writs relating to Hurstingstone.

81. This writ might also be related to *ibid.,* no. 1451. Another listing in the *Ramsey Cartulary,* no. 518, reads: Breve R. Sarum episcopi comite Oxonise et Galfrido de Merlay quod faciant homagium abbate. This cannot be one of Roger's writs since the earldom of Oxford was not created until 1141.

Salisbury.[82] However, 1120 seemed too early for a French charter, and the assize of bread and ale was rarely seen then, either. I brought these problems to the attention of Professor Kathleen Edwards, who is editing the registers of Bishop Roger Martival, the ordinary of Salisbury from 1315 to 1330. She kindly checked and found that that Bishop Roger was at Woodford, Wiltshire, on March 10, 1328.[83] Clearly then, this French grant belongs to him, not to the great twelfth-century bishop and viceroy.

82. *Sarum Documents,* p. 5, no. 6.
83. Also see Susan Reynolds, *The Register of Roger Martival, Bishop of Salisbury 1315–1330,* 3 (Canterbury and York Society, LIX, 1965):202, no. 738, which gives a writ Bishop Martival received at Woodford on March 10, 1328.

Appendix 3

ROGER OF SALISBURY'S FAMILY

HUMPHREY was Bishop Roger's brother. He was mentioned only once, as a witness to a charter the bishop issued in Wales in 1114. Alexander of Lincoln was called Roger's nephew through Roger's brother.[1] Bishop Alexander's mother was named ADA. Her name was given in the Lincoln obit book, and in 1130 she was pardoned thirty shillings for lands in Winford, Dorset.[2] Although Roger could have had more than one brother, Ada was probably Humphrey's wife.

MATILDA OF RAMSBURY was the mother of Bishop Roger's son, Roger the Pauper, and castellan of the viceroy's fortress at Devizes in 1139. She and Roger may have married before he became bishop, but it is extremely unlikely. Their son was certainly born after his father's consecration, and they may have had another son, Adelelm. Orderic Vitalis was the only writer to mention Matilda, whom he depicted as a considerate, strong-willed woman.[3]

ROGER THE PAUPER was the son of Bishop Roger and Matilda of Ramsbury, and, although his birthdate is unknown, he was said to be a very young man in 1139.[4] After his coronation King Stephen rewarded the bishop by making one of his "nephews" royal chancellor and another royal treasurer.[5] Young Roger became chancellor, and as such witnessed more than sixty of Stephen's writs between

1. Charter 4; William of Malmesbury, *H.N.*, p. 25.
2. Gerald of Wales, *Opera*, 7:154; *Pipe Roll*, p. 15.
3. Orderic Vitalis, 4:120–121.
4. William of Malmesbury, *H.N.*, p. 39.
5. *Ibid.*

December 1135 and June 1139, as well as one viceregal writ of the bishop, always signing himself *R.,* or *Roger, the chancellor.*[6] It was only chroniclers writing after 1139 who called him Roger the Pauper (*Pauperus*).[7] It is not clear why they gave him this name; perhaps it referred to his expectations of a bishopric, the normal reward of a chancellor, which were dashed by his father's disgrace. Young Roger played his own part in these events, and it was the threat of hanging him which induced his mother to surrender Devizes castle. He was apparently banished thereafter.[8]

BISHOP ROGER'S RELATIVES were usually rewarded by him with benefices in his chapter and positions in his diocese. There were several men in the Sarum cathedral chapter named Roger, and it is tempting to identify the chancellor with one of them. Roger of Ramsbury, archdeacon of Wiltshire c. 1130–1160, seems a good candidate at first glance, but if Adelelm the treasurer were Roger the Pauper's brother, as seems probable, the chancellor could not have been Roger of Ramsbury, since he and Adelelm of Dorset were not closely related.[9] The chancellor might have been another Salisbury archdeacon, ROGER OF BERKSHIRE, who also died in the mid 1160s.[10] If this suggestion is correct,

6. *Regesta,* 3, index; Charter 25. The *Gesta Stephani,* p. 52, called young Roger the king's "chief secretary" (*summusque illius antigraphus*), a good description of the chancellorship which was not yet the great office it was to become.

7. Orderic Vitalis, 4:120; Florence of Worcester (Continuator's part), 2:108; "Annals of Oseney," in *Annales Monastici,* 4:23.

8. See Chapter 6 for a description of this struggle; John of Hexham, *Historia,* p. 310, reports his exile.

9. A case involving the then canon, Roger of Ramsbury, was transferred from the jurisdiction of his brother, Archdeacon Azo, to that of Archdeacon Adelelm of Dorset in order to avoid a conflict of interest; *Register of St. Osmund,* 1:349, 351. This must have happened after 1129, see Charter 19, Note 53.

10. Between 1136 and 1139 Bishop Roger sent a writ to an unnamed archdeacon of Berkshire and Adelelm the treasurer witnessed it; Charter 22. For Roger of Berkshire's appearances as a witness see *Register of St. Osmund,* 1:218, and *Sarum Documents,* p. 19,

ROGER OF RAMSBURY and his brother AZO, an archdeacon and dean of Salisbury, may have been brothers of Matilda of Ramsbury.

ADELELM was a "nephew," and probably was a son, of Bishop Roger, but his witness as royal treasurer has not appeared on any known writ of Stephen. However, as "Adelelm the king's treasurer" he signed a Lincoln diocesan charter with Bishop Alexander, and as "A. the treasurer" he witnessed a brief writ of Bishop Roger at Winchester.[11] Adelelm was also the archdeacon of Dorset (c. 1129–1165) and the dean of Lincoln (c. 1142–1165).[12]

ALEXANDER and NIGEL were consistently described as nephews of Bishop Roger, and it is likely that they were brothers, although the chronicles never indicated this rela-

where he appears as Robert of Berkshire, probably a scribal error. Interestingly, Roger of Berkshire was also a canon of the Lincoln chapter, Gerald of Wales, *Opera*, 7:156.

11. *Thame Cartulary*, 1:2; Charter 22. The "Annals of Oseney," in *Annales Monastici*, 4:23, described his flight from capture at Oxford in 1139, but characterized him as "Adelelm, the nephew of Bishop Alexander, who was then the treasurer of the king." The reason for this identification is unknown, but perhaps knowing Adelelm's later place in Lincoln affairs the thirteenth century Oseney writer felt bound to establish some direct relation between Adelelm and Bishop Alexander.

12. That the archdeacon and the treasurer are the same individual is demonstrated by the fact that Master Osbert de Hache (Hette) identified himself as a clerk of Archdeacon Adelelm and also witnessed with Adelelm the royal treasurer; *Cirencester Cartulary*, 2:566, *Thame Cartulary*, 1:2. The fact that the archdeacon and dean are the same individual is proved by a writ of Bishop Jocelin of Salisbury attested by "Adelelm the dean of Lincoln and our archdeacon;" Hampshire County Record Office Manuscript, Southwick Priory Register, Number I, fos. 3r.–v. I owe this reference to the generosity of Dr. Brian Kemp of the University of Reading. For Adelelm's appearances as archdeacon see: Charter 19 (where he attests as Athelelm); Charter 20; *Register of St. Osmund*, 1:349, 351; *Sarum Documents*, pp. 28, 29, 31; *Registrum Antiquissimum*, no. 334; *Foliot Charters*, pp. 92, 458; John of Salisbury, *Letters*, pp. 131–132. For Adelelm's appearances as dean see: *Registrum Antiquissimum*, nos. 129, 255, 302–303, 321, 335–336, 346, 576, 614, 797, 939, 1295, 2494; *Foliot Charters*, p. 117; *Eynsham Cartulary*, 1:38, 2:159; Gibbs, *St. Paul's Charters*, p. 156; Gerald of Wales, *Opera*, 7:156.

tionship. It is certainly incorrect to describe them both as Bishop Roger's bastard sons.[13] Alexander was the son of Ada and a brother of Roger, probably Humphrey. Alexander and Nigel studied at Laon together and were both archdeacons at Salisbury. From these positions they went on to bishoprics. Alexander at Lincoln (1123–1148), and Nigel at Ely (1133–1169). Nigel had also been a royal treasurer before his election.

ALEXANDER'S RELATIVES included a brother, DAVID, who became archdeacon of Buckingham in the Lincoln diocese.[14] It is odd that he was never mentioned in connection with Bishop Roger or the diocese of Salisbury. A nephew of Bishop Alexander, WILLIAM, became archdeacon of Northampton. Kathleen Major recently identified him as the son of Osbert the archdeacon and suggested that William, in turn, had a son named PHILIP, who was also a canon of Lincoln.[15] Bishop Alexander also had a niece whose son, ROBERT DE ALVERS, was the heir of an estate held in Northamptonshire of Alan of Brittany.[16]

NIGEL'S RELATIVES included RICHARD FITZ NIGEL, who was born about three years before his father became a bishop. He grew to be royal treasurer beginning in 1158, wrote the famed *Dialogue of the Exchequer,* and served as bishop of London from 1189 to 1199. Richard himself had a son, ROBERT OF BARNEVILLE.[17] Bishop Nigel had another son called WILLIAM THE ENGLISHMAN.[18] Another William, WILLIAM OF ELY, was royal treasurer from 1195 to 1215, but his relationship to Nigel and Richard Fitz Nigel is unclear. He

13. Cantor, *The English,* p. 127.

14. Henry of Huntingdon, p. 303.

15. *Ibid.; Registrum Antiquissimum,* 9:259. He was also called William of St. Clare.

16. Farrar and Clay, *Early Yorkshire Charters,* 4, pt. I, no. 13; *Registrum Antiquissimum,* 2:6. A knight in Bishop Alexander's service was named Ralph de Alvers, *Registrum Antiquissimum,* 2:17, 254; 3:263.

17. For more on Richard Fitz Nigel see Charles Johnson's introduction to his *Dialogue of the Exchequer,* pp. *xi–xxii.*

18. Richard Fitz Nigel, p. *xv; Red Book of the Exchequer,* 1: *xxv.*

had a son, RALPH, and possibly a daughter, AGNES OF ELY.[19]

THE NAME "POOR": Richard Fitz Nigel praised his grand-uncle when he quoted the saying "How fertile is the lean poverty of men," which William Stubbs, the great nineteenth-century historian and bishop, felt indicated that Bishop Roger, as well as his son, was called Roger the Poor (sometimes spelled *le Poer* or *le Poor*). Other historians have also characterized Bishop Roger thus. Stubbs, moreover, felt that this name implied a connection between the great viceroy and two later bishops of Salisbury, Herbert Poore (1194–1217) and his brother, Richard Poore (1217–1229, translated to Durham 1229–1237), sons of Richard of Ilchester, an exchequer clerk and bishop of Winchester (1174–1188).[20] However, no direct relation has been established between Bishop Roger or his family and Richard of Ilchester. Moreover, my investigations do not support any identification of the name *Poor* with Bishop Roger. Nor do I see it as a family name for his descendants. It was not an uncommon cognomen in the twelfth century, but it seems to have had no special meaning for Bishop Roger.

Doubtless, other individuals can be connected with Roger's family, but even the few listed here demonstrate that the bishop founded a dynasty which produced distinguished leaders in the English church and state for more than a century.

19. Henry G. Richardson, "William of Ely, the King's Treasurer, 1195–1215."

20. Richard Fitz Nigel, p. 42; William Stubbs, *Historical Introductions to the Rolls Series,* ed. Arthur Hassel (London, 1902), pp. 145, 299–300 (these are the introductions to Benedict of Peterborough and Roger of Hovedon). Of course Stubbs was not the first one to use the term; John Leland had used it in the sixteenth century; see his *Itinerary,* 2:154. William of Ely did, however, control lands formerly held by Herbert Poore; see Richardson, "William of Ely," p. 60. See also Charles Duggan, "Richard of Ilchester, Royal Servant and Bishop," TRHS, 16 (1966):1–23.

Appendix 4

PARDONS GRANTED TO BISHOP ROGER IN THE PIPE ROLL OF 1130

County	Previous Danegeld	Present Danegeld	Previous City Aid	Present City Aid	Murder Fines
Oxford	100s 2d		72s	48s 8d	
Dorset	£7 6s	£41 10s 6d			29s 5d
					36s 8d
					160s (1 mark)
Wiltshire	£29	£77 16s 9d		15s	4s 11d
					£6 12s
Hampshire			£7 7s 8d	£6 15s 8d	
Surrey		4s			
Herts		13s 6d			
Kent		12s			
Essex		32s			
Staffordshire		40s	3s	3s	19s
Gloucester		25s		3s	
Northants	14s 9d	12s 4d			
Norfolk		1s 6d			
Bucks		22s			
Warwick		38s			
Berkshire		£18 13s 6d			
London			£8 10s		
Middlesex		4s			
Total Present Danegeld Pardons		£148 5s 1d			

Bibliography

THIS BIBLIOGRAPHY is divided into three sections: manuscripts, published editions of medieval sources, and modern studies. The manuscripts, which are chiefly original writs and bound monastic cartularies, are listed alphabetically by their present locations. Published editions of medieval sources are alphabetized by the name of the twelfth century author, or by a commonly used title of the anonymous chronicle, treatise, cartulary, or government record. Collections of documents and modern studies are listed alphabetically by author.

MANUSCRIPTS

BRITISH MUSEUM
  Additional Charters: 8071; 19575
  Additional Manuscript 46487
  Cotton Manuscripts: Claudius B III; Claudius B VI; Cleopatra A VII; Cleopatra E I; Faustina A II; Julius D II; Vespasian E V; Vespasian E XXV; Vespasian F XV; Vitellius A X; Vitellius E XV.
  Egerton Manuscript 3031
  Harley Manuscripts: 742; 1708
  Harley Roll A 3
  Stowe Manuscript 925

CAMBRIDGE UNIVERSITY LIBRARY
  Manuscript Mm. IV, 19

CANTERBURY CATHEDRAL ARCHIVES
  Manuscripts: C 115; C 117

COLLEGE OF ARMS (LONDON)
  Arundel Manuscript 28

OXFORD UNIVERSITY
  Balliol College Manuscript 271
  Bodleian Manuscripts: 3860 (James 23); Digby 96 (*Medita-*

ciones Godwini Cantoris Salesberie ad Rainilvam Reculsam);
Dodsworth 63.
Christ Church Manuscript 160

PUBLIC LIBRARY OF ROUEN (FRANCE)
Manuscript Y 200 (photostat use only)

PUBLIC RECORD OFFICE (LONDON)
Duchy of Lancaster Charter 25/2
Exchequer Manuscripts: 164, 27; 164, 28.

SAINT PAUL'S CATHEDRAL ARCHIVES
Ancient Deeds A/Box 24/1351

SALISBURY DIOCESAN RECORD OFFICE AND CATHEDRAL ARCHIVES
Manuscripts: *Liber Evidentiarum* B; *Liber Evidentiarum* C;
Registrum Rubrum; Vetus Registrum Ecclesie Sarum (Registrum S. Osmundi).

WESTMINSTER ABBEY MUNIMENT ROOM
Manuscripts: 13247; 13251; 13478.

YORK MINSTER LIBRARY
Magnum Registrum Album III

PUBLISHED EDITIONS OF MEDIEVAL SOURCES

Abingdon Chronicle: Joseph Stevenson, ed., *Chronicon Monasterii de Abingdon,* RS 2(1858), 2 vols.
Abelard, *The Story of My Adversities,* ed., J. T. Muckle (Toronto, 1954).
Ailred of Rievaulx, *Relatio de Standardo,* ed. Richard Howlett in *Chronicles of the Reigns of Stephen, Henry II, and Richard I,* RS 82(1886)2:181–199.
Anglo-Saxon Chronicle, ed. Benjamin Thorpe, RS 23(1861), 2 vols. Other editions consulted: John Earle and Charles Plummer, *Two of the Saxon Chronicle Parallel,* 2nd. ed. (Oxford, 1952): Cecily Clark, *The Peterborough Chronicle* (Oxford, 1958): Dorothy Whitelock, David C. Douglas, and Susie I. Tucker, *The Anglo-Saxon Chronicle* (New Brunswick, 1961).
Annales Monastici, ed. Henry Richard Luard, RS 36(1864–1869), 5 vols.

Anselm, *Opera Omnia,* ed. F. S. Schmitt (London, 1946–1961), 6 vols.

Bath Cartularies: William Hunt, ed., *Two Cartularies of the Priory of Saint Peter at Bath,* Somerset Record Society 7(1893).

Battle Chronicle: J. S. Brewer, ed., *Chronicon Monasterii de Bello* (London, 1846). There is a translation by Anthony Lower, *The Chronicle of Battle Abbey from 1066 to 1176* (London, 1851).

Bigelow, Melville Madison, *Placita Anglo-Normannica* (Boston, 1881).

Book of Llan-Dav, ed. J. G. Evans and John Rhys (Oxford, 1893).

Book of the Foundation of St. Bartholomew's Church in London, ed. Norman Moore (London, 1923). There is a translation by E. A. Webb, *The Book of the Foundation of the Church of St. Bartholomew, London* (Oxford, 1923).

Bruton and Montacute Cartularies: *Two Cartularies of the Augustinian Priory of Bruton and the Cluniac Priory of Montacute,* Somerset Record Society 8(1894).

Cartae Antiquae: J. Conway Davies, *The Cartae Antiquae, Rolls 11–20,* Pipe Roll Society Publications, New Series 33 (1960, for the year 1957).

Christina of Markyate: C. H. Talbot, ed., *The Life of Christina of Markyate, a Twelfth Century Recluse* (Oxford, 1959).

Cirencester Cartulary: C. D. Ross, ed., *The Cartulary of Cirencester Abbey, Gloucestershire* (London, 1964), 2 vols.

Constitutio Domus Regis, ed. and trans. Charles Johnson in *The Course of the Exchequer,* Nelson's Medieval Texts (London, 1950).

D'Anisy, Amédée Louis Lechaude, *Extrait des Chartes et Autres Actes Normands ou Anglo-Normands Qui se Trouvent Dans les Archives du Calvados* (Caen, 1834–1835), 2 vols.

Davies, J. Conway, *Episcopal Acts Relating to Welsh Dioceses, 1066–1272* (Cardiff, 1946–1948), 3 vols.

Delisle, Léopold, *Rouleaux des Morts* (Paris, 1866).

Douglas, David C., *Feudal Documents From the Abbey of Bury St. Edmunds* (London, 1932).

———, and Greenway, George W., *English Historical Documents,* 2(London, 1952).

Dugdale, William, *Monasticon Anglicanum,* ed. John Caley, Henry Ellis, Bulkeley Bandinal (London, 1817), 6 vols. in 8 pts.

Eadmer, *H.N.*: Martin Rule, ed., *Eadmeri Historia Novorum in Anglia,* RS 81(1884).

———, *The Life of St. Anselm, Archbishop of Canterbury,* ed. and trans. Richard W. Southern, Nelson's Medieval Texts (London, 1962).

Eynsham Cartulary, ed. H. E. Salter, Oxford Historical Society Publications 49(1907), 51(1908).

Farrar, William, and Clay, Charles T., *Early Yorkshire Charters,* Yorkshire Archaeological Society Record Series (1914–1965), 12 vols.

Florence of Worcester: Benjamin Thorpe, ed., *Florenti Wigorniensis Chronicon Ex Chronicis* (London, 1848–1849), 2 vols.

Foliot Charters: Adrian Morey and C. N. L. Brooke, *The Letters and Charters of Gilbert Foliot* (Cambridge, 1967).

Galbert of Bruges, *The Murder of Charles the Good, Count of Flanders,* ed. and trans. James Bruce Ross (New York, 1967).

Gerald of Wales, *Opera:* J. S. Brewer, James F. Dimock, and George F. Warner, eds., *Giraldus Cambrensis Opera,* RS 21(1861–1891), 8 vols.

Gervase of Canterbury, *Opera:* William Stubbs, ed., *The Historical Works of Gervase of Canterbury,* RS 73(1879–1880), 2 vols.

Gesta Stephani, ed. and trans., K. R. Potter, Nelson's Medieval Texts (London, 1955).

Gibbs, Marion, *Early Charters of the Cathedral Church of St. Paul's, London,* Royal Historical Society Publications, Third Series 58(1939).

Gloucester Cartulary: W. H. Hart, ed., *Historia et Cartularium Monasterii Gloucestriae,* RS 33(1863–1867), 3 vols.

Godstow Register: Andrew Clark, ed., *The Early Register of Godstow Nunnery, Near Oxford,* Early English Text Society 129(1905).

Guibert of Nogent-Sous-Coucy: C. C. Swinton Bland, ed. and trans., *The Autobiography of Guibert Abbot of Nogent-Sous-Coucy* (London, 1925).

Henry of Huntingdon: Thomas Arnold, ed., *Henrici Huntendunensis Historia Anglorum,* RS 74(1879). There is a translation by Thomas Forester, *The History of the English by Henry of Huntingdon,* Bohn's Antiquarian Library (London, 1853).

Herbert of Losinga, *Epistolae:* Robert Anstruther, ed., *Epistolae Herberti de Losinga* (London, 1846). There is a translation by

Edward M. Gouldburn and Henry Symonds, *The Life, Letters, and Sermons of Bishop Herbert de Losinga* (Oxford, 1878), 2 vols.

Herman of Tournai, *De Miraculis S. Mariae Laudunensis*, PL 156, cols. 961–985.

Hildebert of Lavardin, *Opera*, PL 171.

Holtzmann, Walther, *Papsturkunden in England* (Berlin, 1936), 2 vols.

Hugh Candidus, *Chronicle:* W. T. Mellows, ed., *The Chronicle of Hugh Candidus* (Oxford, 1949).

Hugh the Chantor, *The History of the Church of York, 1066–1127,* ed. and trans., Charles Johnson, Nelson's Medieval Texts (London, 1961).

Hunter, Joseph, *Ecclesiastical Documents,* Camden Society 8(1840).

Huntingdon Cartulary: William M. Noble, ed., *The Cartulary of Huntingdon,* Transactions of the Cambridge and Huntingdon Archaeological Society 4(1930).

Jaffee, Philip, *Regesta Pontificum Romanorum,* ed. W. Wattenbach, S. Lowenfeld, F. Kaltenbrunner, and P. Ewald, 2nd. ed. (Leipzig, 1885–1888), 2 vols.

John of Ford, *Wulfric of Haselbury,* ed. Maurice Bell, Somerset Record Society 48(1933).

John of Hexham, *Historia:* Thomas Arnold, ed., *Historia Iohannis Prioris Hagustaldensis Ecclesiae,* in *Symeonis Monachi Opera Omnia,* RS 75(1885)2:284-332.

John of Salisbury, *Letters:* W. J. Millor, H. E. Butler, and C. N. L. Brooke, eds. and trans., *The Letters of John of Salisbury, 1153–1161,* Nelson's Medieval Texts (London, 1955).

———, *Memoirs:* Marjorie Chibnall, ed. and trans., *John of Salisbury's Memoirs of the Papal Court* (also called the *Historia Pontificalis*), Nelson's Medieval Texts (London, 1956).

John of Worcester: John R. H. Weaver, ed., *The Chronicle of John of Worcester, 1118–1146* (Oxford, 1908).

Johnson, Charles, "Some Early Charters of Henry I," in *Historical Essays in Honour of James Tait,* ed. J. G. Edwards, V. H. Galbraith, and E. F. Jacob (Manchester, 1933), pp. 137–143.

Leach, Arthur, *Educational Charters and Documents* (London, 1911).

Lewes Cartulary: L. F. Salzman, ed. and trans., *The Chartulary of the Priory of St. Pancras of Lewes,* Sussex Record Society 38(1932), 40(1934).

Liber Eliensis, ed. E. O. Blake, Royal Historical Society Publications, Third Series 92(1962).

Liber Monasterii de Hyda, ed. Edward Edwards, RS 45(1866).

Liebermann, Felix, *Ungedruckte Anglo-Normannische Geschichtsquellen* (Strassburg, 1879).

Malmesbury Register: J. S. Brewer and Charles Trice Martin, eds., *Registrum Malmesburiense,* RS 72(1879–1880), 2 vols.

Massingbred, W. O., "Lincoln Cathedral Charters," in *Associated Architectural Societies Reports and Papers of the Architectural and Archaeological Society of the County of Lincoln,* 27(1903–1904):1–72.

Matthew Paris, *Historia Anglorum,* ed. Frederic Madden, RS 44(1866–1869), 3 vols.

———, *Chronica Majora,* ed. Henry Richard Luard, RS 57(1872–1883), 7 vols.

Matthew of Westminster, *Flores Historiarum,* ed. Henry Richard Luard, RS 95(1890), 3 vols.

The Memoranda Roll for the Michaelmas Term of the First Year of the Reign of King John (1199–1200), ed. H. G. Richardson, Pipe Roll Society Publications 59(1943).

Offler, H. S., *Durham Episcopal Charters,* Surtees Society Publications 179(1968).

Orderic Vitalis: *Orderici Vitalis Historiae Ecclesiasticae Libri Tredecim,* ed. August Le Prévost (Paris, 1838–1855), 5 vols.

Osbert of Clare, *Letters:* E. W. Williamson, ed., *The Letters of Osbert de Clare, Prior of Westminster* (Oxford, 1929).

Oseney Cartulary: H. E. Salter, ed., *The Cartulary of Oseney Abbey,* Oxford Historical Society Publications 89(1929), 90(1930), 91(1931), 97(1934), 98(1935), 101(1936).

Peter of Blois, *Opera,* PL 207.

Pipe Roll: Joseph Hunter, ed., *Magnus Rotulus Scaccarii, vel Magnus Rotulus Pipae, Anno Tricesimo-primo Regni Henrici Primi* (London, 1833).

Raine, James, ed., *Historians of the Church of York,* RS 71(1886), 3 vols.

Ralph de Diceto: William Stubbs, ed., *The Historical Works of Master Ralph de Diceto, Dean of London,* RS 68(1876), 2 vols.

Ramsey Cartulary: William Henry Hart and Ponsonby A. Lyons, eds., *Cartularium Monasterii de Rameseia,* RS 79(1884–1894), 3 vols.

Ramsey Chronicle: W. Dunn Macray, ed., *Chronicon Abbatiae Rameseiensis,* RS 83(1886).

The Red Book of the Exchequer, ed. Hubert Hall, RS 99(1897), 3 vols.

Regesta 1–4: *Regesta Regum Anglo-Normannorum;* vol. 1, ed. H. W. C. Davis (Oxford, 1913); vol. 2, ed. Charles Johnson and H. A. Cronne (Oxford, 1956); vol. 3, ed. H. A. Cronne and R. H. C. Davis (Oxford, 1968); vol. 4 (facsimilies), ed. H. A. Cronne and R. H. C. Davis (Oxford, 1969).

Register of St. Osmund: W. H. Rich Jones, ed., *Vetus Registrum Sarisberiense, or Registrum S. Osmundi Episcopi,* RS 78(1883–1884), 2 vols.

Registrum Antiquissimum: Charles Wilmer Foster and Kathleen Major, eds., *The Registrum Antiquissimum of the Cathedral Church of Lincoln,* Lincoln Record Society Publications, 27(1931), 28(1933), 29(1935), 32(1937), 34(1940), 41(1950), 46(1953), 51(1958), 62(1968).

Richard Fitz Nigel: Charles Johnson, ed. and trans., *The Course of the Exchequer by Richard Son of Nigel,* Nelson's Medieval Texts (London, 1950).

Richard of Hexham, *Historia de Gestis Stephani et de Bello Standardii,* ed. Richard Howlett, in *Chronicles of the Reigns of Stephen, Henry II, and Richard I,* RS 82(1886)3:139–178.

Robert of Torigni, *Chronicle,* ed. Richard Howlett, in *Chronicles of the Reigns of Stephen, Henry II, and Richard I,* RS 82(1890)4:3–315.

Round, John Horace, *Ancient Charters, Royal and Private Prior to 1200,* Pipe Roll Society Publications 10(1888).

———, *Calendar of Documents Preserved in France Illustrative of the History of Great Britain and Ireland* (London, 1899).

Saint Frideswide Cartulary: Spencer Robert Wigram, ed., *The Cartulary of the Monastery of Saint Frideswide at Oxford,* Oxford Historical Society Publications 28(1895), 31(1896).

Sarum Documents: W. Rich Jones and W. Dunn Macray, eds., *Charters and Documents Illustrating the History of the Cathedral, City, and Diocese of Salisbury in the Twelfth and Thirteenth Centuries,* RS 97(1891).

Stenton, Doris M., "Roger of Salisbury, 'Regni Angliae Procurator'," EHR, 39(1924):79–80.

Stenton, Frank M., "*Acta Episcoporum,*" CHJ, 3(1929):1–15.

Symeon of Durham: Thomas Arnold, ed., *Symeonis Monachi Opera Omnia,* RS 75(1882–1885), 2 vols.

The Thame Cartulary, ed. H. E. Salter, Oxfordshire Record Society 25(1947), 26(1948).

Wharton, Henry, *Anglia Sacra* (London, 1691), 2 vols.

Wilkins, David, *Concilia Magnae Britanniae et Hiberniae* (London, 1737), 4 vols.

William of Malmesbury, *G.P.:* Nicholas E. S. A. Hamilton, ed., *Willelmi Malmesbiriensis Monachi de Gestis Pontificum Anglorum,* RS 52(1870).

――, *G.R.:* William Stubbs, ed., *Willelmi Malmesbiriensis Monachi de Gestis Regum Anglorum,* RS 90(1887-1889), 2 vols.

――, *H.N.:* K. R. Potter, ed. and trans., *The Historia Novella of William of Malmesbury,* Nelson's Medieval Texts (London, 1955).

――, *Treatise on the Miracles of the Virgin Mary,* ed. Peter N. Carter (Oxford University D. Phil. thesis, 1959).

William of Newburgh: Hans Claude Hamilton, ed., *Historia Rerum Anglicarum of William of Newburgh* (London, 1856), 2 vols.

"Winchcombe Annals, 1049-1181," ed. R. R. Darlington, in *A Medieval Miscellany for Doris Mary Stenton,* ed., Patricia Barnes and C. F. Slade, Pipe Roll Society Publications, New Series 26(1962, for 1960):111-137.

Winchester Cartulary: A. W. Goodman, ed., *Cartulary of Winchester Cathedral* (Winchester, 1927).

"Winton Domesday," in *Domesday Book* 4(London, 1816).

Worcester Cartulary: R. R. Darlington, ed., *The Cartulary of Worcester Cathedral Priory (Register I),* Pipe Roll Society Publications, New Series 38(1968, for 1962-1963).

Wood, Anthony, *Survey of the Antiquities of the City of Oxford Composed in 1661-1666,* ed. Andrew Clark, Oxford Historical Society Publications 15(1889), 17(1890).

MODERN STUDIES

Alexander, James W., "Herbert of Norwich, 1091-1119: Studies in the History of Norman England," *Studies in Medieval and Renaissance History* 6(1969):115-232.

Allen, Hope Emily, "On the Author of the *Ancren Riwle,*" PMLA 44(1929):635-680.

Andrew, W. J., *A Numismatic History of the Reign of Henry I,*

1100–1135, in the *Numismatic Chronicle*, Fourth Series 1(1901):1–515.

Appleby, John, *The Troubled Reign of King Stephen* (New York, 1970).

Baddeley, Welbore St. Clair, *A History of Cirencester* (Cirencester, 1924).

Beeler, John, *Warfare in England, 1066–1189* (Ithaca, 1966).

Beresford, M. W., and St. Joseph, J. K. S., *Medieval England: An Aerial Survey* (Cambridge, 1958).

Bethell, Denis, "William of Corbeil and the Canterbury-York Dispute," JEH 19(1968):145–159.

——, "English Black Monks and Episcopal Elections in the 1120's," EHR 84(1969):673–698.

Bishop, Edmund, *Liturgica Historica* (Oxford, 1918).

Bishop, Terrence A. M., *Scriptores Regis* (Oxford, 1961).

Blake, E. O., "The *Historia Eliensis* As a Source for Twelfth Century History," *Bulletin of the Johns Rylands Library* 41(1959):304–327.

Bloch, Marc, *Feudal Society*, trans. L. A. Manyon (London, 1961).

Boase, Thomas S. R., *English Art. 1100–1216* (Oxford, 1953).

Böhmer, Heinrich, *Kirche und Staat in England und in der Normandie im XI. und XII. Jahrhundert* (Leipzig, 1899).

Boivin-Champeaux, Louis, *Notice sur Roger le Grand, évêque de Salisbury et premier ministre d'Angleterre au XIIe siècle* (Evreux, 1878).

Boussard, Jacques, "Les institutions financières de l'Angleterre au XIIe siècle," *Cahiers de Civilisation Médiévale* 1(1958):475–494.

Brett, Martin, "The Organization of the English Secular Church in the Reign of Henry I" (Oxford University D. Phil. thesis, 1968).

Brooke, C. N. L., "Gregorian Reform in Action, Clerical Marriage in England, 1050–1200," CHJ 12(1956):1–22.

——, "Married Men Among the English Higher Clergy, 1066–1200," CHJ 12(1956):187–188.

Brooke, George C. *English Coins,* 3rd ed. (London, 1950).

Brooke, Zachary N., *The English Church and the Papacy From the Conquest to the Reign of John* (Cambridge, 1952).

——, "Lay Investiture and Its Relation to the Conflict of Empire and Papacy," PBA 25(1939):217–249.

——, and Brooke, C. N. L., "Hereford Cathedral Dignitaries in the Twelfth Century," CHJ 8(1944):1–22.

Burridge, A. W., "L'Immaculée Conception dans la théologie de l'Angleterre médiévale," *Revue D'Histoire Ecclésiastique* (Louvain) 32(1936):570–598.

Butcher, W. H., "Roger, Bishop of Salisbury, Chancellor and Justiciar of England, 1102–1139," *The Journal of the British Archaeological Association,* New Series 23(1917):124–136.

Campbell, John C., *Lives of the Lord Chancellors* 1 (New York, 1874).

Cantor, Norman F., *Church, Kingship, and Lay Investiture in England, 1089–1135* (Princeton, 1958).

————, *The English: A History of Politics and Society* (New York, 1967).

————, "The Crisis of Western Monasticism, 1050–1130," AHR 66(1960):47–68.

Chaplais, Pierre, "The Original Charters of Herbert and Gervase, Abbots of Westminster, 1127–1157," in *A Medieval Miscellany for Doris Mary Stenton,* ed. Patricia Barnes and C. F. Slade, Pipe Roll Society Publications New Series 26(1962, for 1960):89–95.

Cheney, Christopher R., *English Bishops' Chanceries, 1100–1250* (Manchester, 1950).

Chew, Helena, *The English Ecclesiastical Tenants-in-Chief and Knight Service* (Oxford, 1932).

Chrimes, S. B., *An Introduction to the Administrative History of Medieval England* (Oxford, 1959).

Clark, Cecily, "The Ecclesiastical Adventurer: Henry of Saint Jean d'Angély," EHR 89(1969):548–560.

Cronne, H. A., "The Royal Forest in the Reign of Henry I," *Essays in British and Irish History in Honour of James Eadie Todd,* ed. H. A. Cronne, T. W. Moody, and D. B. Quinn (London, 1949).

————, "The Office of Local Justiciar in England Under the Norman Kings," *University of Birmingham Historical Journal* 11(1957):18–38.

Crosby, Everett U., "The Organization of the English Episcopate Under Henry I," *Studies in Medieval and Renaissance History* 4(1967):1–89.

Cunnington, R. H., "Devizes Castle: A Suggested Reconstruction," *The Wiltshire Archaeological and Natural History Magazine* 51(1947):496–499.

D'Ancona, Mirella Levi, *The Iconography of the Immaculate Conception in the Middle Ages and Early Renaissance* (New York, 1957).

David, Charles Wendell, *Robert Curthose, Duke of Normandy* (Cambridge, Mass., 1920).

Davis, G. R. C., *Medieval Cartularies of Great Britain: A Short Catalogue* (London, 1958).

Davis, H. Francis, "The Origins of the Devotion to Our Lady's Immaculate Conception," *Dublin Review* 228(1954):375–392.

Davis, H. W. C., "The Anarchy of Stephen's Reign" EHR 18(1903):630–641.

——, "Waldric, the Chancellor of Henry I," EHR 26(1911):84–89.

Davis, R. H. C., *King Stephen, 1135–1154* (Berkeley and Los Angeles, 1967).

——, "The Monks of St. Edmund, 1021–1048," *History*, New Series 40(1955):227–240.

——, "The Authorship of the *Gesta Stephani*," EHR 77(1962):209–233.

——, "*Geoffrey de Mandeville Reconsidered*," EHR 79(1964):299–307.

——, "What Happened in Stephen's Reign," *History*, New Series 49(1964):1–12.

Dickinson, John C., *The Origins of the Austin Canons and Their Introduction into England* (London, 1950).

——, *Monastic Life in Medieval England* (New York, 1962).

van Dijk, S. J. P., "The Origins of the Latin Feast of the Conception of the Blessed Virgin Mary," *Dublin Review* 228(1954):251–267, 428–442.

Dodsworth, William, *An Historical Account of the Episcopal See and Cathedral Church of Sarum, or Salisbury* (Salisbury, 1814).

Dodwell, Barbara, "The Honours of the Bishop of Theford/Norwich in the Late Eleventh and Early Twelfth Centuries," *Norfolk Archaeology* 33(1965):185–200.

Douglas, David C., *William the Conqueror: The Norman Impact Upon England* (Berkeley and Los Angeles, 1964).

Edwards, Kathleen, *English Secular Cathedrals in the Middle Ages,* 2nd ed. (Manchester, 1967).

Ekwall, Eilbert, *Concise Oxford Dictionary of English Place Names,* 4th ed. (Oxford, 1964)

Farmer, Hugh, "William of Malmesbury's Life and Works," JEH 13(1962):39–54.

Fawtier, Robert, *The Capetian Kings of France, 987–1328, trans.* Lionel Butler and R. J. Adam (New York, 1960).

Foreville, Raymonde, and Leclerq Jean, "Un débat sur le sacerdoce des moines au XIIe siècle," *Studia Anselmiana,*
41(1957):8–118.

Fowler, Joseph, *Medieval Sherborne* (Dorchester, 1951).

Fox, Cyril, and Radford, C. A. Ralegh, "Kidwelly Castle, Carmarthenshire, including a survey of the Polychrome Pottery
Found There and Elsewhere in Britain," *Archaeologia* 83
(1933):93–138.

Freeman, Edward, *The History of the Norman Conquest of
England, Its Causes and Its Results,* 6 vols. (Oxford, 1876).

Gough, "Conjectures on an Ancient Tomb in Salisbury Cathedral," *Archaeologia* 2 (1773):188–193.

Graham, Rose, "The Intellectual Influence of English Monasticism Between the Tenth and Twelfth Centuries," TRHS New
Series 17 (1903):23–67.

Greenway, Diana E., ed., *John Le Neve, Fasti Ecclesiae Anglicanae, 1066–1300* 1, *Saint Paul's, London* (London, 1968).

Grinnell-Milne, Duncan, *The Killing of William Rufus: An
Investigation in the New Forest* (New York, 1968).

Haskins, Charles Homer, *Norman Institutions* (Cambridge,
Mass., 1918).

——, *Studies in the History of Medieval Science* (Cambridge,
Mass., 1924).

——, *The Renaissance of the Twelfth Century* (Cambridge,
Mass., 1927).

——, "Adelard of Bath," EHR 26 (1911):491–498.

——, "The Abacus and the King's Curia," EHR 27
(1912):101–106.

Hearne, Thomas, *Remarks and Collections,* ed. C. E. Doble, 3
vols. (Oxford, 1885–1889).

Hodge, Bernulf, *A History of Malmesbury* (Malmesbury,
1969).

Hollister, C. Warren, *The Military Organization of Norman England* (Oxford, 1965).

——, *The Twelfth Century Renaissance* (New York, 1969).

Holmes, Urban T., *Daily Living in the Twelfth Century* (Madison, 1962).

——, "The Anglo-Norman Rhymed Chronicle," in *Linguistic
and Literary Studies in Honor of Helmut A. Hatzfeld,* ed.
Alessandro S. Crisafulli (Washington, 1964), pp. 231–236.

——, "Norman London," *The London and Middlesex Historian* 2 (1966):9–15.

Honeybourne, M. B., "The Sanctuary Boundaries and Environs of Westminster Abbey and the College of St. Martin-le-Grand," *British Archaeological Association Journal* New Series 38 (1933):316–333.

Hope, William H. St. John, "Report on Excavation at Old Sarum Cathedral Church, 1913," *Proceedings of the Society of Antiquaries of London* Second Series 26(1913–1914):100–119.

Hoyt, Robert S., *The Royal Demesne in English Constitutional History, 1066–1272* (Ithaca, 1950).

Hurnard, Naomi D., "The Anglo-Norman Franchises," EHR 64 (1949):289–327, 433–460.

Hurry, Jamieson B., *Reading Abbey* (London, 1901).

Jennings, J. C., "The Origins of the 'Elements Series' of the *Miracles of the Virgin*," *Medieval and Renaissance Studies* 6 (1968):84–94.

Jolliffe, J. E. A., *The Constitutional History of Medieval England,* 2nd ed. (London, 1954).

Jones, William Henry, "The Bishops of Old Sarum, 1075-1225," *The Wiltshire Archaeological and Natural History Magazine* 12 (1878):161–192.

———, *Salisbury* (London, 1880).

Kemp, Brian, "The Foundation of Reading Abbey and the Growth of Its Possessions and Privileges in England in the Twelfth Century" (Reading University Ph.D. thesis, 1966).

———, *Reading Abbey: An Introduction to the History of the Abbey* (Reading, 1968).

———, "The Mother Church of Thatcham," *Berkshire Archaeological Journal* 63 (1967–1968):15–22.

———, "The Monastic Dean of Leominster," EHR 83 (1968):505–515.

Kempe, Alfred John, *Historical Notes on the Collegiate Church of St. Martin-le-Grand, London* (London, 1825).

Ker, Neil R., *English Manuscripts in the Century After the Norman Conquest* (Oxford, 1960).

Knowles, David, *The Religious Houses of Medieval England* (London, 1940).

———, *The Monastic Order in England, 943–1216,* 2nd ed. (Cambridge, 1950).

———, and Hadcock, R. Neville, *Medieval Religious Houses: England and Wales* (London, 1953).

Landon, Lionel, "Everard, Bishop of Norwich," *Proceedings of the Suffolk Institute of Archaeology* 20 (1930):186–198.

La Rue, Gervaise, *Essais Historiques sur la Ville de Caen et son Arrondissement,* 2 vols. (Rouen, 1820).

Leland, John, *Itinerary: 1535-1543,* ed. Lucy Toulmin Smith, 5 vols. (Carbondale, Illinois, 1964; reprint of 1907 ed.).

Le Neve, John, *Fasti Ecclesiae Anglicanae,* ed. Thomas Dufus Hardy, 3 vols (Oxford, 1854).

Le Prévost, August, *Memoirs et Notes de M. August Le Prévost, Pour Servir à l'Histoire de Département de l'Eure,* 2 vols. (Evreux, 1864).

Leyser, Karl, "England and the Empire in the Early Twelfth Century," TRHS Fifth Series 10 (1960):61-85.

Liebermann, Felix, *Einleitung in Den Dialogus de Scaccario* (Gottingen, 1875).

———, *Quadripartitus: Ein Englisches Rechtsbuch von 1114* (Halle, 1892).

Lloyd, John Edward, *A History of Wales,* 2 vols. (London, 1912).

———, *The History of Carmarthenshire,* 2 vols. (Cardiff, 1935-1939).

Lunt, William E., *Papal Revenues in the Middle Ages,* 2 vols. (New York, 1934).

Lyon, Bryce, *A Constitutional and Legal History of Medieval England* (New York, 1960).

———, and Verhulst, A. E., *Medieval Finance: A Comparison of Financial Institutions in Northwestern Europe* (Providence, 1967).

McKisack, May, "London and the Succession to the Crown During the Middle Ages," in *Studies in Medieval History Presented to Frederick Maurice Powicke,* ed. R. W. Hunt, W. A. Pantin, and R. W. Southern (Oxford, 1948), pp. 76-89.

Martin, Charles Trice, *The Record Interpreter* (London, 1910).

Megaw, Isabel, "The Ecclesiastical Policy of Stephen, 1135-1139: A Reinterpretation," in *Essays in British and Irish History in Honour of James Eadie Todd,* ed. H. A. Cronne, T. W. Moody, and D. B. Quinn (London, 1949), pp. 24-46.

Miller, Edward, *The Abbey and Bishopric of Ely* (Cambridge, 1951).

Moore, Norman, *The History of St. Bartholomew's Hospital,* 2 vols. (London, 1918).

Morey, Adrian, and Brooke, C. N. L., *Gilbert Foliot and His Letters* (Cambridge, 1965).

Morris, William Alfred, *The Medieval English Sheriff to 1300* (Manchester, 1927).

Nelson, Lynn H., *The Normans in South Wales, 1070–1171* (Austin, 1966).

Nicholl, Donald, *Thurstan, Archbishop of York (1114–1140)* (York, 1964).

Norgate, Kate, "The Date of the Composition of William of Newburgh's History," EHR 19 (1919):288–297.

Oliver, Edith, *Wiltshire* (London, 1951).

Painter, Sidney, *Studies in the History of the English Feudal Barony* (Baltimore, 1943).

Patterson, Robert B., "William of Malmesbury's Robert of Gloucester, A Re-evaluation of the *Historia Novella*," AHR 70 (1965):983–997.

———, "Stephen's Shaftesbury Charter: Another Case Against William of Malmesbury," *Speculum* 43 (1968):487–492.

Poole, Austin Lane, *From Domesday Book to Magna Carta 1087–1216*, 2nd ed. (Oxford, 1955).

Poole, Reginald Lane, *The Exchequer in the Twelfth Century* (Oxford, 1912).

Preston, A. E., *The Church and Parish of St. Nicholas, Abingdon,* Oxford Historical Society Publications 99 (1935).

Prestwick, J. A., "War and Finance in the Anglo-Norman State," TRHS Fifth Series 4 (1954) :19–43.

Ramsay, James H., *A History of the Revenues of the Kings of England, 1066–1399* 1 (Oxford, 1925).

Reedy, William T., "The Origins of the General Eyre in the Reign of Henry I," *Speculum* 41 (1966):688–725.

Rees, Henry, "Malmesbury: Its Castle and Walls," *Wiltshire Archaeological and Natural History Magazine* 51 (1945): 184–192.

Richardson, Henry G., "Richard Fitzneal and the *Dialogus de Scaccario,*" EHR 43 (1928):161–171, 321–340.

———, "William of Ely, the King's Treasurer, 1195–1215," TRHS Fourth Series 15 (1932):45–91.

———, "Gervase of Tilbury," *History* 46(1961):102–115.

———, and Sayles, George O., *The Governance of Medieval England from the Conquest to Magna Carta* (Edinburgh, 1963).

———, and Sayles, George O., *Law and Legislation from AEthelberht to Magna Carta* (Edinburgh, 1966).

Roberts, George, "Llanthony Priory, Monmouthshire," *Archaeologia Cambrensis* 1 (1846):201–245.

Ross, James Bruce, "Rise and Fall of a Twelfth Century Clan:

The Erembalds and the Murder of Count Charles of Flanders, 1127-1128," *Speculum* 34 (1959):367-390.

Round, John Horace, *Geoffrey de Mandeville: A Study in Anarchy* (London, 1892; reprinted New York, 1960).

————, *Feudal England* (London, 1895).

————, *The Commune of London and Other Studies* (Westminster, 1899).

Saltman, Avrom, *Theobald, Archbishop of Canterbury* (London, 1956).

Shaw, Stebbing, *The History and Antiquities of Staffordshire*, 2 vols. (London, 1789-1801).

Sheehan, Michael, *The Will in Medieval England* (Toronto, 1963).

Shortt, Hugh de S., *Old Sarum* (London, 1965).

————, "Three Early Episcopal Tombs in Salisbury Cathedral," *Wiltshire Archaeological and Natural History Magazine* 57 (1960):217-219.

Southern, Richard W., *The Making of the Middle Ages* (London, 1953).

————, *Saint Anselm and His Biographer: A Study of Monastic Life and Thought, 1059-1130* (Cambridge, 1963).

————, "Ranulf Flambard and Early Anglo-Norman Administration," TRHS Fourth Series 16 (1933), pp. 95-129.

————, "The Canterbury Forgeries," EHR 73(1958):192-227.

————, "The English Origins of the Virgin's Miracles," *Medieval and Renaissance Studies* 4 (1958):176-216.

————, "The Place of England in the Twelfth Century Renaissance," *History* 45 (1960):201-216.

————, "The Place of Henry I in English History," PBA 48(1962):127-170.

Stalley, Roger A., "The Patronage of Roger of Salisbury" (The Courtauld Institute, London, M. A. report, 1969).

Stenton, Doris M., *English Justice Between the Norman Conquest and the Great Charter, 1066-1215* (Philadelphia, 1964).

Stenton, Frank M., *The First Century of English Feudalism: 1066-1166* (Oxford, 1932).

————, *Norman London* (London, 1934).

Stone, Edward, *Devizes Castle: Its History and Romance* (Devizes, 1920).

Stubbs, William, *The Constitutional History of England*, 1, 3rd ed. (Oxford, 1880).

————, *Historical Introductions to the Rolls Series,* ed. Arthur Hassall (London, 1902).

Styles, Dorothy, "The Early History of the King's Chapels in Staffordshire," *Birmingham Archaeological Society Transactions and Proceedings* 60 (1936):56–96.

Tatlock, John S. P., "The English Journey of the Laon Canons," *Speculum* 8 (1933):454–465.

Tellenbach, Gerd, *Church, State and Christian Society at the Time of the Investiture Contest* (Oxford, 1959).

Tout, Thomas F., *Chapters in the Administrative History of Medieval England* 1 (Manchester, 1920).

Turner, George J., "The Sheriff's Farm," TRHS New Series 12(1898):117–151.

Van Caenegem, Raoul C., *Royal Writs in England From the Conquest to Glanville* (London, 1959).

Walker, David, "Miles of Gloucester, Earl of Hereford," *Transactions of the Bristol and Gloucestershire Archaeological Society* 77 (1958):66–84.

———, "The Honours of the Earls of Hereford in the Twelfth Century," *Transactions of the Bristol and Gloucestershire Archaeological Society* 79 (1960):174–213.

Way, Albert, "Contributions Towards the History of Reading Abbey," *Archaeological Journal* 20(1863):281–296, 22(1865):151–161.

Waylen, *Chronicle of Devizes* (London, 1939).

Webb, Clement C., *John of Salisbury* (London, 1932).

Webb, E. A., *The Records of St. Bartholomew's Priory and of the Church and Parish of St. Bartholomew the Great, West Smithfield,* 2 vols (Oxford, 1928).

West, Francis J., *The Justiciarship in England, 1066–1232* (Cambridge, 1966).

White, Geoffrey H., "Financial Administration Under Henry I," TRHS Fourth Series 8(1925):56–79.

———, "The Career of Waleran, Count of Meulan and Earl of Worcester (1104–1166)," TRHS Fourth Series 17(1934):19–49.

———, "The Household of the Norman Kings," TRHS Fourth Series 30(1948):127–155.

Wightman, Wilfrid E., *The Lacy Family in England and Normandy, 1066–1194* (Oxford, 1966).

Williams, Watkin, *Saint Bernard of Clairvaux* (Manchester, 1935).

Zarnecki, George, *The Early Sculpture of Ely Cathedral* (London, 1958).

Index

witnesses charters (4), 232;
(19), 254

Ralph d'Escures, bishop of Rochester, 126, 127; becomes abp.
of Canterbury, 128; death of,
130

Ralph, son of Warin, witnesses
charter (4), 232

Ramsey abbey, 64; cartularies of,
269–270

Ranulf, the chancellor, 61

Ranulf, earl of Chester, 183

Ranulf of Salisbury, and Ely conspiracy, 167

Reading abbey, Berkshire, and
burial of Henry I, 159;
cartularies of, 224, 240;
founded by Henry I, 225,
240; granted Edgar the
minter, 243–244; Gregorian
reforms and, 126; Immacu-
late Conception and, 141;
privileges of, 241; Roger's
role in establishment of, 67–
72, 116; Salisbury diocese
and, 239; see also Hugh,
abbot of Reading

Reading school, 258–259

Redeninge, 60

Redvers, Baldwin de, 163, 169

Reedy, William, 64, 65

Register of St. Osmund, 224, 238,
239

Registrum Rubrum, 270–271

Reinhelm, becomes bishop of
Hereford, 21; refuses consecration by abp. Gerard, 17

Reinni, Roger de, witnesses charter (4), 232

Revel, Robert, 251

Restoldus, the sheriff, 245, 246

Richard, bishop of London, 132

Richard of Devizes, witnesses
charter (19), 254

Richard of Montacute, witnesses
charter (19), 254

Ridel, Geoffrey, 63

Robert of Arundel, witnesses
charter (19), 254

Robert of Bagpuize, 230

Robert of Barneville, 275

Robert, bishop of Bath, and
Gesta Stephani, 7, 156, 188

Robert, bishop of Hereford, and
introduction of abacus to
England, 47–48

Robert, count of Meulan, earl of
Leicester, 71, 132, 170; and
Canterbury-York dispute,
123; excommunicated, 18, 19

Robert, earl of Gloucester and
natural son of Henry I, 97,
147, 160; ambushed by King
Stephen, 166; invades England, 199; and King Ste-
phen's coronation charter,
162; and oath to Empress
Matilda, 149; rumors of his
attack on England, 174; renounces fealty to King Stephen, 168, 169; and Stephen
of Blois, 155

Robert, earl of Leicester, excommunicated, 201–202; and
gifts to Holy Trinity, 251;
and imprisonment of Roger,
181; as twin brother of
Waleran, 170

Robert of Lincoln, witnesses charter (19), 254

Robert, the old steward, witnesses
charter (4), 232

Robert of Sees, witnesses charter
(4), 232

Robert of Torigni, 155

Rochester, bishop of, see Ralph
d'Escures; Ernulf

Rochester, bishopric of, 125

Roger, archdeacon of Salisbury,
witnesses charter (19), 254

Roger of Berkshire, 273

Roger, bishop of Salisbury